# Addison-Wesley Mathematics

**Robert E. Eicholz**
**Phares G. O'Daffer**
**Charles R. Fleenor**

Randall I. Charles
Sharon Young
Carne S. Barnett

▲
Addison-Wesley Publishing Company

Menlo Park, California • Reading, Massachusetts • Don Mills, Ontario • Wokingham, England
Amsterdam • Sydney • Singapore • Tokyo • Madrid • Bogotá • Santiago • San Juan

## ILLUSTRATIONS

**Roberta Holmes** 1–21, 23–32, 179–196

**Ron Lehew** 153–178, 291–312, 339, 340, 342, 344

**Rich Lo** 346, 352, 356, 359

**Kathy McCarthy** 22, 33–64, 134, 146, 148, 197–224, 246, 313–336, 337–339, 341–343

**Jane McCreary** 134, 246

**Carol Nicklaus** 125–133, 135–145, 147, 149–152, 269–280, 283, 285, 288, 289

**Bill Ogden** 95–124, 247–268, 281, 282, 284, 286, 287, 290

**Judy Sakaguchi** 65–94, 225–245

Cover Photograph: © **Vince Streano**

All line illustrations rendered by the Addison-Wesley Technical Graphics Department

ISBN 0-201-26200-2

NOPQRSTUV-WC-892109

# Contents

## CHAPTER 4    DIFFERENCES TO 18

## CHAPTER 5    TIME AND MONEY

## CHAPTER 6    ADDITION: 2-DIGIT NUMBERS

# CHAPTER 7   GEOMETRY AND GRAPHING

# CHAPTER 8   SUBTRACTION: 2-DIGIT NUMBERS

# CHAPTER 9   MEASUREMENT—METRIC UNITS

## CHAPTER 10   3-DIGIT PLACE VALUE

## CHAPTER 11   ADDITION AND SUBTRACTION: 3-DIGIT NUMBERS

## CHAPTER 12   MULTIPLICATION

# CHAPTER 13    FRACTIONS AND CUSTOMARY MEASUREMENT

# TECHNOLOGY RESOURCE BANK

# APPENDIX

# ADDITION AND SUBTRACTION

**How many are there?**

| | | |
|---|---|---|
| **1.** | zero | 0  0  ___  ___  ___ |
| **2.** | one | 1  1  ___  ___  ___ |
| **3.** | two | 2  2  ___  ___  ___ |
| **4.** | three | 3  3  ___  ___  ___ |
| **5.** | four | 4  4  ___  ___  ___ |
| **6.** | five | 5  5  ___  ___  ___ |
| **7.** | six | 6  6  ___  ___  ___ |

**8.**     2

**9.** ___

**10.** ___

**11.** ___

**12.** ___

**13.** ___

How many are there?

1. seven    7    7 _____ _____ _____

2. eight    8    8 _____ _____ _____

3. nine    9    9 _____ _____ _____

4. ten    10    10 _____ _____ _____

5. eleven    11    11 _____ _____ _____

6. twelve    12    12 _____ _____ _____

7. _____

8. _____

9. _____

10. _____

11. _____

12. _____

Name _____

Use counters to find the sums.

**1.**

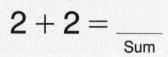

2 + 2 = ____
Sum

**2.**

1 + 2 = ____
Sum

**3.**

1 + 1 = ____
Sum

**4.**

1 + 3 = ____
Sum

**5.**

3 + 2 = ____
Sum

**6.**

2 + 3 = ____
Sum

Addition concept—sums to 5

(three)  **3**

Add.

1.

$$\begin{array}{r}2\\+1\\\hline 3\end{array}$$

2.
$$\begin{array}{r}1\\+3\\\hline 4\end{array}$$

3.
$$\begin{array}{r}2\\+2\\\hline\end{array}$$

4.
$$\begin{array}{r}3\\+1\\\hline\end{array}$$

5.
$$\begin{array}{r}1\\+2\\\hline\end{array}$$

6.
$$\begin{array}{r}2\\+3\\\hline\end{array}$$

7.
$$\begin{array}{r}1\\+4\\\hline\end{array}$$

8.
$$\begin{array}{r}1\\+1\\\hline\end{array}$$

Addition concept—sums to 5

Name _____

Count and add.

**1.** 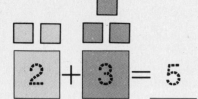 $2 + 3 = 5$

     □ + □ = ___     □ + □ = ___

**2.** □ + □ = ___     □ + □ = ___     □ + □ = ___

**3.** 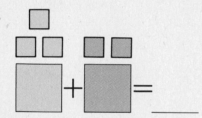 □ + □ = ___     □ + □ = ___     □ + □ = ___

**4.** 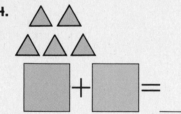 □ + □ = ___     □ + □ = ___     □ + □ = ___

Write the sums.

**5.** $0 + 5 = $ ___         $3 + 2 = $ ___         $2 + 1 = $ ___

**6.** $2 + 2 = $ ___         $2 + 0 = $ ___         $3 + 1 = $ ___

**7.** $1 + 4 = $ ___         $1 + 0 = $ ___         $0 + 0 = $ ___

**8.** $2 + 1 = $ ___         $2 + 3 = $ ___         $0 + 4 = $ ___

Addition concept—sums to 5                 (five) **5**

Count and add.

1.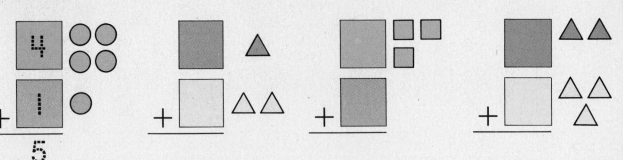

4
+ 1
5

2.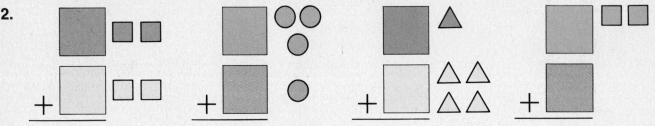

Find the sums.

3. 
$$4 + 1$$   $$1 + 3$$   $$3 + 2$$   $$2 + 2$$   $$1 + 4$$   $$1 + 2$$

4. 
$$1 + 1$$   $$4 + 1$$   $$1 + 3$$   $$2 + 1$$   $$2 + 3$$   $$2 + 2$$

Finish the counting.

2, 3, ___, ___          9, 8, ___, ___

7, 8, ___, ___          3, 2, ___, ___

Addition concept—sums to 5

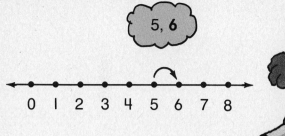

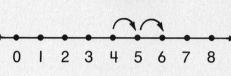

5, 6

4, 5, 6

0 1 2 3 4 5 6 7 8

0 1 2 3 4 5 6 7 8

$5 + 1 = \underline{6}$

$4 + 2 = \underline{6}$

Add.

0 1 2 3 4 5 6 7 8 9 10 11 12

1. $8 + 1 = \underline{\hphantom{00}}$     $6 + 2 = \underline{\hphantom{00}}$     $1 + 1 = \underline{\hphantom{00}}$

2. $4 + 2 = \underline{\hphantom{00}}$     $5 + 2 = \underline{\hphantom{00}}$     $7 + 1 = \underline{\hphantom{00}}$

3. $2 + 1 = \underline{\hphantom{00}}$     $4 + 1 = \underline{\hphantom{00}}$     $9 + 1 = \underline{\hphantom{00}}$

4. $3 + 2 = \underline{\hphantom{00}}$     $6 + 1 = \underline{\hphantom{00}}$     $2 + 2 = \underline{\hphantom{00}}$

5. $7 + 1 = \underline{\hphantom{00}}$     $9 + 2 = \underline{\hphantom{00}}$     $3 + 1 = \underline{\hphantom{00}}$

6. $4 + 2 = \underline{\hphantom{00}}$     $2 + 2 = \underline{\hphantom{00}}$     $6 + 2 = \underline{\hphantom{00}}$

7. $5 + 1 = \underline{\hphantom{00}}$     $1 + 2 = \underline{\hphantom{00}}$     $8 + 1 = \underline{\hphantom{00}}$

8. $7 + 2 = \underline{\hphantom{00}}$     $8 + 2 = \underline{\hphantom{00}}$     $9 + 2 = \underline{\hphantom{00}}$

Adding 1 and 2—counting on

$$\begin{array}{r} 6 \\ +1 \\ \hline 7 \end{array} \qquad \begin{array}{r} 1 \\ +6 \\ \hline 7 \end{array} \qquad\qquad \begin{array}{r} 5 \\ +2 \\ \hline 7 \end{array} \qquad \begin{array}{r} 2 \\ +5 \\ \hline 7 \end{array}$$

**Find the sums.**

1.
$$\begin{array}{r} 7 \\ +2 \\ \hline \end{array} \quad \begin{array}{r} 2 \\ +7 \\ \hline \end{array} \qquad \begin{array}{r} 8 \\ +2 \\ \hline \end{array} \quad \begin{array}{r} 2 \\ +8 \\ \hline \end{array} \qquad \begin{array}{r} 6 \\ +2 \\ \hline \end{array} \quad \begin{array}{r} 2 \\ +6 \\ \hline \end{array}$$

2.
$$\begin{array}{r} 2 \\ +6 \\ \hline \end{array} \quad \begin{array}{r} 1 \\ +6 \\ \hline \end{array} \qquad \begin{array}{r} 9 \\ +2 \\ \hline \end{array} \quad \begin{array}{r} 2 \\ +1 \\ \hline \end{array} \qquad \begin{array}{r} 8 \\ +1 \\ \hline \end{array} \quad \begin{array}{r} 2 \\ +9 \\ \hline \end{array}$$

3.
$$\begin{array}{r} 1 \\ +5 \\ \hline \end{array} \quad \begin{array}{r} 4 \\ +2 \\ \hline \end{array} \qquad \begin{array}{r} 5 \\ +1 \\ \hline \end{array} \quad \begin{array}{r} 2 \\ +2 \\ \hline \end{array} \qquad \begin{array}{r} 7 \\ +2 \\ \hline \end{array} \quad \begin{array}{r} 1 \\ +9 \\ \hline \end{array}$$

4.
$$\begin{array}{r} 5 \\ +2 \\ \hline \end{array} \quad \begin{array}{r} 8 \\ +2 \\ \hline \end{array} \qquad \begin{array}{r} 6 \\ +2 \\ \hline \end{array} \quad \begin{array}{r} 1 \\ +7 \\ \hline \end{array} \qquad \begin{array}{r} 7 \\ +2 \\ \hline \end{array} \quad \begin{array}{r} 2 \\ +8 \\ \hline \end{array}$$

## SKILLKEEPER

Write the times.

 :00

_____     _____     _____

Order property

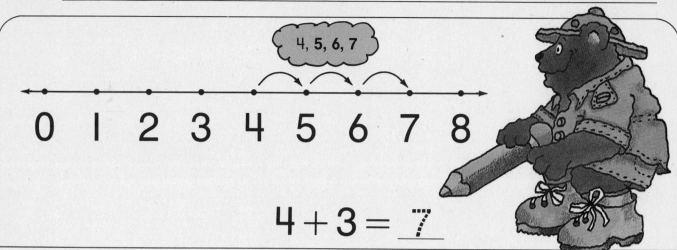

4, 5, 6, 7

0 1 2 3 4 5 6 7 8

$4 + 3 = \underline{7}$

Add 3.

0 1 2 3 4 5 6 7 8 9 10 11 12

1. $5 + 3 = \underline{\phantom{00}}$    $2 + 3 = \underline{\phantom{00}}$    $1 + 3 = \underline{\phantom{00}}$

2. $7 + 3 = \underline{\phantom{00}}$    $9 + 3 = \underline{\phantom{00}}$    $6 + 3 = \underline{\phantom{00}}$

3. $8 + 3 = \underline{\phantom{00}}$    $3 + 3 = \underline{\phantom{00}}$    $5 + 3 = \underline{\phantom{00}}$

4. $6 + 3 = \underline{\phantom{00}}$    $4 + 3 = \underline{\phantom{00}}$    $8 + 3 = \underline{\phantom{00}}$

Find the sums.

5.
$$\begin{array}{r} 7 \\ +2 \\ \hline \end{array} \quad \begin{array}{r} 9 \\ +3 \\ \hline \end{array} \quad \begin{array}{r} 4 \\ +3 \\ \hline \end{array} \quad \begin{array}{r} 1 \\ +8 \\ \hline \end{array} \quad \begin{array}{r} 6 \\ +2 \\ \hline \end{array} \quad \begin{array}{r} 1 \\ +5 \\ \hline \end{array}$$

6.
$$\begin{array}{r} 9 \\ +1 \\ \hline \end{array} \quad \begin{array}{r} 7 \\ +1 \\ \hline \end{array} \quad \begin{array}{r} 4 \\ +2 \\ \hline \end{array} \quad \begin{array}{r} 1 \\ +6 \\ \hline \end{array} \quad \begin{array}{r} 3 \\ +5 \\ \hline \end{array} \quad \begin{array}{r} 5 \\ +2 \\ \hline \end{array}$$

7.
$$\begin{array}{r} 8 \\ +2 \\ \hline \end{array} \quad \begin{array}{r} 3 \\ +1 \\ \hline \end{array} \quad \begin{array}{r} 6 \\ +3 \\ \hline \end{array} \quad \begin{array}{r} 3 \\ +3 \\ \hline \end{array} \quad \begin{array}{r} 3 \\ +7 \\ \hline \end{array} \quad \begin{array}{r} 8 \\ +3 \\ \hline \end{array}$$

Find the sums.

1.
$$3 + 6$$    $$2 + 1$$    $$9 + 2$$    $$1 + 3$$

2.
$$2 + 2$$    $$2 + 3$$    $$3 + 1$$    $$3 + 7$$    $$6 + 2$$    $$1 + 4$$

3.
$$1 + 7$$    $$9 + 1$$    $$2 + 6$$    $$8 + 3$$    $$2 + 8$$    $$8 + 1$$

4.
$$2 + 6$$    $$3 + 2$$    $$1 + 2$$    $$1 + 3$$    $$5 + 2$$    $$5 + 3$$

5.
$$2 + 7$$    $$6 + 3$$    $$4 + 3$$    $$2 + 9$$    $$4 + 2$$    $$1 + 6$$

## THINK MATH

There are 5 fish in all.
How many are inside the castle?

_____ fish

Practice the facts

$2 + 0 = \underline{2}$

Add 0.

1.  $4 + 0 = \underline{\quad}$          $0 + 5 = \underline{\quad}$          $0 + 0 = \underline{\quad}$

2.  $0 + 3 = \underline{\quad}$          $7 + 0 = \underline{\quad}$          $6 + 0 = \underline{\quad}$

3.  $0 + 8 = \underline{\quad}$          $1 + 0 = \underline{\quad}$          $0 + 9 = \underline{\quad}$

Find the sums.

4.
$$\begin{array}{r} 4 \\ +0 \\ \hline \end{array} \qquad \begin{array}{r} 0 \\ +8 \\ \hline \end{array} \qquad \begin{array}{r} 0 \\ +0 \\ \hline \end{array} \qquad \begin{array}{r} 0 \\ +2 \\ \hline \end{array} \qquad \begin{array}{r} 9 \\ +0 \\ \hline \end{array} \qquad \begin{array}{r} 0 \\ +6 \\ \hline \end{array}$$

5.
$$\begin{array}{r} 6 \\ +1 \\ \hline \end{array} \qquad \begin{array}{r} 2 \\ +8 \\ \hline \end{array} \qquad \begin{array}{r} 4 \\ +0 \\ \hline \end{array} \qquad \begin{array}{r} 3 \\ +6 \\ \hline \end{array} \qquad \begin{array}{r} 7 \\ +2 \\ \hline \end{array} \qquad \begin{array}{r} 0 \\ +7 \\ \hline \end{array}$$

6.
$$\begin{array}{r} 2 \\ +5 \\ \hline \end{array} \qquad \begin{array}{r} 9 \\ +0 \\ \hline \end{array} \qquad \begin{array}{r} 1 \\ +8 \\ \hline \end{array} \qquad \begin{array}{r} 8 \\ +3 \\ \hline \end{array} \qquad \begin{array}{r} 2 \\ +9 \\ \hline \end{array} \qquad \begin{array}{r} 7 \\ +0 \\ \hline \end{array}$$

Add.

1.
$$8 + 2$$   $$9 + 0$$   $$2 + 1$$   $$1 + 8$$

2.
$$3 + 9$$   $$1 + 3$$   $$9 + 2$$   $$0 + 6$$   $$4 + 1$$   $$1 + 9$$

3.
$$3 + 5$$   $$2 + 2$$   $$7 + 3$$   $$3 + 0$$   $$3 + 2$$   $$2 + 7$$

4. Write the sums and color.

10 Yellow

9 Green

8 Blue

7 Red

$$9 + 1$$   $$0 + 9$$   $$3 + 7$$

$$7 + 0$$   $$4 + 3$$

$$2 + 7$$   $$2 + 6$$   $$8 + 1$$

$$2 + 5$$   $$1 + 6$$

$$8 + 2$$   $$6 + 3$$   $$5 + 5$$

Practice the facts

## Problem Solving    Name _____

**1.** Tell a story. Answer the question. How many are there in all?

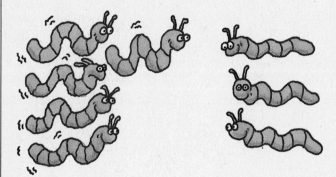

_____ worms

**2.** How many are there altogether?

_____ fish

**3.** How many are there now?

_____ birds

**4.** How many are there in all?

_____ shells

**5.** How many are there in all?

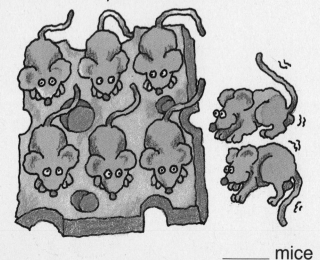

_____ mice

**6.** How many are there altogether?

_____ lions

Problem solving—tell a story

## Problem Solving

Solve.

1. Jim has 3 balloons.

   Nina has 4 balloons.

   How many are there in all? __7__ balloons

$$\begin{array}{r} 3 \\ + 4 \\ \hline 7 \end{array}$$

2. 

   Lisa caught 5 fish.

   Ted caught 2 fish.

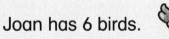

   How many are there in all? _____ fish

3. 

   Pat has 3 birds.

   Joan has 6 birds.

   How many birds are there altogether? _____ birds

4. 

   Penny found 3 leaves.

   C. J. found 3 leaves.

   How many is this altogether? _____ leaves

Problem solving—short sentence

Name _____

## Use counters to find the differences.

**1.**

$3 - 2 =$ _____
Difference

**2.**

$4 - 1 =$ _____
Difference

**3.**

$5 - 1 =$ _____
Difference

**4.**

$4 - 3 =$ _____
Difference

**5.**

$5 - 3 =$ _____
Difference

**6.**

$5 - 2 =$ _____
Difference

Subtraction concept—differences related to sums to 5

Subtract.

1.

$$\begin{array}{r} 5 \\ -\ 2 \\ \hline 3 \end{array}$$

2.

$$\begin{array}{r} 4 \\ -\ 1 \\ \hline 3 \end{array}$$

3.

$$\begin{array}{r} 3 \\ -\ 2 \\ \hline \end{array}$$

4.

$$\begin{array}{r} 4 \\ -\ 2 \\ \hline \end{array}$$

5.

$$\begin{array}{r} 5 \\ -\ 1 \\ \hline \end{array}$$

6.

$$\begin{array}{r} 5 \\ -\ 3 \\ \hline \end{array}$$

7.

$$\begin{array}{r} 4 \\ -\ 3 \\ \hline \end{array}$$

8.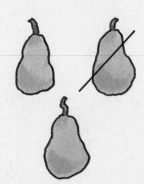

$$\begin{array}{r} 3 \\ -\ 1 \\ \hline \end{array}$$

Subtraction concept—differences related to sums to 5

Name _____

Use the pictures. Subtract.

1.  5 − 3 = _2_        3 − 1 = ___        4 − 1 = ___

2.  5 − 4 = ___        4 − 2 = ___        5 − 2 = ___

3.  3 − 3 = ___        2 − 1 = ___        5 − 1 = ___

4.  4 − 3 = ___        4 − 0 = ___        3 − 2 = ___

Find the differences.

5.  3 − 1 = ___        5 − 1 = ___        5 − 0 = ___

6.  2 − 0 = ___        1 − 1 = ___        0 − 0 = ___

7.  4 − 1 = ___        3 − 2 = ___        5 − 5 = ___

8.  5 − 2 = ___        2 − 2 = ___        3 − 0 = ___

9.  4 − 4 = ___        2 − 1 = ___        4 − 3 = ___

Subtraction concept—differences related to sums to 5        (seventeen)  17

Cross out and subtract.

1.
$$5 - 2 = \underset{\text{(3)}}{}$$     $$3 - 3$$     $$4 - 2$$     $$5 - 3$$

2.
$$5 - 1$$     $$4 - 1$$     $$3 - 1$$     $$4 - 3$$

Find the differences.

3.
$$5 - 4$$     $$5 - 1$$     $$3 - 1$$     $$4 - 1$$     $$4 - 2$$     $$4 - 3$$

4.
$$4 - 2$$     $$2 - 2$$     $$3 - 2$$     $$5 - 5$$     $$4 - 1$$     $$5 - 4$$

5.
$$5 - 1$$     $$5 - 3$$     $$4 - 2$$     $$4 - 3$$     $$2 - 1$$     $$3 - 2$$

## SKILLKEEPER

Add.

$$8 + 1$$     $$5 + 3$$     $$4 + 2$$     $$7 + 3$$     $$3 + 4$$     $$3 + 3$$

Subtraction concept—differences related to sums to 5

6 − 1 = 5

7 − 2 = 5

Subtract.

0  1  2  3  4  5  6  7  8  9  10  11  12

1.  6 − 1 = ___        3 − 2 = ___        7 − 2 = ___

2.  4 − 1 = ___        11 − 2 = ___       8 − 1 = ___

3.  2 − 2 = ___        9 − 1 = ___        5 − 2 = ___

4.  3 − 1 = ___        4 − 2 = ___        10 − 2 = ___

5.  6 − 2 = ___        9 − 2 = ___        1 − 1 = ___

6.  7 − 1 = ___        10 − 1 = ___       4 − 1 = ___

7.  2 − 1 = ___        8 − 2 = ___        5 − 1 = ___

8.  1 − 1 = ___        10 − 2 = ___       6 − 2 = ___

Subtracting 1 and 2—counting back

Subtract.

1.
$$8 - 1$$  $$6 - 2$$  $$10 - 2$$  $$7 - 1$$

2.
$$6 - 2$$  $$5 - 1$$  $$9 - 1$$  $$5 - 2$$

3.
$$8 - 2$$  $$7 - 1$$  $$10 - 1$$  $$8 - 1$$  $$7 - 2$$  $$9 - 2$$

4.
$$5 - 1$$  $$10 - 2$$  $$8 - 1$$  $$2 - 2$$  $$11 - 2$$  $$5 - 2$$

5.
$$6 - 1$$  $$7 - 1$$  $$7 - 2$$  $$9 - 1$$  $$4 - 2$$  $$8 - 2$$

---

## THINK MATH

What number was subtracted?

$$9 - \boxed{\phantom{0}} = 8$$    $$7 - \boxed{\phantom{0}} = 5$$    $$8 - \boxed{\phantom{0}} = 6$$    $$6 - \boxed{\phantom{0}} = 5$$

Practice the facts

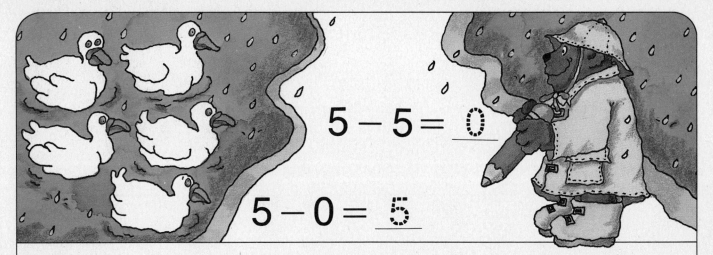

$$5 - 5 = \underline{0}$$

$$5 - 0 = \underline{5}$$

Subtract.

1. $4 - 0 = \underline{\phantom{0}}$  $\qquad$  $3 - 3 = \underline{\phantom{0}}$  $\qquad$  $1 - 0 = \underline{\phantom{0}}$

2. $9 - 9 = \underline{\phantom{0}}$  $\qquad$  $6 - 0 = \underline{\phantom{0}}$  $\qquad$  $7 - 7 = \underline{\phantom{0}}$

3. $8 - 0 = \underline{\phantom{0}}$  $\qquad$  $2 - 0 = \underline{\phantom{0}}$  $\qquad$  $0 - 0 = \underline{\phantom{0}}$

Find the differences.

4.
$$\begin{array}{r} 7 \\ -2 \\ \hline \end{array} \qquad \begin{array}{r} 8 \\ -1 \\ \hline \end{array} \qquad \begin{array}{r} 6 \\ -6 \\ \hline \end{array} \qquad \begin{array}{r} 9 \\ -3 \\ \hline \end{array} \qquad \begin{array}{r} 9 \\ -9 \\ \hline \end{array} \qquad \begin{array}{r} 10 \\ -1 \\ \hline \end{array}$$

5.
$$\begin{array}{r} 10 \\ -3 \\ \hline \end{array} \qquad \begin{array}{r} 6 \\ -2 \\ \hline \end{array} \qquad \begin{array}{r} 7 \\ -0 \\ \hline \end{array} \qquad \begin{array}{r} 10 \\ -10 \\ \hline \end{array} \qquad \begin{array}{r} 8 \\ -0 \\ \hline \end{array} \qquad \begin{array}{r} 12 \\ -3 \\ \hline \end{array}$$

6.
$$\begin{array}{r} 11 \\ -2 \\ \hline \end{array} \qquad \begin{array}{r} 7 \\ -0 \\ \hline \end{array} \qquad \begin{array}{r} 8 \\ -3 \\ \hline \end{array} \qquad \begin{array}{r} 8 \\ -8 \\ \hline \end{array} \qquad \begin{array}{r} 9 \\ -0 \\ \hline \end{array} \qquad \begin{array}{r} 11 \\ -3 \\ \hline \end{array}$$

Zero in subtraction

Ring the names for
the number on top.

5

7 − 2
8 − 2
9 − 3
6 − 1

6

(8 − 2)
10 − 3
9 − 3
7 − 2

7

9 − 2
10 − 2
8 − 1
7 − 1

8

2 + 6
8 + 0
7 + 2

8

8 − 1
10 − 2
9 − 1
8 − 0

9

0 + 9
8 + 2
3 + 6
7 + 2

10

7 + 3
3 + 5
9 + 0
2 + 8

Different names for the same number

Name _____

Add or subtract.

1.
$$\begin{array}{r} 6 \\ +2 \\ \hline \end{array}$$
$$\begin{array}{r} 3 \\ +6 \\ \hline \end{array}$$
$$\begin{array}{r} 3 \\ +7 \\ \hline \end{array}$$
$$\begin{array}{r} 1 \\ +6 \\ \hline \end{array}$$

2.
$$\begin{array}{r} 9 \\ -2 \\ \hline \end{array}$$
$$\begin{array}{r} 10 \\ -1 \\ \hline \end{array}$$
$$\begin{array}{r} 6 \\ -2 \\ \hline \end{array}$$
$$\begin{array}{r} 9 \\ -3 \\ \hline \end{array}$$
$$\begin{array}{r} 8 \\ -2 \\ \hline \end{array}$$
$$\begin{array}{r} 7 \\ -3 \\ \hline \end{array}$$

3.
$$\begin{array}{r} 3 \\ +3 \\ \hline \end{array}$$
$$\begin{array}{r} 6 \\ -3 \\ \hline \end{array}$$
$$\begin{array}{r} 6 \\ +3 \\ \hline \end{array}$$
$$\begin{array}{r} 8 \\ -2 \\ \hline \end{array}$$
$$\begin{array}{r} 10 \\ -3 \\ \hline \end{array}$$
$$\begin{array}{r} 3 \\ +5 \\ \hline \end{array}$$

4.
$$\begin{array}{r} 11 \\ -2 \\ \hline \end{array}$$
$$\begin{array}{r} 3 \\ +4 \\ \hline \end{array}$$
$$\begin{array}{r} 12 \\ -3 \\ \hline \end{array}$$
$$\begin{array}{r} 3 \\ +8 \\ \hline \end{array}$$
$$\begin{array}{r} 10 \\ -2 \\ \hline \end{array}$$
$$\begin{array}{r} 2 \\ +7 \\ \hline \end{array}$$

5.
$$\begin{array}{r} 3 \\ +5 \\ \hline \end{array}$$
$$\begin{array}{r} 8 \\ -0 \\ \hline \end{array}$$
$$\begin{array}{r} 6 \\ +0 \\ \hline \end{array}$$
$$\begin{array}{r} 7 \\ -2 \\ \hline \end{array}$$
$$\begin{array}{r} 9 \\ -3 \\ \hline \end{array}$$
$$\begin{array}{r} 5 \\ +2 \\ \hline \end{array}$$

## THINK MATH

What is her name?
It has five letters.
It ends with y.

Sleepy

Softy

Snobby

Fluff

Practice the facts

(twenty-five)  **25**

**1.** Add to finish the flowers.

**2.** Subtract to finish the flowers.

**3.** Try making your own flowers.

Practice the facts

Name _____

**1.** Write the number.

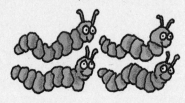   

_____     _____     _____     _____

Add or subtract.

**2.** $3 + 2 =$ _____     $2 + 2 =$ _____     $0 + 3 =$ _____

**3.**
$$\begin{array}{cc} 5 \\ +2 \\ \hline \end{array} \quad \begin{array}{cc} 7 \\ +1 \\ \hline \end{array} \quad \begin{array}{cc} 6 \\ +3 \\ \hline \end{array} \quad \begin{array}{cc} 9 \\ +2 \\ \hline \end{array} \quad \begin{array}{cc} 8 \\ +1 \\ \hline \end{array} \quad \begin{array}{cc} 4 \\ +3 \\ \hline \end{array}$$

**4.**
$$\begin{array}{cc} 3 \\ -1 \\ \hline \end{array} \quad \begin{array}{cc} 5 \\ -4 \\ \hline \end{array} \quad \begin{array}{cc} 4 \\ -2 \\ \hline \end{array} \quad \begin{array}{cc} 3 \\ -3 \\ \hline \end{array} \quad \begin{array}{cc} 1 \\ -0 \\ \hline \end{array} \quad \begin{array}{cc} 5 \\ -1 \\ \hline \end{array}$$

**5.**
$$\begin{array}{cc} 11 \\ -2 \\ \hline \end{array} \quad \begin{array}{cc} 8 \\ -3 \\ \hline \end{array} \quad \begin{array}{cc} 9 \\ -1 \\ \hline \end{array} \quad \begin{array}{cc} 7 \\ -2 \\ \hline \end{array} \quad \begin{array}{cc} 10 \\ -2 \\ \hline \end{array} \quad \begin{array}{cc} 11 \\ -3 \\ \hline \end{array}$$

**6.** Solve.

Bill has 3 kites.

Sara has 2 kites.

How many kites is this in all?

_____ kites

Name _____

# CUMULATIVE REVIEW

**How many are there?**

1.
   - ○ 1
   - ● 2
   - ○ 3

2.
   - ○ 7
   - ○ 8
   - ○ 9

3.
   - ○ four
   - ○ three
   - ○ one

4.
   - ○ four
   - ○ three
   - ○ one

**Add or subtract.**

5.
$$6 + 3$$
   - ○ 3
   - ○ 12
   - ○ 9

6.
$$9 + 2$$
   - ○ 11
   - ○ 10
   - ○ 7

7.
$$5 - 1$$
   - ○ 4
   - ○ 6
   - ○ 7

8.
$$9 - 3$$
   - ○ 3
   - ○ 5
   - ○ 6

9. **Solve.**

   Doug had 8 flowers.

   He gave away 2.

   How many does he have now?

   - ○ 6
   - ○ 7
   - ○ 8

# ANOTHER LOOK

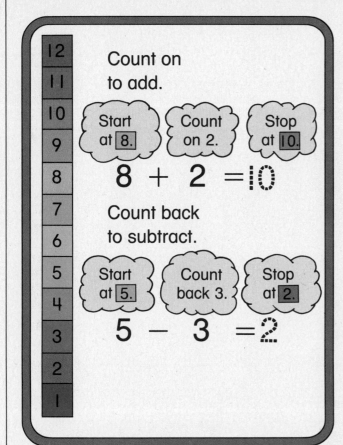

Count on to add.

Start at 8.    Count on 2.    Stop at 10.

8 + 2 = 10

Count back to subtract.

Start at 5.    Count back 3.    Stop at 2.

5 − 3 = 2

Add.

**1.**

Count on →

|  5  |  6  |  9  |
|-----|-----|-----|
| + 2 | + 2 | + 3 |
|  7  |     |     |

**2.**

| 4 | 8 | 7 |
|-----|-----|-----|
| + 3 | + 3 | + 2 |

Subtract.

**3.**

Count back →

|  7  |  9  | 10  |
|-----|-----|-----|
| − 2 | − 3 | − 1 |
|  5  |     |     |

**4.**

| 10 | 11 | 8 |
|-----|-----|-----|
| − 2 | − 3 | − 3 |

Add or subtract.

**5.**

| 4 | 7 | 5 | 5 | 2 | 6 |
|-----|-----|-----|-----|-----|-----|
| +2 | +2 | +2 | +0 | +3 | +2 |

**6.**

| 7 | 10 | 8 | 6 | 11 | 10 |
|-----|-----|-----|-----|-----|-----|
| −3 | −2 | −3 | −1 | −3 | −3 |

**7.**

| 3 | 8 | 5 | 10 | 4 | 9 |
|-----|-----|-----|-----|-----|-----|
| +5 | −2 | +3 | −3 | +2 | −3 |

# ENRICHMENT

Give the missing signs, + or −.

1. $5 \oplus 3 = 8$     $7 \ominus 3 = 4$     $4 \oplus 2 = 6$

2. $10 \bigcirc 2 = 8$     $9 \bigcirc 2 = 7$     $2 \bigcirc 7 = 9$

3. $7 \bigcirc 3 = 10$     $3 \bigcirc 3 = 0$     $8 \bigcirc 3 = 5$

4. $9 \bigcirc 3 = 6$     $12 \bigcirc 3 = 9$     $3 \bigcirc 6 = 9$

5. $4 \bigcirc 3 = 7$     $9 \bigcirc 2 = 11$     $10 \bigcirc 3 = 7$

Give the missing signs.
= is equal to
≠ is not equal to

6. $6 + 3 \bigcirc= 9$     $5 - 1 \bigcirc\neq 6$     $8 - 3 \bigcirc\neq 4$

7. $10 - 2 \bigcirc 7$     $8 + 2 \bigcirc 10$     $4 + 2 \bigcirc 6$

8. $9 - 2 \bigcirc 7$     $3 + 9 \bigcirc 11$     $5 + 0 \bigcirc 6$

9. $7 - 2 \bigcirc 4$     $4 - 1 \bigcirc 3$     $8 - 2 \bigcirc 6$

10. $3 + 5 \bigcirc 8$     $7 + 3 \bigcirc 10$     $10 - 2 \bigcirc 8$

Name _____

# PLACE VALUE AND COUNTING

Count the tens. Say the word.

 I ten
ten

 3 tens
That is
thirty.

 2 tens
twenty

 3 tens
thirty

 4 tens
forty

 5 tens
fifty

 6 tens
sixty

 7 tens
seventy

 8 tens
eighty

 9 tens
ninety

How many tens are there?

1. forty = _____ tens         sixty = _____ tens         seventy = _____ tens

2. thirty = _____ tens         eighty = _____ tens         twenty = _____ tens

3. seventy = _____ tens         fifty = _____ tens         ten = _____ ten

4. ninety = _____ tens         twenty = _____ tens         forty = _____ tens

Decade names

Color to match.

1.
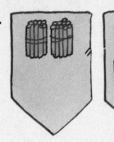     

eighty    forty    twenty    sixty    seventy    thirty

2.

forty    seventy    twenty    ninety    fifty    eighty

2 tens    4 tens    7 tens    5 tens    8 tens    9 tens

Give the word.

3.  3 tens = ___thirty___          6 tens = _____

4.  5 tens = _____          2 tens = _____

5.  8 tens = _____          4 tens = _____

Name _____

___2___ tens and ___3___ ones = __23__     ___3___ tens and ___2___ ones = __32__

## How many are there?

**1.**

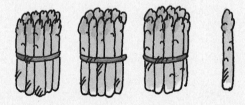

_____ tens and _____ ones

**2.**

_____ tens and _____ ones

**3.**

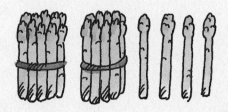

_____ tens and _____ one

**4.**

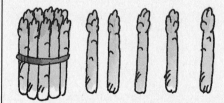

_____ ten and _____ ones

**5.**

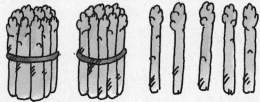

_____ tens and _____ ones

**6.**

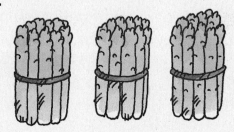

_____ tens and _____ ones

**1.** How many are there? Ring tens.

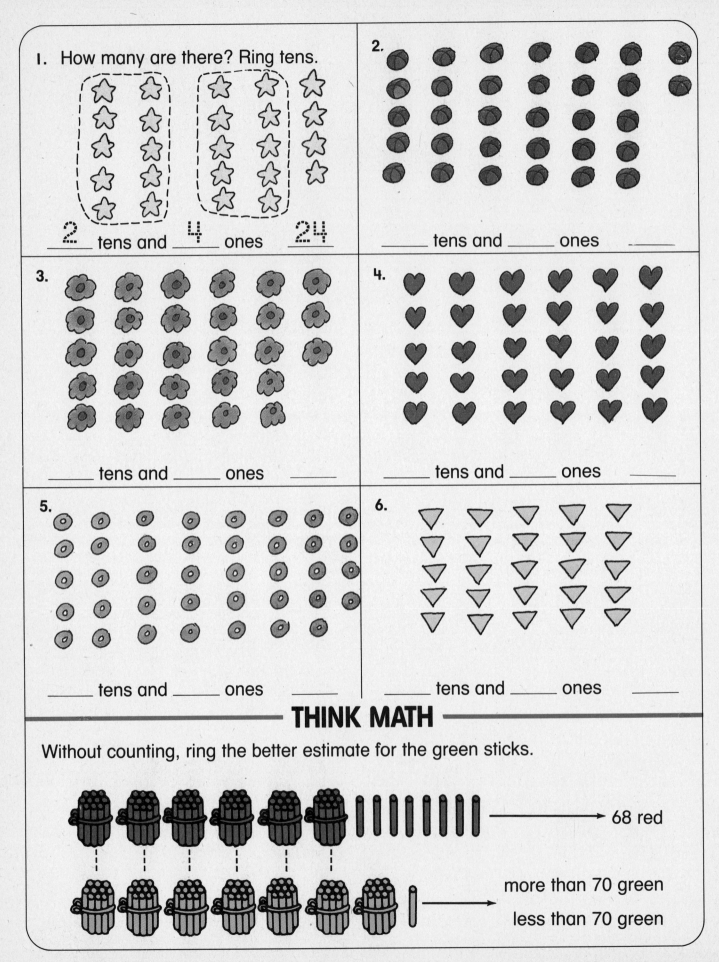

__2__ tens and __4__ ones   __24__

**2.** _____ tens and _____ ones _____

**3.** _____ tens and _____ ones

**4.** _____ tens and _____ ones _____

**5.** _____ tens and _____ ones _____

**6.** _____ tens and _____ ones _____

## THINK MATH

Without counting, ring the better estimate for the green sticks.

⟶ 68 red

more than 70 green

less than 70 green

Two-digit place value

Name _____

**1. What does the red digit mean?**

( 7 tens ) 7 ones

**2.**

3 tens        3 ones

**3.**

4 tens        4 ones

**4.**

8 tens        8 ones

**5.**

5 tens        5 ones

**6.**

2 tens        2 ones

**7.**

2 tens        2 ones

**8.**

3 tens        3 ones

**9.**

1 ten        1 one

**10.**

2 tens        2 ones

**11.**

2 tens        2 ones

**12.**

3 tens        3 ones

Place value understanding

(thirty-seven) **37**

How many are there?

**1.**

__2__ tens

__4__ ones

__24__ In all

**2.**

__3__ tens

__2__ ones

__32__ In all

**3.**

__2__ tens

__3__ ones

__23__ In all

**4.**

_____ tens

_____ ones

_____ In all

**5.**

_____ tens

_____ ones

_____ In all

**6.**

_____ tens

_____ ones

_____ In all

**7.**

_____ tens

_____ ones

_____ In all

**8.**

_____ tens

_____ ones

_____ In all

**9.**

_____ tens

_____ ones

_____ In all

## SKILLKEEPER

Add or subtract.

$$5 + 3$$  $$9 - 3$$  $$3 + 7$$  $$8 - 1$$  $$2 - 0$$  $$6 + 2$$

Place value understanding

Write how many there are.
Then read the name.

There are 23 in all.

23
twenty-three

**1.**

32
thirty-two

**2.**

_____
twenty-four

**3.**

_____
forty-one

**4.**

_____
fifty-two

**5.**

_____
twenty-two

**6.**

_____
forty-three

**7.**

_____
thirty-one

**8.**

_____
thirty-four

**9.**

_____
fifty-one

Number names

**1. Color to match.**

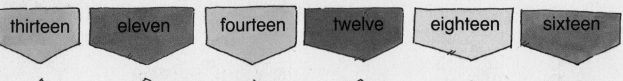

| thirteen | eleven | fourteen | twelve | eighteen | sixteen |

| 11 | 14 | 13 | 16 | 12 | 18 |

Write the number.

2. twenty-six  _26_        forty-eight  _____        thirty-seven  _____

3. fifty-eight  _____        eighty-three  _____        sixty-four  _____

4. ninety-three  _____        fifty-one  _____        eighty-nine  _____

5. seventy-two  _____        forty-four  _____        ninety-five  _____

6. fifty-seven  _____        eighty-four  _____        seventy-six  _____

7. thirty-three  _____        twenty-eight  _____        sixty-one  _____

## SKILLKEEPER

Add or subtract.

$$\begin{array}{r} 7 \\ +3 \\ \hline \end{array} \qquad \begin{array}{r} 12 \\ -3 \\ \hline \end{array} \qquad \begin{array}{r} 9 \\ +2 \\ \hline \end{array} \qquad \begin{array}{r} 6 \\ +2 \\ \hline \end{array} \qquad \begin{array}{r} 10 \\ -2 \\ \hline \end{array} \qquad \begin{array}{r} 7 \\ -3 \\ \hline \end{array}$$

Number names

Name _____

Dimes and pennies are like tens and ones.

I penny     I dime

I cent
I¢

10 cents
10¢

 10 ones    same as    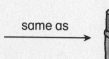 I ten

 10 pennies    same as     I dime

---

## How many are there?

1.

| Tens | Ones |
|------|------|
|      |      |

_____24_____

## How much money is there?

2.

| Dimes | Pennies |
|-------|---------|
|       |         |

_____24_____ ¢

---

3.

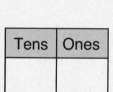

| Tens | Ones |
|------|------|
|      |      |

_____

4.

| Dimes | Pennies |
|-------|---------|
|       |         |

_____ ¢

---

z

2-digit numbers—dimes and pennies

z

(forty-one) 41

# How much money is there?

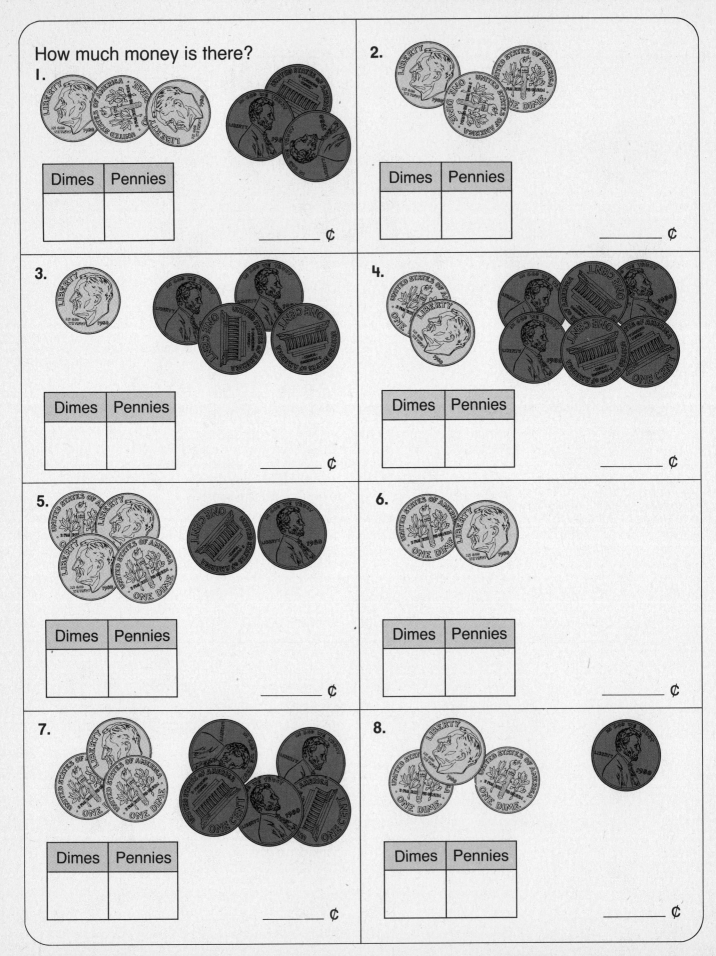

1.

| Dimes | Pennies |
|-------|---------|
|       |         |

_____ ¢

2.

| Dimes | Pennies |
|-------|---------|
|       |         |

_____ ¢

3.

| Dimes | Pennies |
|-------|---------|
|       |         |

_____ ¢

4.

| Dimes | Pennies |
|-------|---------|
|       |         |

_____ ¢

5.

| Dimes | Pennies |
|-------|---------|
|       |         |

_____ ¢

6.

| Dimes | Pennies |
|-------|---------|
|       |         |

_____ ¢

7.

| Dimes | Pennies |
|-------|---------|
|       |         |

_____ ¢

8.

| Dimes | Pennies |
|-------|---------|
|       |         |

_____ ¢

2-digit numerals—dimes and pennies

32

33
One more

29

30
One more

When you count by ones,
the **next** number after 32 is 33.

32, 33

When you count by ones,
the **next** number after 29 is 30.

29, 30

Draw one more. Write the number.

**1.**

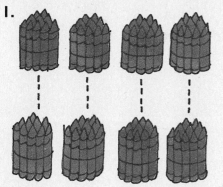

40

41

40, _____

**2.**

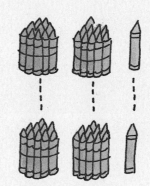

21

21, _____

**3.**

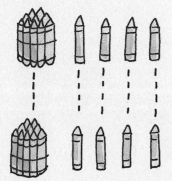

14

14, _____

**4.**

23

23, _____

Give the number that is one more.

1. 44, <u>45</u>     28, ___     49, ___

2. 37, ___     69, ___     51, ___

3. 96, ___     80, ___     56, ___     19, ___

4. 87, ___     79, ___     76, ___     89, ___

Give the number that comes next.

5. 23, 24, 25, 26, <u>27</u>     38, 39, 40, 41, ___

6. 16, 17, 18, 19, ___     60, 61, 62, 63, ___

7. 84, 85, 86, 87, ___     92, 93, 94, 95, ___

8. 76, 77, 78, 79, ___     27, 28, 29, 30, ___

## THINK MATH

Jim is in front.
Jan is in front of Peg.
Who is in the middle?

_____

Counting—one more

Name _____

39

| 39 | **40**<br>After | **27**<br>Before | 28 |

---

## Give the page that comes **after**.

1.  53    _____<br>After

2.  49    _____<br>After

3.  85    _____<br>After

4.  79    _____<br>After

5.  23    _____<br>After

## Give the page that comes **before**.

6. _____<br>Before     48

7. _____<br>Before    60

8. _____<br>Before     36

9. _____<br>Before    78

10. _____<br>Before     18

Counting—after and before

**1. What number comes after?**

37, ___

56, ___

49, ___

70, ___

69, ___

57, ___

30, ___

89, ___

19, ___

54, ___

**2. What number comes before?**

___, 26

___, 67

___, 40

___, 25

___, 88

___, 70

___, 65

___, 10

___, 28

___, 80

**3. What number comes between?**

26, ___, 28

37, ___, 39

39, ___, 41

42, ___, 44

59, ___, 61

93, ___, 95

68, ___, 70

82, ___, 84

29, ___, 31

50, ___, 52

## SKILLKEEPER

Count the pennies.

___ ¢

___ ¢

___ ¢

Counting—before, after, and between

Name _____

Finish each row.

one more  one more  one more  one more  one more  one more  one more  one more

| 0 | 1 | 2 | 3 | | | | | |

| 9 | 10 | 11 | 12 | | | | | |

| 18 | 19 | 20 | | | | | | |

| 27 | 28 | | | | | | | |

| 36 | 37 | | | | | | | |

| 45 | 46 | | | | | | | |

| 54 | 55 | | | | | | | |

Counting on a number line

(forty-seven)  **47**

Complete the table. Finish the counting.

| 1 | 2 | 3 | 4 | 5 | | | | 9 | 10 |
|---|---|---|---|---|---|---|---|---|----|
| 11 | 12 | | | | | | | | |
| 21 | | | | | | | | | 30 |
| | | | 34 | | | | | | |
| | | | | | | 47 | | | |
| 51 | | | | | | | | | |
| | | | | | | | | | 70 |
| | | | | | 76 | | | | |
| | | | | | | | 88 | | |
| | | | | | | | | | 100 |

Color the boxes with

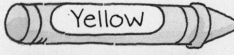

1. 7 in the ones' place    Yellow

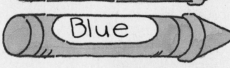

2. 3 in the tens' place    Blue

3. tens' and ones' place the same    Red

What boxes have 2 colors? _____

Name _____

Count on to find how many in all.

**1.**   __32__ cans

**2.**

_____ eggs

**3.**

_____ pennies

**4.**

_____ crayons

**5.**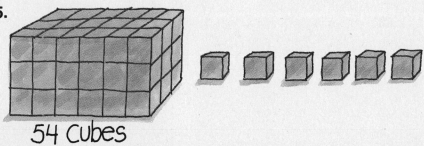

_____ cubes

Counting on

(forty-nine) **49**

Connect the dots. Begin with 27.

## THINK MATH

Ring the correct number.
It comes after 25.
It comes before 45.

48          23

84          32

**1.** Count the pennies. Skip count by 2s.

2 _____ 4 _____ 6 _____ _____ _____ _____ _____

**2.** Skip count by 3s.

3 _____ 6 _____ 9 _____ _____ _____ _____

**3.** Connect the dots. Skip count by 2s.

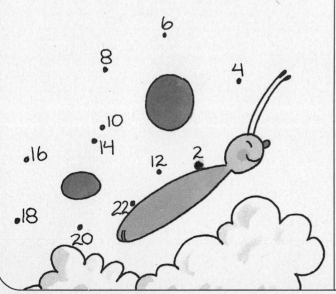

6
8
4
.10
.16 .14 12 2
.18 22
20

**4.** Skip count by 3s.

6•   3•
9•
12•
15•
18•   21
24•

**1.** Skip count by 5s. Color the boxes.

| 1 | 2 | 3 | 4 | 5 | 6 | 7 | 8 | 9 | 10 |
|---|---|---|---|---|---|---|---|---|----|
| 11 | 12 | 13 | 14 | | 16 | 17 | 18 | 19 | |
| 21 | 22 | 23 | 24 | | 26 | 27 | 28 | 29 | |
| 31 | 32 | 33 | 34 | | 36 | 37 | 38 | 39 | |

**2.** A dime is 10 cents. Skip count by 10s.

10   20   30   __   __   __   __   __

---

## SKILLKEEPER

Add or subtract.

$$
\begin{array}{cccccc}
3 & 8 & 5 & 10 & 9 & 2 \\
+7 & -3 & +1 & -2 & -0 & +6 \\
\hline
\end{array}
$$

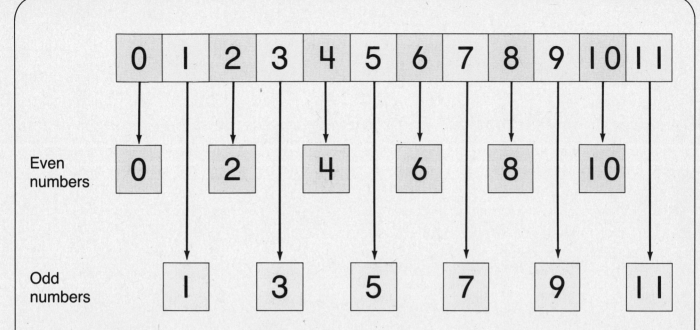

Even numbers

Odd numbers

Finish each row.

1. | 0 | 2 | 4 | 6 | 8 | 10 | 12 | 14 | | | | | |

2. | 1 | 3 | 5 | 7 | | | | | | | | | |

3. | 30 | 32 | 34 | 36 | | | | | | | | | |

4. | 41 | 43 | 45 | 47 | | | | | | | | | |

Even and odd numbers

1. Count on. Use **even** numbers.

60, 62, ___, ___, ___, ___, ___, ___, ___

24, ___, ___, ___, ___, ___, ___, ___, ___

78, ___, ___, ___, ___, ___, ___, ___, ___

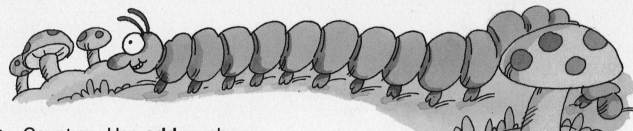

2. Count on. Use **odd** numbers.

27, 29, ___, ___, ___, ___, ___, ___, ___

51, ___, ___, ___, ___, ___, ___, ___, ___

73, ___, ___, ___, ___, ___, ___, ___, ___

3. Put a ring ◯ around the even numbers.
   Put a box ☐ around the odd numbers.

72          25          91          67          6          21

        34              83          58              49

14          26          13          50

Even and odd numbers

Name _____

5 is greater than 3.

$$5 > 3$$

3 is less than 5.

$$3 < 5$$

1. Fill in the blanks.

_6_ is greater than _____.

_____ is less than _____.

_____ > _____

_____ < _____

Put > or < in each ◯.

2. **8 ⊙ 3**
is greater than

**5 ⊙ 7**
is less than

**8 ◯ 7**
is greater than

3. **80 ◯ 30**
is greater than

**50 ◯ 70**
is less than

**80 ◯ 70**
is greater than

4. **28 ◯ 23**
is greater than

**25 ◯ 27**
is less than

**27 ◯ 28**
is less than

5. **86 ◯ 36**

**56 ◯ 76**

**86 ◯ 76**

Put > or < in each ◯.

1. 40 ◯ 20      60 ◯ 30      20 ◯ 70

2. 46 ◯ 26      62 ◯ 32      28 ◯ 78

3. 3 ◯ 8        9 ◯ 4        7 ◯ 2

4. 63 ◯ 68      49 ◯ 44      37 ◯ 32

5. 58 ◯ 61      27 ◯ 32      44 ◯ 39

6. 67 ◯ 59      83 ◯ 69      72 ◯ 58

Fill in the blanks. Use the numbers in the ring.

7. ( 68, 72, 59 )      8. ( 41, 36, 28 )      9. ( 91, 82, 78 )

_59_ , _68_ , _____    _____ , _____ , _____    _____ , _____ , _____
Smallest        Largest   Smallest        Largest   Smallest        Largest

## THINK MATH

Put >, <, or = in each ◯.          Write your own.

6 + 2 ◯ 7 + 1                      5 + 3 = _____

9 + 3 ◯ 9 + 4                      6 + 2 < _____

9 − 3 ◯ 9 − 4                      6 − 2 > _____

first
1st
second
2nd
third
3rd
fourth
4th
fifth
5th
sixth
6th
seventh
7th
eighth
8th
ninth
9th
tenth
10th

**1.** Ring.  third [Red]  sixth [Green]     eighth [Blue]  tenth [Orange]

first                                                                    tenth

**2.** Ring. second [Blue]  fifth [Red]     seventh [Orange]  ninth [Purple]

first                                                                    tenth

Ordinals to tenth

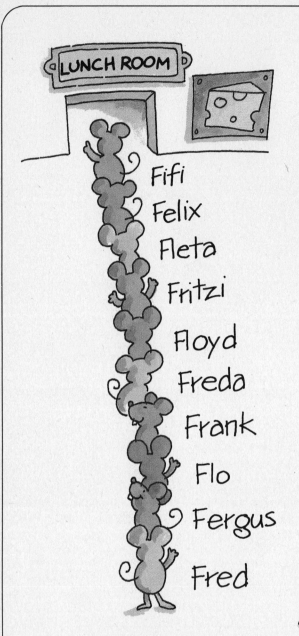

Fifi is first in line.
Who is

1. fifth? _____

2. eighth? _____

3. third? _____

4. ninth? _____

Floyd lives on the first floor.
Ring the floor for

5. Flo      seventh      eight      ninth

6. Frank      first      second      third

7. Fleta      eighth      ninth      tenth

8. Fifi      fifth      sixth      seventh

Ordinals to tenth

How many clowns can you
put in an empty wagon?

Use the code to find the answer.

O  ___  ___ .  ___  ___  ___  ___  ___
fifteenth  fourteenth  fifth  first  sixth  twentieth  fifth  eighteenth

___  ___  ___  ___  ___  ___
twentieth  eighth  first  twentieth  ninth  twentieth

___  ___  ___  ___  ___
ninth  nineteenth  fourteenth  fifteenth  twentieth

___  ___  ___  ___  ___ .
fifth  thirteenth  sixteenth  twentieth  twenty-fifth

Code

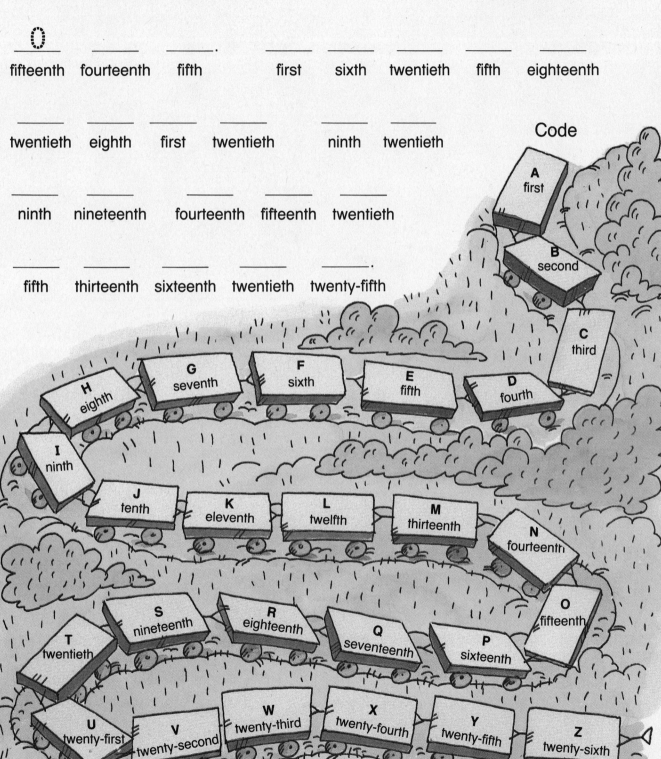

Ordinals to twenty-sixth

## Problem-Solving Strategy

Find all the ways to Grandma's house.

__Red__ road, then __green__ road.

__Red__ road, then _____ road.

_____ road, then _____ road.

_____ road, then _____ road.

Problem solving strategy—make a list

Name _____

## CHAPTER REVIEW/TEST

**1.** How many are there?

| Tens | Ones |
|------|------|
|      |      |

_____

| Tens | Ones |
|------|------|
|      |      |

_____

| Tens | Ones |
|------|------|
|      |      |

_____

**2.** How much money is there?

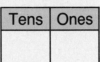

_____ ¢

| Dimes | Pennies |
|-------|---------|
|       |         |

**3.** Give the number.

After                    Before                    Between

39, _____          _____, 56          79, _____, 81

**4.** Finish the row.

26,  27,  _____,  _____,  _____,  _____,  _____,  _____

**5.** Finish the counting.

5, 10, _____, _____          3, 6, _____, _____          10, 20, _____, _____

**6.** Ring the even numbers.

36      72      65      81      90      45      28

**7.** Put > or < in each ◯.

37 ◯ 41          82 ◯ 79          65 ◯ 56

**8.** Ring the 8th and the 13th letters.

A B C D E F G H I J K L M N O P

Name _____

# CUMULATIVE REVIEW

Add.

1.
$$\begin{array}{r} 2 \\ +3 \\ \hline \end{array}$$
○ 1
○ 5
○ 4

2.
$1 + 4 =$
○ 5
○ 3
○ 2

3.
$9 + 3 =$
○ 12
○ 0
○ 10

4.
$$\begin{array}{r} 6 \\ +3 \\ \hline \end{array}$$
○ 11
○ 3
○ 9

Subtract.

5.
$$\begin{array}{r} 4 \\ -0 \\ \hline \end{array}$$
○ 4
○ 3
○ 5

6.
$$\begin{array}{r} 5 \\ -4 \\ \hline \end{array}$$
○ 9
○ 3
○ 1

7.
$$\begin{array}{r} 12 \\ -3 \\ \hline \end{array}$$
○ 11
○ 9
○ 12

8.
$$\begin{array}{r} 11 \\ -2 \\ \hline \end{array}$$
○ 10
○ 8
○ 9

9. Solve.

Rosalie planted 8 carrots.

Jasper planted 3 carrots.

How many carrots did they

plant in all?

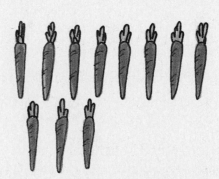

○ 13

○ 11

○ 5

# ANOTHER LOOK

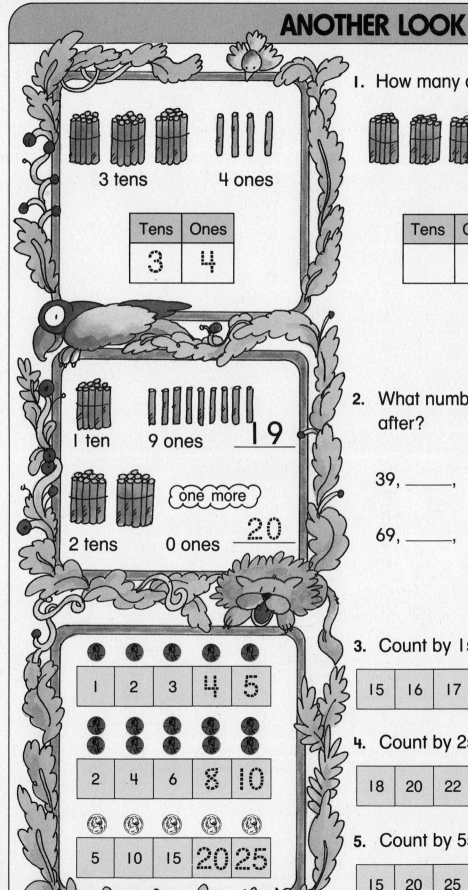

3 tens      4 ones

| Tens | Ones |
|------|------|
| 3    | 4    |

1 ten      9 ones      19

one more

2 tens      0 ones      20

| 1 | 2 | 3 | 4 | 5 |
|---|---|---|---|---|

| 2 | 4 | 6 | 8 | 10 |
|---|---|---|---|---|

| 5 | 10 | 15 | 20 | 25 |
|---|----|----|----|----|

**1.** How many are there?

| Tens | Ones |
|------|------|
|      |      |

**2.** What number comes after?

39, _____,     49, _____,     59, _____

69, _____,     79, _____,     89, _____

**3.** Count by 1s.

| 15 | 16 | 17 |  |  |  |  |
|----|----|----|--|--|--|--|

**4.** Count by 2s.

| 18 | 20 | 22 |  |  |  |  |
|----|----|----|--|--|--|--|

**5.** Count by 5s.

| 15 | 20 | 25 |  |  |  |  |
|----|----|----|--|--|--|--|

# ENRICHMENT

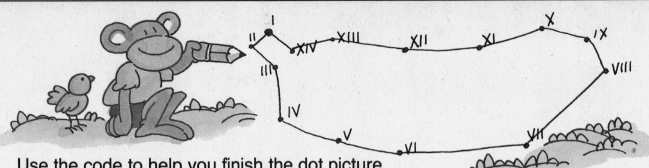

Use the code to help you finish the dot picture.
This code uses Roman numerals.

| | |
|---|---|
| 1 | I |
| 2 | II |
| 3 | III |
| 4 | IV |
| 5 | V |
| 6 | VI |
| 7 | VII |
| 8 | VIII |
| 9 | IX |
| 10 | X |
| 11 | XI |
| 12 | XII |
| 13 | XIII |
| 14 | XIV |
| 15 | XV |
| 16 | XVI |
| 17 | XVII |
| 18 | XVIII |
| 19 | XIX |
| 20 | XX |

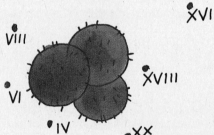

**3**  Name _____

Find the sums.

**1.**

$2 + 2 = \underline{\quad}$

**2.** These are doubles.

$3 + 3 = \underline{\quad}$

**3.**
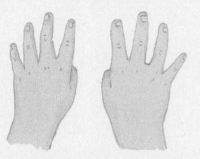

$4 + 4 = \underline{\quad}$

**4.**

$5 + 5 = \underline{\quad}$

Add.

**5.**  $3 + 3 = \underline{\quad}$     $2 + 2 = \underline{\quad}$     $1 + 1 = \underline{\quad}$

**6.**  $5 + 5 = \underline{\quad}$     $4 + 4 = \underline{\quad}$     $0 + 0 = \underline{\quad}$

**7.**
$$\begin{array}{r} 3 \\ +3 \\ \hline \end{array} \qquad \begin{array}{r} 1 \\ +1 \\ \hline \end{array} \qquad \begin{array}{r} 4 \\ +4 \\ \hline \end{array} \qquad \begin{array}{r} 0 \\ +0 \\ \hline \end{array} \qquad \begin{array}{r} 2 \\ +2 \\ \hline \end{array} \qquad \begin{array}{r} 5 \\ +5 \\ \hline \end{array}$$

**8.**
$$\begin{array}{r} 4 \\ +4 \\ \hline \end{array} \qquad \begin{array}{r} 0 \\ +0 \\ \hline \end{array} \qquad \begin{array}{r} 2 \\ +2 \\ \hline \end{array} \qquad \begin{array}{r} 5 \\ +5 \\ \hline \end{array} \qquad \begin{array}{r} 1 \\ +1 \\ \hline \end{array} \qquad \begin{array}{r} 3 \\ +3 \\ \hline \end{array}$$

Doubles—2, 3, 4, 5

Add.

1.
$$\begin{array}{r} 0 \\ +\,0 \\ \hline \end{array}\qquad \begin{array}{r} 1 \\ +\,1 \\ \hline \end{array}\qquad \begin{array}{r} 2 \\ +\,2 \\ \hline \end{array}\qquad \begin{array}{r} 3 \\ +\,3 \\ \hline \end{array}\qquad \begin{array}{r} 4 \\ +\,4 \\ \hline \end{array}$$

2.  $5 + 5 =$ ____     $2 + 2 =$ ____     $4 + 4 =$ ____

3.  $1 + 1 =$ ____     $0 + 0 =$ ____     $3 + 3 =$ ____

Find the sums. Ring doubles.

4.
$$\left(\begin{array}{r} 4 \\ +\,4 \\ \hline \end{array}\right)\quad \begin{array}{r} 5 \\ +\,2 \\ \hline \end{array}\quad \begin{array}{r} 8 \\ +\,3 \\ \hline \end{array}\quad \begin{array}{r} 1 \\ +\,1 \\ \hline \end{array}\quad \begin{array}{r} 3 \\ +\,3 \\ \hline \end{array}\quad \begin{array}{r} 3 \\ +\,7 \\ \hline \end{array}$$

5.
$$\begin{array}{r} 5 \\ +\,5 \\ \hline \end{array}\quad \begin{array}{r} 2 \\ +\,9 \\ \hline \end{array}\quad \begin{array}{r} 0 \\ +\,0 \\ \hline \end{array}\quad \begin{array}{r} 1 \\ +\,7 \\ \hline \end{array}\quad \begin{array}{r} 6 \\ +\,2 \\ \hline \end{array}\quad \begin{array}{r} 2 \\ +\,2 \\ \hline \end{array}$$

6.
$$\begin{array}{r} 4 \\ +\,3 \\ \hline \end{array}\quad \begin{array}{r} 2 \\ +\,2 \\ \hline \end{array}\quad \begin{array}{r} 5 \\ +\,1 \\ \hline \end{array}\quad \begin{array}{r} 2 \\ +\,6 \\ \hline \end{array}\quad \begin{array}{r} 5 \\ +\,5 \\ \hline \end{array}\quad \begin{array}{r} 7 \\ +\,2 \\ \hline \end{array}$$

## THINK MATH

Jan needs 1 more penny to have 50 cents.
How much does she have now?

_____ cents

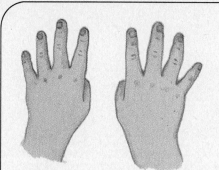

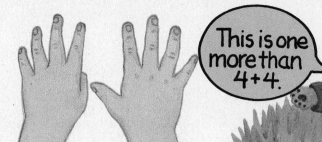

$4 + 4 = \underline{8} \rightarrow 4 + 5 = \underline{9}$

**Add.**

1. 
$$\begin{array}{r} 3 \\ +3 \\ \hline \end{array} \rightarrow \begin{array}{r} 3 \\ +4 \\ \hline \end{array}$$

2. 
$$\begin{array}{r} 5 \\ +5 \\ \hline \end{array} \rightarrow \begin{array}{r} 5 \\ +6 \\ \hline \end{array}$$

3. 
$$\begin{array}{r} 2 \\ +2 \\ \hline \end{array} \rightarrow \begin{array}{r} 2 \\ +3 \\ \hline \end{array}$$

4. 
$$\begin{array}{r} 4 \\ +4 \\ \hline \end{array} \rightarrow \begin{array}{r} 5 \\ +4 \\ \hline \end{array}$$

**Add.**

5. 
$$\begin{array}{r} 4 \\ +4 \\ \hline \end{array} \quad \begin{array}{r} 4 \\ +5 \\ \hline \end{array} \quad \begin{array}{r} 2 \\ +2 \\ \hline \end{array} \quad \begin{array}{r} 3 \\ +2 \\ \hline \end{array} \quad \begin{array}{r} 5 \\ +5 \\ \hline \end{array} \quad \begin{array}{r} 5 \\ +6 \\ \hline \end{array}$$

6. 
$$\begin{array}{r} 3 \\ +3 \\ \hline \end{array} \quad \begin{array}{r} 4 \\ +3 \\ \hline \end{array} \quad \begin{array}{r} 5 \\ +5 \\ \hline \end{array} \quad \begin{array}{r} 6 \\ +5 \\ \hline \end{array} \quad \begin{array}{r} 1 \\ +1 \\ \hline \end{array} \quad \begin{array}{r} 2 \\ +1 \\ \hline \end{array}$$

7. 
$$\begin{array}{r} 2 \\ +3 \\ \hline \end{array} \quad \begin{array}{r} 4 \\ +5 \\ \hline \end{array} \quad \begin{array}{r} 5 \\ +6 \\ \hline \end{array} \quad \begin{array}{r} 3 \\ +4 \\ \hline \end{array} \quad \begin{array}{r} 1 \\ +2 \\ \hline \end{array} \quad \begin{array}{r} 6 \\ +5 \\ \hline \end{array}$$

Doubles plus one

Add.

1.
$$2 + 1$$    $$4 + 4$$    $$3 + 2$$    $$5 + 5$$    $$2 + 2$$    $$4 + 5$$

2.
$$3 + 3$$    $$1 + 3$$    $$7 + 2$$    $$2 + 6$$    $$3 + 4$$    $$4 + 1$$

3.
$$2 + 2$$    $$3 + 1$$    $$2 + 3$$    $$5 + 4$$    $$4 + 3$$    $$5 + 6$$

4.
$$2 + 5$$    $$5 + 5$$    $$5 + 4$$    $$1 + 2$$    $$1 + 4$$    $$5 + 5$$

5.
$$6 + 3$$    $$7 + 2$$    $$4 + 3$$    $$3 + 3$$    $$1 + 8$$    $$2 + 2$$

6.
$$4 + 4$$    $$9 + 0$$    $$5 + 3$$    $$5 + 5$$    $$7 + 1$$    $$5 + 6$$

      Doubles plus one

Name _____

Find the sums.

**1.**

$6 + 6 =$ _____

Here are more doubles.

**2.**

$7 + 7 =$ _____

**3.**

CRAYONS

$8 + 8 =$ _____

**4.**

$9 + 9 =$ _____

Add.

**5.** $5 + 5 =$ _____ $\quad$ $7 + 7 =$ _____ $\quad$ $6 + 6 =$ _____

**6.** $3 + 3 =$ _____ $\quad$ $9 + 9 =$ _____ $\quad$ $8 + 8 =$ _____

**7.**
$$\begin{array}{r}4 \\ +4 \\ \hline\end{array} \qquad \begin{array}{r}8 \\ +8 \\ \hline\end{array} \qquad \begin{array}{r}2 \\ +2 \\ \hline\end{array} \qquad \begin{array}{r}7 \\ +7 \\ \hline\end{array} \qquad \begin{array}{r}6 \\ +6 \\ \hline\end{array} \qquad \begin{array}{r}9 \\ +9 \\ \hline\end{array}$$

**8.**
$$\begin{array}{r}3 \\ +3 \\ \hline\end{array} \qquad \begin{array}{r}8 \\ +8 \\ \hline\end{array} \qquad \begin{array}{r}5 \\ +5 \\ \hline\end{array} \qquad \begin{array}{r}9 \\ +9 \\ \hline\end{array} \qquad \begin{array}{r}4 \\ +4 \\ \hline\end{array} \qquad \begin{array}{r}7 \\ +7 \\ \hline\end{array}$$

Doubles—6, 7, 8, 9

Add.

1.
$$4 + 4$$  $$5 + 5$$  $$6 + 6$$  $$7 + 7$$  $$8 + 8$$  $$9 + 9$$

2.  $8 + 8 =$ ___    $6 + 6 =$ ___    $7 + 7 =$ ___

3.  $9 + 9 =$ ___    $5 + 5 =$ ___    $4 + 4 =$ ___

Find the sums. Ring doubles.

4.
$$7 + 7$$  $$8 + 8$$  $$2 + 8$$  $$9 + 9$$  $$6 + 6$$  $$7 + 3$$

5.
$$9 + 2$$  $$6 + 6$$  $$9 + 9$$  $$3 + 6$$  $$7 + 7$$  $$8 + 8$$

6.
$$6 + 1$$  $$5 + 5$$  $$6 + 5$$  $$4 + 4$$  $$4 + 5$$  $$7 + 3$$

## THINK MATH

Tom spent 7¢.
Ring the things
he bought.

Doubles—6, 7, 8, 9

This is one more than 6+6.

$$6 + 6 = 12 \rightarrow 6 + 7 = 13$$

Add.

**1.** $\begin{array}{r} 5 \\ + 5 \\ \hline 10 \end{array}$ → $\begin{array}{r} 6 \\ + 5 \\ \hline 11 \end{array}$

**2.** $\begin{array}{r} 4 \\ + 4 \\ \hline \end{array}$ → $\begin{array}{r} 4 \\ + 5 \\ \hline \end{array}$

**3.** $\begin{array}{r} 8 \\ + 8 \\ \hline \end{array}$ → $\begin{array}{r} 8 \\ + 9 \\ \hline \end{array}$

**4.** $\begin{array}{r} 7 \\ + 7 \\ \hline \end{array}$ → $\begin{array}{r} 8 \\ + 7 \\ \hline \end{array}$

Add.

**5.** $\begin{array}{r} 4 \\ + 4 \\ \hline \end{array}$ $\begin{array}{r} 5 \\ + 4 \\ \hline \end{array}$ $\begin{array}{r} 8 \\ + 8 \\ \hline \end{array}$ $\begin{array}{r} 9 \\ + 8 \\ \hline \end{array}$ $\begin{array}{r} 5 \\ + 5 \\ \hline \end{array}$ $\begin{array}{r} 5 \\ + 6 \\ \hline \end{array}$

**6.** $\begin{array}{r} 7 \\ + 7 \\ \hline \end{array}$ $\begin{array}{r} 7 \\ + 8 \\ \hline \end{array}$ $\begin{array}{r} 6 \\ + 6 \\ \hline \end{array}$ $\begin{array}{r} 6 \\ + 7 \\ \hline \end{array}$ $\begin{array}{r} 8 \\ + 8 \\ \hline \end{array}$ $\begin{array}{r} 8 \\ + 9 \\ \hline \end{array}$

**7.** $\begin{array}{r} 5 \\ + 6 \\ \hline \end{array}$ $\begin{array}{r} 9 \\ + 8 \\ \hline \end{array}$ $\begin{array}{r} 6 \\ + 7 \\ \hline \end{array}$ $\begin{array}{r} 7 \\ + 8 \\ \hline \end{array}$ $\begin{array}{r} 4 \\ + 5 \\ \hline \end{array}$ $\begin{array}{r} 3 \\ + 4 \\ \hline \end{array}$

More doubles plus one

Color to match.

1.

| 6 + 6 | 6 + 7 | 8 + 8 | 8 + 9 | 7 + 7 | 7 + 8 |

| 16 | 12 | 13 | 14 | 15 | 17 |

Find the sums.

2.
$$
\begin{array}{r} 7 \\ +6 \\ \hline \end{array}
\qquad
\begin{array}{r} 6 \\ +5 \\ \hline \end{array}
\qquad
\begin{array}{r} 5 \\ +5 \\ \hline \end{array}
\qquad
\begin{array}{r} 8 \\ +7 \\ \hline \end{array}
\qquad
\begin{array}{r} 1 \\ +8 \\ \hline \end{array}
\qquad
\begin{array}{r} 2 \\ +3 \\ \hline \end{array}
$$

3.
$$
\begin{array}{r} 8 \\ +8 \\ \hline \end{array}
\qquad
\begin{array}{r} 6 \\ +3 \\ \hline \end{array}
\qquad
\begin{array}{r} 8 \\ +3 \\ \hline \end{array}
\qquad
\begin{array}{r} 6 \\ +5 \\ \hline \end{array}
\qquad
\begin{array}{r} 4 \\ +5 \\ \hline \end{array}
\qquad
\begin{array}{r} 8 \\ +9 \\ \hline \end{array}
$$

4.
$$
\begin{array}{r} 6 \\ +6 \\ \hline \end{array}
\qquad
\begin{array}{r} 9 \\ +9 \\ \hline \end{array}
\qquad
\begin{array}{r} 7 \\ +8 \\ \hline \end{array}
\qquad
\begin{array}{r} 2 \\ +2 \\ \hline \end{array}
\qquad
\begin{array}{r} 6 \\ +7 \\ \hline \end{array}
\qquad
\begin{array}{r} 2 \\ +8 \\ \hline \end{array}
$$

5.
$$
\begin{array}{r} 7 \\ +2 \\ \hline \end{array}
\qquad
\begin{array}{r} 7 \\ +7 \\ \hline \end{array}
\qquad
\begin{array}{r} 5 \\ +6 \\ \hline \end{array}
\qquad
\begin{array}{r} 7 \\ +8 \\ \hline \end{array}
\qquad
\begin{array}{r} 6 \\ +2 \\ \hline \end{array}
\qquad
\begin{array}{r} 9 \\ +2 \\ \hline \end{array}
$$

## SKILLKEEPER

Subtract.

$$
\begin{array}{r} 10 \\ -2 \\ \hline \end{array}
\qquad
\begin{array}{r} 11 \\ -3 \\ \hline \end{array}
\qquad
\begin{array}{r} 9 \\ -3 \\ \hline \end{array}
\qquad
\begin{array}{r} 10 \\ -1 \\ \hline \end{array}
\qquad
\begin{array}{r} 12 \\ -3 \\ \hline \end{array}
\qquad
\begin{array}{r} 8 \\ -1 \\ \hline \end{array}
$$

More doubles plus one

Find the sums.

1.
$$7 + 8$$   $$4 + 4$$   $$9 + 2$$   $$5 + 6$$   $$7 + 7$$

2.
$$6 + 6$$   $$5 + 5$$   $$7 + 6$$   $$3 + 7$$   $$2 + 2$$   $$9 + 9$$

3.
$$7 + 2$$   $$8 + 8$$   $$3 + 8$$   $$5 + 4$$   $$6 + 6$$   $$9 + 1$$

4.
$$8 + 7$$   $$3 + 3$$   $$2 + 6$$   $$5 + 5$$   $$8 + 2$$   $$8 + 8$$

5.
$$9 + 9$$   $$6 + 7$$   $$4 + 4$$   $$3 + 9$$   $$7 + 7$$   $$6 + 5$$

6.

| Add 2. | |
|---|---|
| 8 | 10 |
| 6 | |
| 9 | |
| 5 | |
| 7 | |

7.

| Add 1. | |
|---|---|
| 7 | |
| 9 | |
| 6 | |
| 5 | |
| 8 | |

8.

| Add 3. | |
|---|---|
| 6 | |
| 9 | |
| 5 | |
| 8 | |
| 7 | |

Practice the facts

(seventy-three) 73

What are the children saying?

Add. Use the code.
Write the letter under the answer.

**1.**

$$\begin{array}{r} 6 \\ +0 \\ \hline 6 \end{array} \quad \begin{array}{r} 2 \\ +7 \\ \hline \end{array} \quad \begin{array}{r} 9 \\ +2 \\ \hline \end{array} \quad \begin{array}{r} 2 \\ +6 \\ \hline \end{array}$$

R __ __ __

**2.**

$$\begin{array}{r} 3 \\ +3 \\ \hline \end{array} \quad \begin{array}{r} 4 \\ +5 \\ \hline \end{array} \quad \begin{array}{r} 5 \\ +6 \\ \hline \end{array} \quad \begin{array}{r} 4 \\ +4 \\ \hline \end{array} \quad \begin{array}{r} 6 \\ +7 \\ \hline \end{array} \quad \begin{array}{r} 6 \\ +6 \\ \hline \end{array} \quad \begin{array}{r} 1 \\ +8 \\ \hline \end{array} \quad \begin{array}{r} 9 \\ +8 \\ \hline \end{array} \quad \begin{array}{r} 6 \\ +3 \\ \hline \end{array} \quad \begin{array}{r} 3 \\ +4 \\ \hline \end{array}$$

__ __ __ __ __ __ __ __ __ __ .

**3.**

$$\begin{array}{r} 7 \\ +8 \\ \hline \end{array} \quad \begin{array}{r} 9 \\ +3 \\ \hline \end{array} \quad \begin{array}{r} 7 \\ +7 \\ \hline \end{array} \quad \begin{array}{r} 7 \\ +3 \\ \hline \end{array} \quad \begin{array}{r} 5 \\ +4 \\ \hline \end{array} \quad \begin{array}{r} 7 \\ +6 \\ \hline \end{array} \quad \begin{array}{r} 7 \\ +2 \\ \hline \end{array} \quad \begin{array}{r} 3 \\ +8 \\ \hline \end{array} \quad \begin{array}{r} 5 \\ +3 \\ \hline \end{array}$$

__ __ __ __ __ __ __ __ __

**4.**

$$\begin{array}{r} 3 \\ +6 \\ \hline \end{array} \quad \begin{array}{r} 7 \\ +1 \\ \hline \end{array} \quad \begin{array}{r} 3 \\ +9 \\ \hline \end{array} \quad \begin{array}{r} 8 \\ +8 \\ \hline \end{array} \quad \begin{array}{r} 2 \\ +3 \\ \hline \end{array} \quad \begin{array}{r} 5 \\ +5 \\ \hline \end{array} \quad \begin{array}{r} 4 \\ +2 \\ \hline \end{array} \quad \begin{array}{r} 9 \\ +9 \\ \hline \end{array} \quad \begin{array}{r} 8 \\ +1 \\ \hline \end{array} \quad \begin{array}{r} 2 \\ +5 \\ \hline \end{array}$$

__ __ __ __ __ __ __ __ __ __ .

**Code**

| 5 | 6 | 7 | 8 | 9 | 10 | 11 | 12 | 13 | 14 | 15 | 16 | 17 | 18 |
|---|---|---|---|---|----|----|----|----|----|----|----|----|----|
| H | R | Y | N | A | E | I | O | G | M | C | T | W | D |

Practice the facts

Find the sums.

1. $4 + 5 =$ ___          $5 + 6 =$ ___

2. $6 + 6 =$ ___          $6 + 7 =$ ___

3. $8 + 3 =$ ___          $4 + 5 =$ ___

4. $9 + 9 =$ ___          $7 + 3 =$ ___          $8 + 7 =$ ___

5. $9 + 1 =$ ___          $2 + 9 =$ ___          $8 + 8 =$ ___

6.
$$\begin{array}{r} 7 \\ +8 \\ \hline \end{array} \quad \begin{array}{r} 8 \\ +9 \\ \hline \end{array} \quad \begin{array}{r} 9 \\ +1 \\ \hline \end{array} \quad \begin{array}{r} 3 \\ +5 \\ \hline \end{array} \quad \begin{array}{r} 7 \\ +7 \\ \hline \end{array} \quad \begin{array}{r} 2 \\ +7 \\ \hline \end{array}$$

7.
$$\begin{array}{r} 9 \\ +9 \\ \hline \end{array} \quad \begin{array}{r} 5 \\ +6 \\ \hline \end{array} \quad \begin{array}{r} 3 \\ +9 \\ \hline \end{array} \quad \begin{array}{r} 4 \\ +4 \\ \hline \end{array} \quad \begin{array}{r} 2 \\ +9 \\ \hline \end{array} \quad \begin{array}{r} 6 \\ +6 \\ \hline \end{array}$$

8.
$$\begin{array}{r} 6 \\ +3 \\ \hline \end{array} \quad \begin{array}{r} 5 \\ +5 \\ \hline \end{array} \quad \begin{array}{r} 2 \\ +8 \\ \hline \end{array} \quad \begin{array}{r} 7 \\ +6 \\ \hline \end{array} \quad \begin{array}{r} 8 \\ +8 \\ \hline \end{array} \quad \begin{array}{r} 6 \\ +5 \\ \hline \end{array}$$

## SKILLKEEPER

Subtract.

$$\begin{array}{r} 10 \\ -3 \\ \hline \end{array} \quad \begin{array}{r} 11 \\ -2 \\ \hline \end{array} \quad \begin{array}{r} 12 \\ -3 \\ \hline \end{array} \quad \begin{array}{r} 10 \\ -1 \\ \hline \end{array} \quad \begin{array}{r} 11 \\ -3 \\ \hline \end{array} \quad \begin{array}{r} 10 \\ -2 \\ \hline \end{array}$$

Practice the facts

## Problem Solving

Solve.

1. Dick had 11 crayons.

   He lost 2 of them.

   How many does he have now? __9__ crayons

   $$\begin{array}{r} 11 \\ -\ 2 \\ \hline 9 \end{array}$$

2. Don ate 5 crackers.

   Fay ate 6 crackers.

   How many did they eat in all? _____ crackers

3. Rita saw 9 cars.

   Then she saw 8 more cars.

   How many cars did Rita see in all? _____ cars

4. Ann caught 8 fish.

   3 fish got away.

   How many does she have now? _____ fish

Problem solving—short sentence

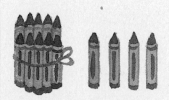 

This is
one less than
10+4.

$10 + 4 = \underline{14}$     $9 + 4 = \underline{13}$

Add.

**1.**

$$\begin{array}{r} 10 \\ + 5 \\ \hline 15 \end{array}$$ → $$\begin{array}{r} 9 \\ + 5 \\ \hline 14 \end{array}$$ I less than 10 + 5

$$\begin{array}{r} 10 \\ + 6 \\ \hline 16 \end{array}$$ → $$\begin{array}{r} 9 \\ + 6 \\ \hline \end{array}$$ I less than 10 + 6

**2.**

$$\begin{array}{r} 10 \\ + 7 \\ \hline 17 \end{array}$$ → $$\begin{array}{r} 9 \\ + 7 \\ \hline \end{array}$$ I less than 10 + 7

$$\begin{array}{r} 10 \\ + 8 \\ \hline 18 \end{array}$$ → $$\begin{array}{r} 9 \\ + 8 \\ \hline \end{array}$$ I less than 10 + 8

**3.**

$$\begin{array}{r} 9 \\ + 5 \\ \hline \end{array}$$     $$\begin{array}{r} 9 \\ + 7 \\ \hline \end{array}$$     $$\begin{array}{r} 9 \\ + 3 \\ \hline \end{array}$$     $$\begin{array}{r} 9 \\ + 6 \\ \hline \end{array}$$     $$\begin{array}{r} 9 \\ + 4 \\ \hline \end{array}$$     $$\begin{array}{r} 9 \\ + 8 \\ \hline \end{array}$$

**4.**

$$\begin{array}{r} 4 \\ + 9 \\ \hline \end{array}$$     $$\begin{array}{r} 9 \\ + 6 \\ \hline \end{array}$$     $$\begin{array}{r} 7 \\ + 9 \\ \hline \end{array}$$     $$\begin{array}{r} 9 \\ + 5 \\ \hline \end{array}$$     $$\begin{array}{r} 3 \\ + 9 \\ \hline \end{array}$$     $$\begin{array}{r} 9 \\ + 4 \\ \hline \end{array}$$

**5.**

$$\begin{array}{r} 9 \\ + 8 \\ \hline \end{array}$$     $$\begin{array}{r} 9 \\ + 3 \\ \hline \end{array}$$     $$\begin{array}{r} 9 \\ + 6 \\ \hline \end{array}$$     $$\begin{array}{r} 9 \\ + 4 \\ \hline \end{array}$$     $$\begin{array}{r} 9 \\ + 7 \\ \hline \end{array}$$     $$\begin{array}{r} 9 \\ + 5 \\ \hline \end{array}$$

An addend of nine

Add.

1.  $\begin{array}{r} 6 \\ +6 \\ \hline \end{array}$   $\begin{array}{r} 8 \\ +8 \\ \hline \end{array}$   $\begin{array}{r} 4 \\ +4 \\ \hline \end{array}$   $\begin{array}{r} 9 \\ +9 \\ \hline \end{array}$   $\begin{array}{r} 5 \\ +5 \\ \hline \end{array}$

2.  $\begin{array}{r} 8 \\ +7 \\ \hline \end{array}$   $\begin{array}{r} 6 \\ +5 \\ \hline \end{array}$   $\begin{array}{r} 8 \\ +9 \\ \hline \end{array}$   $\begin{array}{r} 4 \\ +5 \\ \hline \end{array}$   $\begin{array}{r} 7 \\ +8 \\ \hline \end{array}$   $\begin{array}{r} 6 \\ +7 \\ \hline \end{array}$

3.  $\begin{array}{r} 9 \\ +6 \\ \hline \end{array}$   $\begin{array}{r} 8 \\ +9 \\ \hline \end{array}$   $\begin{array}{r} 4 \\ +9 \\ \hline \end{array}$   $\begin{array}{r} 9 \\ +5 \\ \hline \end{array}$   $\begin{array}{r} 3 \\ +9 \\ \hline \end{array}$   $\begin{array}{r} 9 \\ +7 \\ \hline \end{array}$

4.  $\begin{array}{r} 6 \\ +7 \\ \hline \end{array}$   $\begin{array}{r} 7 \\ +7 \\ \hline \end{array}$   $\begin{array}{r} 9 \\ +7 \\ \hline \end{array}$   $\begin{array}{r} 5 \\ +5 \\ \hline \end{array}$   $\begin{array}{r} 4 \\ +4 \\ \hline \end{array}$   $\begin{array}{r} 5 \\ +9 \\ \hline \end{array}$

5.  $\begin{array}{r} 8 \\ +9 \\ \hline \end{array}$   $\begin{array}{r} 9 \\ +5 \\ \hline \end{array}$   $\begin{array}{r} 4 \\ +9 \\ \hline \end{array}$   $\begin{array}{r} 5 \\ +4 \\ \hline \end{array}$   $\begin{array}{r} 8 \\ +8 \\ \hline \end{array}$   $\begin{array}{r} 9 \\ +8 \\ \hline \end{array}$

6.  $\begin{array}{r} 6 \\ +9 \\ \hline \end{array}$   $\begin{array}{r} 9 \\ +9 \\ \hline \end{array}$   $\begin{array}{r} 6 \\ +5 \\ \hline \end{array}$   $\begin{array}{r} 6 \\ +6 \\ \hline \end{array}$   $\begin{array}{r} 8 \\ +7 \\ \hline \end{array}$   $\begin{array}{r} 9 \\ +3 \\ \hline \end{array}$

An addend of nine

Find the sums.

1.

| 4 | 5 | 6 | 7 | 8 |
|---|---|---|---|---|
| +4 | +4 | +4 | +4 | +4 |

These are the new facts.

2.

| 5 | 6 | 7 | 8 |
|---|---|---|---|
| +5 | +5 | +5 | +5 |

3.

| 6 | 7 | 8 |
|---|---|---|
| +6 | +6 | +6 |

4.

| 6 | 4 | 7 | 4 | 8 | 4 |
|---|---|---|---|---|---|
| +4 | +6 | +4 | +7 | +4 | +8 |

5.

| 7 | 5 | 8 | 5 | 8 | 6 |
|---|---|---|---|---|---|
| +5 | +7 | +5 | +8 | +6 | +8 |

6.

| 4 | 8 | 5 | 6 | 6 | 8 |
|---|---|---|---|---|---|
| +7 | +5 | +7 | +4 | +8 | +4 |

The last six facts

Add.

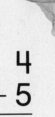

1.
$$\begin{array}{r} 5 \\ +7 \\ \hline \end{array}$$
$$\begin{array}{r} 4 \\ +7 \\ \hline \end{array}$$
$$\begin{array}{r} 8 \\ +5 \\ \hline \end{array}$$

2.
$$\begin{array}{r} 7 \\ +6 \\ \hline \end{array}$$
$$\begin{array}{r} 7 \\ +4 \\ \hline \end{array}$$
$$\begin{array}{r} 9 \\ +6 \\ \hline \end{array}$$
$$\begin{array}{r} 4 \\ +5 \\ \hline \end{array}$$

3.
$$\begin{array}{r} 9 \\ +7 \\ \hline \end{array}$$
$$\begin{array}{r} 9 \\ +9 \\ \hline \end{array}$$
$$\begin{array}{r} 8 \\ +6 \\ \hline \end{array}$$
$$\begin{array}{r} 6 \\ +5 \\ \hline \end{array}$$
$$\begin{array}{r} 5 \\ +9 \\ \hline \end{array}$$
$$\begin{array}{r} 4 \\ +6 \\ \hline \end{array}$$

4.
$$\begin{array}{r} 7 \\ +7 \\ \hline \end{array}$$
$$\begin{array}{r} 5 \\ +7 \\ \hline \end{array}$$
$$\begin{array}{r} 9 \\ +8 \\ \hline \end{array}$$
$$\begin{array}{r} 5 \\ +8 \\ \hline \end{array}$$
$$\begin{array}{r} 6 \\ +4 \\ \hline \end{array}$$
$$\begin{array}{r} 8 \\ +8 \\ \hline \end{array}$$

5.
$$\begin{array}{r} 7 \\ +2 \\ \hline \end{array}$$
$$\begin{array}{r} 6 \\ +4 \\ \hline \end{array}$$
$$\begin{array}{r} 6 \\ +8 \\ \hline \end{array}$$
$$\begin{array}{r} 8 \\ +4 \\ \hline \end{array}$$
$$\begin{array}{r} 4 \\ +7 \\ \hline \end{array}$$
$$\begin{array}{r} 7 \\ +5 \\ \hline \end{array}$$

## SKILLKEEPER

Fill in the blanks.

| Dimes | Pennies |
|-------|---------|
| 2     |         |

_____ ¢

| Dimes | Pennies |
|-------|---------|
|       |         |

_____ ¢

The last six facts

Add.

1.
$$\begin{array}{r} 4 \\ +9 \\ \hline \end{array} \qquad \begin{array}{r} 7 \\ +8 \\ \hline \end{array} \qquad \begin{array}{r} 6 \\ +3 \\ \hline \end{array} \qquad \begin{array}{r} 7 \\ +4 \\ \hline \end{array} \qquad \begin{array}{r} 9 \\ +8 \\ \hline \end{array}$$

2.
$$\begin{array}{r} 6 \\ +6 \\ \hline \end{array} \qquad \begin{array}{r} 7 \\ +9 \\ \hline \end{array} \qquad \begin{array}{r} 6 \\ +4 \\ \hline \end{array} \qquad \begin{array}{r} 7 \\ +7 \\ \hline \end{array} \qquad \begin{array}{r} 9 \\ +2 \\ \hline \end{array} \qquad \begin{array}{r} 7 \\ +6 \\ \hline \end{array}$$

3.
$$\begin{array}{r} 5 \\ +5 \\ \hline \end{array} \qquad \begin{array}{r} 3 \\ +5 \\ \hline \end{array} \qquad \begin{array}{r} 8 \\ +8 \\ \hline \end{array} \qquad \begin{array}{r} 5 \\ +2 \\ \hline \end{array} \qquad \begin{array}{r} 6 \\ +7 \\ \hline \end{array} \qquad \begin{array}{r} 8 \\ +2 \\ \hline \end{array}$$

4.
$$\begin{array}{r} 5 \\ +6 \\ \hline \end{array} \qquad \begin{array}{r} 3 \\ +9 \\ \hline \end{array} \qquad \begin{array}{r} 4 \\ +4 \\ \hline \end{array} \qquad \begin{array}{r} 5 \\ +7 \\ \hline \end{array} \qquad \begin{array}{r} 9 \\ +9 \\ \hline \end{array} \qquad \begin{array}{r} 0 \\ +9 \\ \hline \end{array}$$

5.

| Add 8 | | | | |
|---|---|---|---|---|
| 8 | 6 | 9 | 5 | 7 |
| 16 | | | | |

6.

| Add 7 | | | | |
|---|---|---|---|---|
| 6 | 9 | 7 | 5 | 8 |
| | | | | |

## THINK MATH

Give the missing numbers.

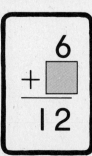

$$\begin{array}{r} 6 \\ +\boxed{\phantom{0}} \\ \hline 12 \end{array} \qquad \begin{array}{r} \boxed{\phantom{0}} \\ +7 \\ \hline 15 \end{array} \qquad \begin{array}{r} 9 \\ +\boxed{\phantom{0}} \\ \hline 14 \end{array}$$

Why shouldn't you tell jokes
while ice skating?

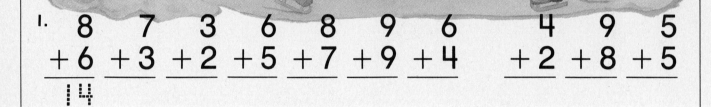

1.
$$8 \atop +6$$  $$7 \atop +3$$  $$3 \atop +2$$  $$6 \atop +5$$  $$8 \atop +7$$  $$9 \atop +9$$  $$6 \atop +4$$  $$4 \atop +2$$  $$9 \atop +8$$  $$5 \atop +5$$

14

B ___ ___ ___ ___ ___ ___ ___ ___ ___

2.
$$9 \atop +3$$  $$2 \atop +3$$  $$5 \atop +5$$  $$2 \atop +5$$  $$8 \atop +4$$  $$9 \atop +7$$  $$8 \atop +9$$  $$3 \atop +3$$

___ ___ ___ ___ ___ ___ ___ ___

3.
$$4 \atop +1$$  $$4 \atop +4$$  $$9 \atop +2$$  $$5 \atop +0$$  $$8 \atop +5$$  $$9 \atop +6$$  $$4 \atop +5$$

___ ___ ___ ___ ___ ___ ___.

**Code**

| 5 | 6 | 7 | 8 | 9 | 10 | 11 | 12 | 13 | 14 | 15 | 16 | 17 | 18 |
|---|---|---|---|---|----|----|----|----|----|----|----|----|----|
| C | T | M | R | P | E  | A  | I  | K  | B  | U  | G  | H  | S  |

Practice the facts

Add.

1.
$$\begin{array}{r} 6 \\ +9 \\ \hline \end{array}$$
$$\begin{array}{r} 7 \\ +3 \\ \hline \end{array}$$
$$\begin{array}{r} 6 \\ +8 \\ \hline \end{array}$$
$$\begin{array}{r} 7 \\ +4 \\ \hline \end{array}$$
$$\begin{array}{r} 8 \\ +9 \\ \hline \end{array}$$

2.
$$\begin{array}{r} 3 \\ +9 \\ \hline \end{array}$$
$$\begin{array}{r} 9 \\ +7 \\ \hline \end{array}$$
$$\begin{array}{r} 8 \\ +6 \\ \hline \end{array}$$
$$\begin{array}{r} 7 \\ +5 \\ \hline \end{array}$$
$$\begin{array}{r} 8 \\ +7 \\ \hline \end{array}$$
$$\begin{array}{r} 9 \\ +4 \\ \hline \end{array}$$

3.
$$\begin{array}{r} 5 \\ +9 \\ \hline \end{array}$$
$$\begin{array}{r} 6 \\ +7 \\ \hline \end{array}$$
$$\begin{array}{r} 3 \\ +5 \\ \hline \end{array}$$
$$\begin{array}{r} 9 \\ +9 \\ \hline \end{array}$$
$$\begin{array}{r} 5 \\ +4 \\ \hline \end{array}$$
$$\begin{array}{r} 4 \\ +9 \\ \hline \end{array}$$

4.
$$\begin{array}{r} 9 \\ +6 \\ \hline \end{array}$$
$$\begin{array}{r} 5 \\ +6 \\ \hline \end{array}$$
$$\begin{array}{r} 7 \\ +9 \\ \hline \end{array}$$
$$\begin{array}{r} 7 \\ +7 \\ \hline \end{array}$$
$$\begin{array}{r} 8 \\ +4 \\ \hline \end{array}$$
$$\begin{array}{r} 7 \\ +8 \\ \hline \end{array}$$

5.
$$\begin{array}{r} 8 \\ +5 \\ \hline \end{array}$$
$$\begin{array}{r} 9 \\ +8 \\ \hline \end{array}$$
$$\begin{array}{r} 5 \\ +8 \\ \hline \end{array}$$
$$\begin{array}{r} 4 \\ +6 \\ \hline \end{array}$$
$$\begin{array}{r} 8 \\ +8 \\ \hline \end{array}$$
$$\begin{array}{r} 9 \\ +5 \\ \hline \end{array}$$

## THINK MATH

Use these cards two at a time ⟶

How many different numbers can you write?

_____   _____   _____   _____   _____   _____

Practice the facts

# Problem Solving

Solve.

**1.**

Tina saw 7 dogs.

Then she saw 4 more.

How many dogs did Tina see altogether? __11__ dogs

$$\begin{array}{r} 7 \\ + 4 \\ \hline 11 \end{array}$$

**2.**

Larry had 9 keys.

He lost 2 of them.

How many keys does he have left? _____ keys

**3.**

Betty had 7 plants.

She bought 9 new plants.

How many does she have in all? _____ plants

**4.**

Bill bought 10 eggs.

He broke 3 of them.

How many eggs does he have left? _____ eggs

Problem solving—short sentence

Jan has 2 fish.

Ted has 4 fish.

Sue has 3 fish.

$$\begin{array}{r} 2 \\ 4 \quad 6 \\ + 3 \\ \hline 9 \end{array}$$

6 + 3

How many are there in all? __9__ fish

Add.
1.

$$\begin{array}{r} 2 \\ 3 \quad 5 \\ + 3 \\ \hline \end{array}$$  $$\begin{array}{r} 2 \\ 5 \quad 7 \\ + 4 \\ \hline \end{array}$$  $$\begin{array}{r} 4 \\ 2 \quad 6 \\ + 4 \\ \hline \end{array}$$  $$\begin{array}{r} 3 \\ 6 \quad 9 \\ + 2 \\ \hline \end{array}$$  $$\begin{array}{r} 3 \\ 2 \quad 5 \\ + 6 \\ \hline \end{array}$$  $$\begin{array}{r} 2 \\ 5 \quad 7 \\ + 4 \\ \hline \end{array}$$

2.

$$\begin{array}{r} 4 \\ 4 \\ + 4 \\ \hline \end{array}$$  $$\begin{array}{r} 2 \\ 1 \\ + 5 \\ \hline \end{array}$$  $$\begin{array}{r} 5 \\ 1 \\ + 7 \\ \hline \end{array}$$  $$\begin{array}{r} 3 \\ 2 \\ + 5 \\ \hline \end{array}$$  $$\begin{array}{r} 1 \\ 2 \\ + 6 \\ \hline \end{array}$$  $$\begin{array}{r} 4 \\ 5 \\ + 2 \\ \hline \end{array}$$

3.

$$\begin{array}{r} 3 \\ 1 \\ + 8 \\ \hline \end{array}$$  $$\begin{array}{r} 6 \\ 1 \\ + 7 \\ \hline \end{array}$$  $$\begin{array}{r} 2 \\ 6 \\ + 0 \\ \hline \end{array}$$  $$\begin{array}{r} 5 \\ 2 \\ + 3 \\ \hline \end{array}$$  $$\begin{array}{r} 1 \\ 2 \\ + 7 \\ \hline \end{array}$$  $$\begin{array}{r} 5 \\ 4 \\ + 0 \\ \hline \end{array}$$

Three addends

$$\begin{array}{r} 4 \\ 3 \\ +5 \\ \hline 12 \end{array} \; 7$$

Check
$$\begin{array}{r} 4 \\ 3 \\ +5 \\ \hline 12 \end{array} \; 8$$

Add.

**1.**

$$\begin{array}{r} 4 \\ 3 \\ +2 \\ \hline \end{array} \; 7$$

Check
$$\begin{array}{r} 4 \\ 3 \\ +2 \\ \hline \end{array} \; 5$$

$$\begin{array}{r} 5 \\ 2 \\ +4 \\ \hline \end{array} \; 7$$

Check
$$\begin{array}{r} 5 \\ 2 \\ +4 \\ \hline \end{array} \; 6$$

$$\begin{array}{r} 2 \\ 3 \\ 1 \\ +5 \\ \hline \end{array} \; 6$$

Check
$$\begin{array}{r} 3 \\ 2 \\ 1 \\ +5 \\ \hline \end{array} \; 8$$

Add and check.

**2.**

$$\begin{array}{r} 5 \\ 3 \\ +2 \\ \hline \end{array}$$

$$\begin{array}{r} 3 \\ 3 \\ +4 \\ \hline \end{array}$$

$$\begin{array}{r} 1 \\ 4 \\ +3 \\ \hline \end{array}$$

$$\begin{array}{r} 4 \\ 1 \\ +5 \\ \hline \end{array}$$

$$\begin{array}{r} 3 \\ 3 \\ +5 \\ \hline \end{array}$$

$$\begin{array}{r} 4 \\ 3 \\ +5 \\ \hline \end{array}$$

**3.**

$$\begin{array}{r} 2 \\ 3 \\ 1 \\ +4 \\ \hline \end{array}$$

$$\begin{array}{r} 2 \\ 1 \\ 2 \\ +4 \\ \hline \end{array}$$

$$\begin{array}{r} 1 \\ 3 \\ 1 \\ +3 \\ \hline \end{array}$$

$$\begin{array}{r} 2 \\ 2 \\ 4 \\ +3 \\ \hline \end{array}$$

$$\begin{array}{r} 4 \\ 3 \\ 2 \\ +4 \\ \hline \end{array}$$

$$\begin{array}{r} 2 \\ 4 \\ 1 \\ +3 \\ \hline \end{array}$$

Three or more addends and check

Name _____

Ring the names for the numbers on top.

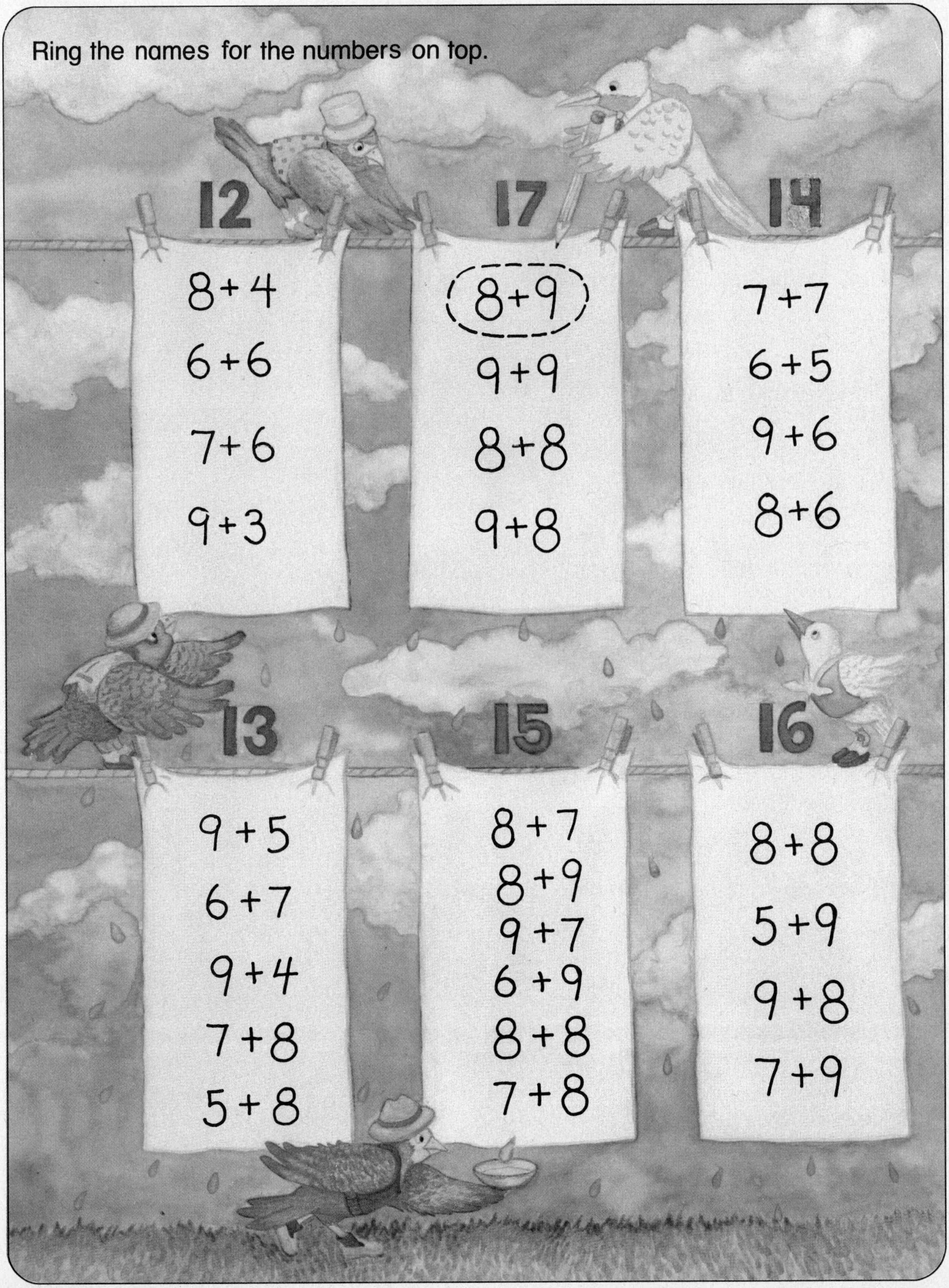

**12**

8 + 4
6 + 6
7 + 6
9 + 3

**17**

(8 + 9)
9 + 9
8 + 8
9 + 8

**14**

7 + 7
6 + 5
9 + 6
8 + 6

**13**

9 + 5
6 + 7
9 + 4
7 + 8
5 + 8

**15**

8 + 7
8 + 9
9 + 7
6 + 9
8 + 8
7 + 8

**16**

8 + 8
5 + 9
9 + 8
7 + 9

Different names for the same number

# Problem Solving

Draw more pictures or mark out some. Solve the problems.

**1.**

Doris has 7 oranges.

She bought 3 more.

How many does she have now? _____ oranges

$$7 + 3 \over 10$$

**2.**

Don picked 6 apples.

He ate 2 of them.

How many does he have left? _____ apples

**3.**

Patty ate 3 pears.

Sue ate 2 pears.

How many did they eat in all? _____ pears

**4.**

Bill has 7 bananas.

He gave away 2 bananas.

How many does he have left? _____ bananas

Problem solving—short sentence

Name _____

**Add.**

**1.**

| 8 | 9 | 7 | 7 | 5 |
|---|---|---|---|---|
| +8 | +2 | +9 | +3 | +8 |

**2.**

| 9 | 6 | 7 | 6 | 9 | 8 |
|---|---|---|---|---|---|
| +6 | +2 | +6 | +3 | +9 | +4 |

**3.**

| 7 | 3 | 9 | 6 | 4 | 9 |
|---|---|---|---|---|---|
| +7 | +4 | +4 | +8 | +5 | +5 |

**4.**

| 5 | 8 | 4 | 5 | 4 | 7 |
|---|---|---|---|---|---|
| +7 | +9 | +6 | +8 | +7 | +8 |

**5.**

| 9 | 5 | 8 | 6 | 9 | 9 |
|---|---|---|---|---|---|
| +8 | +6 | +4 | +6 | +9 | +5 |

**6.**

| 5 | 3 | 6 | 5 | 6 | 7 |
|---|---|---|---|---|---|
| 2 | 4 | 2 | 3 | 2 | 1 |
| +1 | +2 | +4 | +6 | +5 | +6 |

Practice the facts                    (eighty-nine) **89**

## Problem Solving

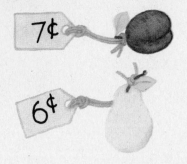

7 ¢

+ 6 ¢
-------------
13 ¢

**What is the total cost?**

**1.**

8 ¢

+ 6 ¢
-------------
14 ¢

**2.**

_____ ¢

_____ ¢

_____ ¢

**3.**

_____ ¢

_____ ¢

_____ ¢

**4.**

_____ ¢

_____ ¢

_____ ¢

**5.**

_____ ¢

_____ ¢

_____ ¢

**6.**

_____ ¢

_____ ¢

_____ ¢

_____ ¢

Problem solving—using data from a price tag

Name _____

## CHAPTER REVIEW/TEST

Add.

1.
| 5 | 2 | 4 | 3 | 3 | 4 |
|---|---|---|---|---|---|
| +5 | +2 | +4 | +3 | +4 | +5 |

2.
| 5 | 2 | 7 | 9 | 6 | 8 |
|---|---|---|---|---|---|
| +6 | +3 | +7 | +9 | +6 | +8 |

3.
| 7 | 8 | 6 | 7 | 8 | 9 |
|---|---|---|---|---|---|
| +8 | +9 | +7 | +5 | +6 | +7 |

4.
| 7 | 9 | 8 | 9 | 8 | 9 |
|---|---|---|---|---|---|
| +4 | +4 | +5 | +6 | +4 | +5 |

5.
| 4 | 5 | 2 | 6 | 3 | 4 |
|---|---|---|---|---|---|
| 3 | 4 | 2 | 2 | 5 | 3 |
| +3 | +3 | +4 | +4 | +1 | +5 |

6. Solve.

Pam has 5 fish.

Paul has 7 fish.

How many do they have altogether? _____ fish

# CUMULATIVE REVIEW

Add or subtract.

1.
$$\begin{array}{r} 6 \\ +1 \\ \hline \end{array}$$
○ 6
○ 7
○ 5

2.
$$\begin{array}{r} 3 \\ +2 \\ \hline \end{array}$$
○ 5
○ 1
○ 7

3.
$$\begin{array}{r} 11 \\ -2 \\ \hline \end{array}$$
○ 12
○ 13
○ 9

4.
$$\begin{array}{r} 10 \\ -3 \\ \hline \end{array}$$
○ 7
○ 9
○ 13

5. How many tens are there?

○ 40
○ 3
○ 4

What number is next?

6. 35, 36, _____
○ 38
○ 40
○ 37

7. 2, 4, 6, _____
○ 7
○ 8
○ 9

8. Which is the second letter?

A, B, C
○ A
○ B
○ C

9. Solve.

Edla fed 8 cats.
Then she fed 3 cats.
How many cats did
she feed altogether?

○ 11
○ 13
○ 5

# ANOTHER LOOK

| 11 | 12 |
|---|---|
| 6 + 5 | 6 + 6 |
| 7 + 4 | 7 + 5 |
| 8 + 3 | 8 + 4 |
| 9 + 2 | 9 + 3 |

| 13 | 14 |
|---|---|
| 7 + 6 | 7 + 7 |
| 8 + 5 | 8 + 6 |
| 9 + 4 | 9 + 5 |

| 15 | 16 |
|---|---|
| 8 + 7 | 8 + 8 |
| 9 + 6 | 9 + 7 |

| 17 | 18 |
|---|---|
| 9 + 8 | 9 + 9 |

Add.

1.
$$6 + 8 \qquad 6 + 6 \qquad 8 + 9$$

2.
$$7 + 9 \qquad 3 + 9 \qquad 3 + 8$$

3.
$$7 + 6 \qquad 8 + 5 \qquad 6 + 9$$

4.
$$9 + 2 \qquad 9 + 8 \qquad 7 + 4$$

5.
$$5 + 8 \qquad 9 + 6 \qquad 5 + 6$$

6.
$$8 + 7 \qquad 4 + 7 \qquad 9 + 9$$

7.
$$5 + 7 \qquad 7 + 7 \qquad 9 + 5$$

Name _____

# ENRICHMENT

Grade Mike's paper.

Right ✔

Wrong ✘

$$\begin{array}{r} 8 \\ 7 \\ +\,2 \\ \hline 17 \end{array}$$

Think 10 + 7

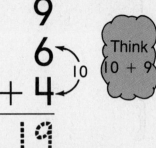

$$\begin{array}{r} 9 \\ 6 \\ +\,4 \\ \hline 19 \end{array}$$

Think 10 + 9

Add. Look for 10.  Mike

1. $\begin{array}{r} 7 \\ 6 \\ +\,3 \\ \hline 16 \end{array}$ ✔
2. $\begin{array}{r} 8 \\ 5 \\ +\,5 \\ \hline 17 \end{array}$ ✘
3. $\begin{array}{r} 6 \\ 8 \\ +\,4 \\ \hline 18 \end{array}$
4. $\begin{array}{r} 3 \\ 2 \\ +\,8 \\ \hline 14 \end{array}$
5. $\begin{array}{r} 5 \\ 6 \\ +\,5 \\ \hline 16 \end{array}$

6. $\begin{array}{r} 1 \\ 7 \\ +\,9 \\ \hline 17 \end{array}$
7. $\begin{array}{r} 6 \\ 3 \\ +\,7 \\ \hline 17 \end{array}$
8. $\begin{array}{r} 8 \\ 5 \\ +\,2 \\ \hline 15 \end{array}$
9. $\begin{array}{r} 9 \\ 4 \\ +\,6 \\ \hline 19 \end{array}$
10. $\begin{array}{r} 7 \\ 3 \\ +\,8 \\ \hline 17 \end{array}$

11. $\begin{array}{r} 4 \\ 8 \\ 3 \\ +\,2 \\ \hline 17 \end{array}$
12. $\begin{array}{r} 4 \\ 2 \\ 6 \\ +\,7 \\ \hline 18 \end{array}$
13. $\begin{array}{r} 3 \\ 5 \\ 5 \\ +\,4 \\ \hline 16 \end{array}$
14. $\begin{array}{r} 7 \\ 5 \\ 3 \\ +\,4 \\ \hline 19 \end{array}$
15. $\begin{array}{r} 2 \\ 6 \\ 6 \\ +\,4 \\ \hline 18 \end{array}$

Score: Number right _____

Number wrong _____

Enrichment—mental math

## DIFFERENCES TO 18

How many are there in each part?
Subtract.

Parts of 6

**1.**

_3_        _3_

$6 - 3 =$ ___

**2.**

___        ___

$6 - 4 =$ ___        $6 - 2 =$ ___

**3.**

___        ___

$6 - 5 =$ ___        $6 - 1 =$ ___

Subtract.

**4.**
$$\begin{array}{r} 6 \\ -4 \\ \hline \end{array} \qquad \begin{array}{r} 6 \\ -1 \\ \hline \end{array} \qquad \begin{array}{r} 6 \\ -6 \\ \hline \end{array} \qquad \begin{array}{r} 6 \\ -3 \\ \hline \end{array} \qquad \begin{array}{r} 6 \\ -5 \\ \hline \end{array} \qquad \begin{array}{r} 6 \\ -0 \\ \hline \end{array}$$

**5.**
$$\begin{array}{r} 6 \\ -2 \\ \hline \end{array} \qquad \begin{array}{r} 6 \\ -0 \\ \hline \end{array} \qquad \begin{array}{r} 6 \\ -4 \\ \hline \end{array} \qquad \begin{array}{r} 6 \\ -6 \\ \hline \end{array} \qquad \begin{array}{r} 6 \\ -1 \\ \hline \end{array} \qquad \begin{array}{r} 6 \\ -3 \\ \hline \end{array}$$

How many are there in each part?
Subtract.

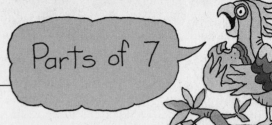

1.

4 _____    3 _____

$7 - 4 =$ _____    $7 - 3 =$ _____

2.

_____    _____

$7 - 5 =$ _____    $7 - 2 =$ _____

3.

_____    _____

$7 - 6 =$ _____    $7 - 1 =$ _____

Subtract.

4.
$$\begin{array}{r} 7 \\ -3 \\ \hline \end{array} \qquad \begin{array}{r} 7 \\ -1 \\ \hline \end{array} \qquad \begin{array}{r} 7 \\ -7 \\ \hline \end{array} \qquad \begin{array}{r} 7 \\ -2 \\ \hline \end{array} \qquad \begin{array}{r} 7 \\ -0 \\ \hline \end{array} \qquad \begin{array}{r} 7 \\ -4 \\ \hline \end{array}$$

5.
$$\begin{array}{r} 7 \\ -5 \\ \hline \end{array} \qquad \begin{array}{r} 7 \\ -6 \\ \hline \end{array} \qquad \begin{array}{r} 7 \\ -4 \\ \hline \end{array} \qquad \begin{array}{r} 7 \\ -0 \\ \hline \end{array} \qquad \begin{array}{r} 7 \\ -1 \\ \hline \end{array} \qquad \begin{array}{r} 7 \\ -2 \\ \hline \end{array}$$

Subtracting from 7

Name _____

How many are there in each part?
Subtract.

 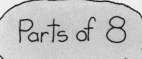

**1.**

4      4

$8 - 4 =$ ____

**2.**

____     ____

$8 - 5 =$ ____     $8 - 3 =$ ____

**3.**

____     ____

$8 - 6 =$ ____     $8 - 2 =$ ____

**4.**

____     ____

$8 - 7 =$ ____     $8 - 1 =$ ____

Subtract.

**5.**

| 8 | 8 | 8 | 8 | 8 | 8 |
|---|---|---|---|---|---|
| −3 | −1 | −6 | −4 | −0 | −2 |

**6.**

| 8 | 8 | 8 | 8 | 8 | 8 |
|---|---|---|---|---|---|
| −7 | −5 | −8 | −2 | −3 | −1 |

Subtracting from 8

How many are there in each part?
Subtract.

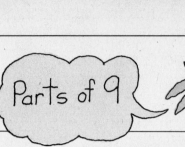 Parts of 9

**1.**

5      4

$9 - 5 =$ ___      $9 - 4 =$ ___

**2.**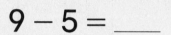

___      ___

$9 - 6 =$ ___      $9 - 3 =$ ___

**3.**

___      ___

$9 - 7 =$ ___      $9 - 2 =$ ___

**4.**

___      ___

$9 - 8 =$ ___      $9 - 1 =$ ___

Subtract.

**5.**

$$\begin{array}{r} 9 \\ -5 \\ \hline \end{array} \quad \begin{array}{r} 9 \\ -1 \\ \hline \end{array} \quad \begin{array}{r} 9 \\ -2 \\ \hline \end{array} \quad \begin{array}{r} 9 \\ -6 \\ \hline \end{array} \quad \begin{array}{r} 9 \\ -4 \\ \hline \end{array} \quad \begin{array}{r} 9 \\ -3 \\ \hline \end{array}$$

**6.**

$$\begin{array}{r} 9 \\ -9 \\ \hline \end{array} \quad \begin{array}{r} 9 \\ -7 \\ \hline \end{array} \quad \begin{array}{r} 9 \\ -0 \\ \hline \end{array} \quad \begin{array}{r} 9 \\ -5 \\ \hline \end{array} \quad \begin{array}{r} 9 \\ -8 \\ \hline \end{array} \quad \begin{array}{r} 9 \\ -2 \\ \hline \end{array}$$

How many are there in each part?
Subtract.

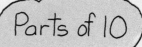

Parts of 10

1.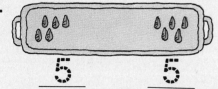
$$10 - 5 = \underline{\phantom{00}}$$

2.
$$10 - 6 = \underline{\phantom{00}} \qquad 10 - 4 = \underline{\phantom{00}}$$

3.
$$10 - 7 = \underline{\phantom{00}} \qquad 10 - 3 = \underline{\phantom{00}}$$

4.
$$10 - 8 = \underline{\phantom{00}} \qquad 10 - 2 = \underline{\phantom{00}}$$

5.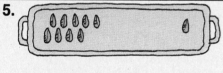
$$10 - 9 = \underline{\phantom{00}} \qquad 10 - 1 = \underline{\phantom{00}}$$

Subtract.

6.
$$\begin{array}{r} 10 \\ -\ 6 \\ \hline \end{array} \qquad \begin{array}{r} 10 \\ -\ 5 \\ \hline \end{array} \qquad \begin{array}{r} 10 \\ -\ 1 \\ \hline \end{array} \qquad \begin{array}{r} 10 \\ -\ 3 \\ \hline \end{array} \qquad \begin{array}{r} 10 \\ -\ 4 \\ \hline \end{array} \qquad \begin{array}{r} 10 \\ -\ 2 \\ \hline \end{array}$$

7.
$$\begin{array}{r} 10 \\ -\ 8 \\ \hline \end{array} \qquad \begin{array}{r} 10 \\ -\ 9 \\ \hline \end{array} \qquad \begin{array}{r} 10 \\ -\ 7 \\ \hline \end{array} \qquad \begin{array}{r} 10 \\ -\ 5 \\ \hline \end{array} \qquad \begin{array}{r} 10 \\ -\ 6 \\ \hline \end{array} \qquad \begin{array}{r} 10 \\ -\ 1 \\ \hline \end{array}$$

Subtract.

**1.**

$$\begin{array}{r} 6 \\ -1 \\ \hline \end{array} \qquad \begin{array}{r} 9 \\ -3 \\ \hline \end{array} \qquad \begin{array}{r} 10 \\ -8 \\ \hline \end{array} \qquad \begin{array}{r} 5 \\ -3 \\ \hline \end{array}$$

**2.**

$$\begin{array}{r} 10 \\ -4 \\ \hline \end{array} \qquad \begin{array}{r} 8 \\ -6 \\ \hline \end{array} \qquad \begin{array}{r} 6 \\ -4 \\ \hline \end{array} \qquad \begin{array}{r} 9 \\ -6 \\ \hline \end{array} \qquad \begin{array}{r} 7 \\ -2 \\ \hline \end{array} \qquad \begin{array}{r} 8 \\ -0 \\ \hline \end{array}$$

**3.**

$$\begin{array}{r} 9 \\ -5 \\ \hline \end{array} \qquad \begin{array}{r} 7 \\ -3 \\ \hline \end{array} \qquad \begin{array}{r} 8 \\ -7 \\ \hline \end{array} \qquad \begin{array}{r} 10 \\ -1 \\ \hline \end{array} \qquad \begin{array}{r} 6 \\ -2 \\ \hline \end{array} \qquad \begin{array}{r} 9 \\ -7 \\ \hline \end{array}$$

**4.**

$$\begin{array}{r} 8 \\ -5 \\ \hline \end{array} \qquad \begin{array}{r} 10 \\ -7 \\ \hline \end{array} \qquad \begin{array}{r} 7 \\ -1 \\ \hline \end{array} \qquad \begin{array}{r} 6 \\ -0 \\ \hline \end{array} \qquad \begin{array}{r} 9 \\ -2 \\ \hline \end{array} \qquad \begin{array}{r} 10 \\ -5 \\ \hline \end{array}$$

**5.**

$$\begin{array}{r} 9 \\ -4 \\ \hline \end{array} \qquad \begin{array}{r} 7 \\ -4 \\ \hline \end{array} \qquad \begin{array}{r} 8 \\ -3 \\ \hline \end{array} \qquad \begin{array}{r} 7 \\ -6 \\ \hline \end{array} \qquad \begin{array}{r} 10 \\ -9 \\ \hline \end{array} \qquad \begin{array}{r} 6 \\ -3 \\ \hline \end{array}$$

## SKILLKEEPER

What time is it?

_____   _____   _____   _____

Practice the facts

Name _____

How many are there in each part?
Subtract.

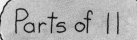 Parts of 11

**1.**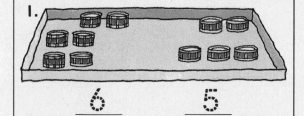

6    5
___  ___

$11 - 6 = \underline{\hspace{1cm}}$    $11 - 5 = \underline{\hspace{1cm}}$

**2.**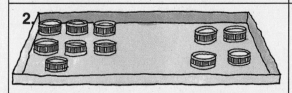

___  ___

$11 - 7 = \underline{\hspace{1cm}}$    $11 - 4 = \underline{\hspace{1cm}}$

**3.**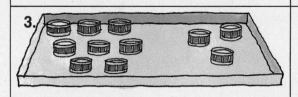

___  ___

$11 - 8 = \underline{\hspace{1cm}}$    $11 - 3 = \underline{\hspace{1cm}}$

**4.**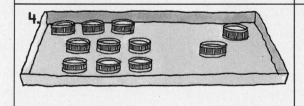

___  ___

$11 - 9 = \underline{\hspace{1cm}}$    $11 - 2 = \underline{\hspace{1cm}}$

Subtract.

**5.**
$$\begin{array}{cccccc} 11 & 11 & 11 & 11 & 11 & 11 \\ -\ 4 & -\ 5 & -\ 9 & -\ 8 & -\ 6 & -\ 7 \\ \hline \end{array}$$

**6.**
$$\begin{array}{cccccc} 11 & 11 & 11 & 11 & 11 & 11 \\ -\ 2 & -\ 3 & -\ 6 & -\ 5 & -\ 4 & -\ 8 \\ \hline \end{array}$$

How many are there in each part?
Subtract.

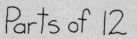

Parts of 12

**1.**

$\underset{6}{\rule{1.5cm}{0.4pt}}$    $\underset{6}{\rule{1.5cm}{0.4pt}}$

$12 - 6 = \underline{\hspace{1.5cm}}$

**2.**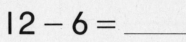

$\underline{\hspace{1.5cm}}$    $\underline{\hspace{1.5cm}}$

$12 - 7 = \underline{\hspace{1cm}}$    $12 - 5 = \underline{\hspace{1cm}}$

**3.**

$\underline{\hspace{1.5cm}}$    $\underline{\hspace{1.5cm}}$

$12 - 8 = \underline{\hspace{1cm}}$    $12 - 4 = \underline{\hspace{1cm}}$

**4.**

$\underline{\hspace{1.5cm}}$    $\underline{\hspace{1.5cm}}$

$12 - 9 = \underline{\hspace{1cm}}$    $12 - 3 = \underline{\hspace{1cm}}$

Subtract.

**5.**
$$\begin{array}{cc} 12 \\ -\ 5 \\ \hline \end{array} \qquad \begin{array}{cc} 12 \\ -\ 8 \\ \hline \end{array} \qquad \begin{array}{cc} 12 \\ -\ 4 \\ \hline \end{array} \qquad \begin{array}{cc} 12 \\ -\ 9 \\ \hline \end{array} \qquad \begin{array}{cc} 12 \\ -\ 6 \\ \hline \end{array} \qquad \begin{array}{cc} 12 \\ -\ 7 \\ \hline \end{array}$$

**6.**
$$\begin{array}{cc} 12 \\ -\ 3 \\ \hline \end{array} \qquad \begin{array}{cc} 12 \\ -\ 7 \\ \hline \end{array} \qquad \begin{array}{cc} 12 \\ -\ 8 \\ \hline \end{array} \qquad \begin{array}{cc} 12 \\ -\ 4 \\ \hline \end{array} \qquad \begin{array}{cc} 12 \\ -\ 5 \\ \hline \end{array} \qquad \begin{array}{cc} 12 \\ -\ 6 \\ \hline \end{array}$$

Subtracting from 12

This is a fact family

11

8    3

$8 + 3 = 11$    $3 + 8 = 11$

$11 - 3 = 8$    $11 - 8 = 3$

Write the fact family number sentences.

**1.**

12

5    7

___ + ___ = 12    ___ + ___ = 12

___ − ___ = 5    ___ − ___ = 7

**2.**

11

4    7

___ + ___ = 11    ___ + ___ = 11

___ − ___ = 4    ___ − ___ = 7

**3.**

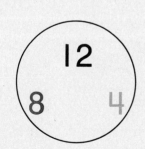

12

8    4

___ + ___ = 12    ___ + ___ = 12

___ − ___ = 8    ___ − ___ = 4

Fact families

Subtract.

1.  $\begin{array}{r} 12 \\ -\ 6 \\ \hline \end{array}$  $\begin{array}{r} 11 \\ -\ 6 \\ \hline \end{array}$  $\begin{array}{r} 10 \\ -\ 4 \\ \hline \end{array}$  $\begin{array}{r} 11 \\ -\ 8 \\ \hline \end{array}$

2.  $\begin{array}{r} 8 \\ -\ 6 \\ \hline \end{array}$  $\begin{array}{r} 12 \\ -\ 8 \\ \hline \end{array}$  $\begin{array}{r} 11 \\ -\ 3 \\ \hline \end{array}$  $\begin{array}{r} 12 \\ -\ 9 \\ \hline \end{array}$  $\begin{array}{r} 11 \\ -\ 9 \\ \hline \end{array}$  $\begin{array}{r} 10 \\ -\ 6 \\ \hline \end{array}$

3.  $\begin{array}{r} 9 \\ -\ 4 \\ \hline \end{array}$  $\begin{array}{r} 11 \\ -\ 7 \\ \hline \end{array}$  $\begin{array}{r} 12 \\ -\ 7 \\ \hline \end{array}$  $\begin{array}{r} 11 \\ -\ 6 \\ \hline \end{array}$  $\begin{array}{r} 8 \\ -\ 8 \\ \hline \end{array}$  $\begin{array}{r} 12 \\ -\ 5 \\ \hline \end{array}$

4.  $\begin{array}{r} 11 \\ -\ 5 \\ \hline \end{array}$  $\begin{array}{r} 8 \\ -\ 0 \\ \hline \end{array}$  $\begin{array}{r} 12 \\ -\ 6 \\ \hline \end{array}$  $\begin{array}{r} 10 \\ -\ 3 \\ \hline \end{array}$  $\begin{array}{r} 11 \\ -\ 3 \\ \hline \end{array}$  $\begin{array}{r} 12 \\ -\ 4 \\ \hline \end{array}$

5.  $\begin{array}{r} 10 \\ -\ 5 \\ \hline \end{array}$  $\begin{array}{r} 11 \\ -\ 8 \\ \hline \end{array}$  $\begin{array}{r} 12 \\ -\ 3 \\ \hline \end{array}$  $\begin{array}{r} 9 \\ -\ 7 \\ \hline \end{array}$  $\begin{array}{r} 12 \\ -\ 8 \\ \hline \end{array}$  $\begin{array}{r} 11 \\ -\ 4 \\ \hline \end{array}$

## THINK MATH

7 birds were on the wires.
4 of them did not fly away.
How many birds flew away?

_____ birds

Practice the facts

Name _____

How many are there in each part?
Subtract.

**1.**

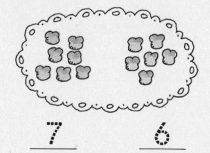

7   6

$13 - 7 =$ ___   $13 - 6 =$ ___

**2.**

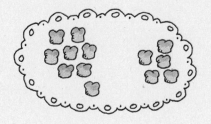

___   ___

$13 - 8 =$ ___   $13 - 5 =$ ___

**3.**

___   ___

$13 - 9 =$ ___   $13 - 4 =$ ___

Subtract.

**4.**

$$\begin{array}{c} 13 \\ -\ 6 \\ \hline \end{array} \qquad \begin{array}{c} 13 \\ -\ 8 \\ \hline \end{array} \qquad \begin{array}{c} 13 \\ -\ 4 \\ \hline \end{array} \qquad \begin{array}{c} 13 \\ -\ 9 \\ \hline \end{array} \qquad \begin{array}{c} 13 \\ -\ 5 \\ \hline \end{array} \qquad \begin{array}{c} 13 \\ -\ 7 \\ \hline \end{array}$$

**5.**

$$\begin{array}{c} 13 \\ -\ 4 \\ \hline \end{array} \qquad \begin{array}{c} 13 \\ -\ 8 \\ \hline \end{array} \qquad \begin{array}{c} 13 \\ -\ 6 \\ \hline \end{array} \qquad \begin{array}{c} 13 \\ -\ 7 \\ \hline \end{array} \qquad \begin{array}{c} 13 \\ -\ 5 \\ \hline \end{array} \qquad \begin{array}{c} 13 \\ -\ 9 \\ \hline \end{array}$$

Subtracting from 13

How many are there in each part?
Subtract.

Parts of 14

**1.**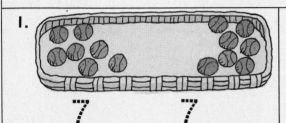

7      7

$14 - 7 = \underline{\hspace{1cm}}$

**2.**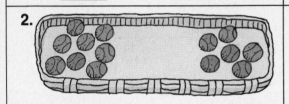

$14 - 8 = \underline{\hspace{1cm}}$     $14 - 6 = \underline{\hspace{1cm}}$

**3.**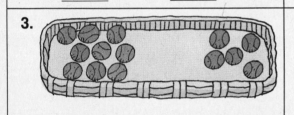

$14 - 9 = \underline{\hspace{1cm}}$     $14 - 5 = \underline{\hspace{1cm}}$

**4.** Subtract.

$$\begin{array}{cccccc} 14 & 14 & 14 & 14 & 14 & 14 \\ -\ 6 & -\ 8 & -\ 9 & -\ 5 & -\ 7 & -\ 8 \\ \hline \end{array}$$

## SKILLKEEPER

Ring the coins you need.

## Write the fact family number sentences.

**1.**

$8 + 5 = 13$     $5 + 8 = 13$

$13 - 5 = 8$     $13 - 8 = 5$

**2.**

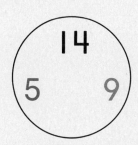

___ + ___ = $14$     ___ + ___ = $14$

___ - ___ = $5$     ___ - ___ = $9$

**3.**

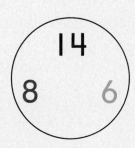

___ + ___ = $14$     ___ + ___ = $14$

___ - ___ = $8$     ___ - ___ = $6$

**4.**

___ + ___ = $13$     ___ + ___ = $13$

___ - ___ = $7$     ___ - ___ = $6$

More fact families     (one hundred seven) **107**

Subtract.

1.  
$$13 - 9$$ $$14 - 8$$ $$12 - 8$$ $$13 - 6$$

2.  
$$10 - 3$$ $$13 - 5$$ $$14 - 9$$ $$12 - 6$$ $$13 - 8$$ $$14 - 7$$

3.  
$$11 - 6$$ $$14 - 5$$ $$13 - 4$$ $$14 - 8$$ $$11 - 2$$ $$13 - 6$$

4.  
$$13 - 7$$ $$14 - 6$$ $$12 - 5$$ $$13 - 9$$ $$14 - 5$$ $$10 - 8$$

5.  
$$11 - 4$$ $$13 - 8$$ $$14 - 7$$ $$12 - 3$$ $$13 - 4$$ $$14 - 9$$

## THINK MATH

Write the missing numbers on the computer sheet.

$$6 + \underline{\quad} = 9 \qquad 4 + \underline{\quad} = 7 \qquad 9 + \underline{\quad} = 16$$

$$8 - \underline{\quad} = 6 \qquad 7 - \underline{\quad} = 2 \qquad 12 - \underline{\quad} = 4$$

Practice the facts

**1. Take-away story**

5 carrots were in the yard.
The rabbits ate 3 carrots.
How many carrots were left?

$5 - 3 =$ _____ carrots

**2. Compare story**

5 carrots were in the yard.
3 rabbits were in the yard.
How many more carrots than
rabbits is this?

$5 - 3 =$ _____ more carrots

**3. Take-away story**

7 nuts were under the tree.
The squirrels ate 4 nuts.
How many nuts were left?

$7 - 4 =$ _____ nuts

**4. Compare story**

7 nuts were under the tree.
4 squirrels were under the tree.
How many more nuts than
squirrels were there?

$7 - 4 =$ _____ more nuts

# Problem Solving

Solve.

**1.**

6 bugs were on the pond.
The fish ate 3 bugs.
How many bugs were left?

$$\begin{array}{r} 6 \\ -\ 3 \\ \hline 3 \end{array}$$

_____ bugs

**2.**

6 bugs were on the pond.
There were 3 fish
in the pond.
How many more bugs
than fish were there?

_____ more bugs

**3.**

3 frogs were on one rock.
4 frogs were on another rock.
How many frogs is this in all?

_____ frogs

**4.**

Karen saw 7 fish.
3 swam away.
How many fish were left?

_____ fish

Problem solving—short sentence

How many are there in each part?
Subtract.

Parts of 15

**1.**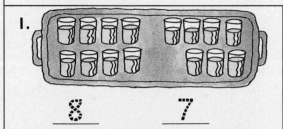

8 _____     7 _____

$15 - 8 =$ _____    $15 - 7 =$ _____

**2.**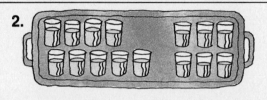

_____

$15 - 9 =$ _____    $15 - 6 =$ _____

**3.**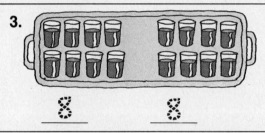

8 _____     8 _____

$16 - 8 =$ _____

Parts of 16

**4.**

_____

$16 - 9 =$ _____    $16 - 7 =$ _____

Subtract.

**5.**
$$\begin{array}{cc} 15 \\ -\ 7 \\ \hline \end{array} \quad \begin{array}{cc} 16 \\ -\ 7 \\ \hline \end{array} \quad \begin{array}{cc} 15 \\ -\ 6 \\ \hline \end{array} \quad \begin{array}{cc} 15 \\ -\ 9 \\ \hline \end{array} \quad \begin{array}{cc} 16 \\ -\ 8 \\ \hline \end{array} \quad \begin{array}{cc} 16 \\ -\ 9 \\ \hline \end{array}$$

**6.**
$$\begin{array}{cc} 15 \\ -\ 8 \\ \hline \end{array} \quad \begin{array}{cc} 15 \\ -\ 9 \\ \hline \end{array} \quad \begin{array}{cc} 16 \\ -\ 8 \\ \hline \end{array} \quad \begin{array}{cc} 16 \\ -\ 7 \\ \hline \end{array} \quad \begin{array}{cc} 15 \\ -\ 7 \\ \hline \end{array} \quad \begin{array}{cc} 16 \\ -\ 9 \\ \hline \end{array}$$

How many are there in each part?
Subtract.

Parts of 17

**1.**

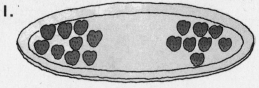

_____    _____

$17 - 9 =$ _____    $17 - 8 =$ _____

Parts of 18

**2.**

_____    _____

$18 - 9 =$ _____

**3.** Subtract.

$$\begin{array}{cc} 17 \\ -\ 9 \\ \hline \end{array} \qquad \begin{array}{cc} 16 \\ -\ 7 \\ \hline \end{array} \qquad \begin{array}{cc} 18 \\ -\ 9 \\ \hline \end{array} \qquad \begin{array}{cc} 15 \\ -\ 7 \\ \hline \end{array} \qquad \begin{array}{cc} 17 \\ -\ 8 \\ \hline \end{array} \qquad \begin{array}{cc} 16 \\ -\ 9 \\ \hline \end{array}$$

## SKILLKEEPER

Add.

$$\begin{array}{cc} 9 \\ +\ 7 \\ \hline \end{array} \qquad \begin{array}{cc} 8 \\ +\ 7 \\ \hline \end{array} \qquad \begin{array}{cc} 9 \\ +\ 6 \\ \hline \end{array} \qquad \begin{array}{cc} 8 \\ +\ 8 \\ \hline \end{array} \qquad \begin{array}{cc} 7 \\ +\ 8 \\ \hline \end{array} \qquad \begin{array}{cc} 6 \\ +\ 7 \\ \hline \end{array}$$

Subtract.

**1.**

| 13 | 16 | 11 | 14 |
|---|---|---|---|
| − 6 | − 7 | − 7 | − 6 |

**2.**

| 11 | 15 | 13 | 12 | 17 | 14 |
|---|---|---|---|---|---|
| − 6 | − 6 | − 8 | − 5 | − 8 | − 9 |

**3.**

| 16 | 13 | 18 | 14 | 15 | 12 |
|---|---|---|---|---|---|
| − 9 | − 5 | − 9 | − 7 | − 9 | − 7 |

**4.**

| 13 | 17 | 15 | 12 | 16 | 14 |
|---|---|---|---|---|---|
| − 7 | − 9 | − 8 | − 6 | − 8 | − 8 |

**5.**

| 15 | 13 | 12 | 11 | 14 | 13 |
|---|---|---|---|---|---|
| − 7 | − 9 | − 4 | − 5 | − 5 | − 4 |

**6.**

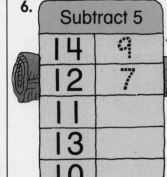

| Subtract 5 | | Subtract 7 | | Subtract 8 | | Subtract 6 | |
|---|---|---|---|---|---|---|---|
| 14 | 9 | 15 | | 11 | | 12 | |
| 12 | 7 | 13 | | 15 | | 10 | |
| 11 | | 16 | | 10 | | 14 | |
| 13 | | 12 | | 16 | | 13 | |
| 10 | | 14 | | 17 | | 15 | |

Practice the facts

# Problem Solving

Solve.

**1.** How many are there in all?

7 blue fish

8 gold fish

$$\begin{array}{r} 7 \\ + 8 \\ \hline 15 \end{array}$$

_____ fish

**2.** How many more red apples than green apples are there?

14 red apples

6 green apples

_____ more

**3.** How many are there in all?

9 frogs

4 turtles

_____ in all

**4.** How many more cars than bicycles are there?

7 bicycles

13 cars

_____ more

**5.** How many more blue birds than red birds are there?

15 blue birds

8 red birds

_____ more

**6.** How many are there altogether?

8 blue flowers

8 red flowers

_____ flowers

Problem solving—data card

Name _____

Subtract.

1.

$$\begin{array}{r}14\\-\ 7\\\hline\end{array}$$   $$\begin{array}{r}16\\-\ 7\\\hline\end{array}$$   $$\begin{array}{r}13\\-\ 7\\\hline\end{array}$$   $$\begin{array}{r}11\\-\ 6\\\hline\end{array}$$   $$\begin{array}{r}17\\-\ 8\\\hline\end{array}$$

2.

$$\begin{array}{r}13\\-\ 8\\\hline\end{array}$$   $$\begin{array}{r}12\\-\ 5\\\hline\end{array}$$   $$\begin{array}{r}15\\-\ 6\\\hline\end{array}$$   $$\begin{array}{r}11\\-\ 3\\\hline\end{array}$$   $$\begin{array}{r}14\\-\ 5\\\hline\end{array}$$   $$\begin{array}{r}12\\-\ 7\\\hline\end{array}$$

3.

$$\begin{array}{r}11\\-\ 5\\\hline\end{array}$$   $$\begin{array}{r}12\\-\ 4\\\hline\end{array}$$   $$\begin{array}{r}18\\-\ 9\\\hline\end{array}$$   $$\begin{array}{r}14\\-\ 9\\\hline\end{array}$$   $$\begin{array}{r}16\\-\ 8\\\hline\end{array}$$   $$\begin{array}{r}13\\-\ 6\\\hline\end{array}$$

4.

$$\begin{array}{r}11\\-\ 4\\\hline\end{array}$$   $$\begin{array}{r}15\\-\ 9\\\hline\end{array}$$   $$\begin{array}{r}13\\-\ 9\\\hline\end{array}$$   $$\begin{array}{r}14\\-\ 6\\\hline\end{array}$$   $$\begin{array}{r}17\\-\ 9\\\hline\end{array}$$   $$\begin{array}{r}11\\-\ 7\\\hline\end{array}$$

5.

$$\begin{array}{r}12\\-\ 9\\\hline\end{array}$$   $$\begin{array}{r}14\\-\ 8\\\hline\end{array}$$   $$\begin{array}{r}16\\-\ 9\\\hline\end{array}$$   $$\begin{array}{r}13\\-\ 5\\\hline\end{array}$$   $$\begin{array}{r}15\\-\ 7\\\hline\end{array}$$   $$\begin{array}{r}12\\-\ 3\\\hline\end{array}$$

6. Subtract to finish the flowers.

How do firefly races start?

Add or subtract. Use the code.
Write the letter under the answer.

**1.**

| 3 | 17 | 6 | 7 | 5 | 8 | 3 |
|---|----|---|---|---|---|---|
| +4 | − 9 | +7 | +5 | +3 | +9 | +9 |

S __ __ __ __ __ __

**2.**

| 15 | 14 | 6 | 14 | | 6 | 6 | 13 | 9 | 3 |
|----|----|---|----|---|---|---|----|---|---|
| − 8 | − 8 | +4 | − 7 | | +5 | +6 | − 7 | +7 | +7 |

__ __ __ __ , " __ __ __ __ __ ,

**3.**

| 2 | 8 | 18 | | 7 | 9 | 16 | 9 |
|---|---|----|---|---|---|----|---|
| +5 | +4 | − 9 | | +7 | +6 | − 8 | +9 |

__ __ __ , __ __ __ __ ."

**Code**

| 6 | 7 | 8 | 9 | 10 | 11 | 12 | 13 | 14 | 15 | 16 | 17 | 18 |
|---|---|---|---|----|----|----|----|----|----|----|----|----|
| A | S | O | T | Y | R | E | M | G | L | D | N | W |

Practice the facts

Add or subtract.

1.
$$5 + 8$$
$$9 + 7$$
$$8 + 3$$
$$4 + 9$$

2.
$$5 + 9$$
$$7 + 5$$
$$7 + 7$$
$$9 + 9$$
$$2 + 9$$
$$7 + 8$$

3.
$$11 - 7$$
$$15 - 6$$
$$12 - 7$$
$$16 - 7$$
$$13 - 4$$
$$10 - 3$$

4.
$$14 - 7$$
$$13 - 5$$
$$17 - 9$$
$$12 - 8$$
$$15 - 8$$
$$12 - 3$$

5.
$$8 + 6$$
$$11 - 8$$
$$8 + 9$$
$$14 - 8$$
$$11 - 5$$
$$8 + 8$$

## THINK MATH

Pretend you close your eyes.
Reach in the jar and get 12 beads.
How many red and how many black
do you think you would get?

_____ red    _____ black

Practice the facts

Solve.

1. 15 frogs were on a log.
7 jumped off.
How many were left?

$$\begin{array}{r} 15 \\ -\ 7 \\ \hline 8 \end{array}$$

frog

_____ frogs

2. There were 7 ducks
in one pond.
6 ducks were in
another pond.
How many ducks is
this in all?

duck

_____ ducks

3. Maria fed 16 squirrels.
Dave fed 9 squirrels.
How many more
squirrels did Maria
feed?

squirrel

_____ more

4. Dan saw 8 rabbits.
Patty saw 9 rabbits.
How many rabbits
did they see in all?

rabbit

_____ rabbits

5. Donna caught 14 fish.
Fay caught 6 fish.
How many more did
Donna catch than Fay?

fish

_____ more

6. Use your own number.
11 birds were in the tree.
_____ birds flew away.
How many were still
in the tree?

11

bird

_____ birds

Problem solving—short sentence

Name _____

Add or subtract.

1.
$$\begin{array}{r} 9 \\ +6 \\ \hline \end{array}$$
$$\begin{array}{r} 12 \\ -4 \\ \hline \end{array}$$
$$\begin{array}{r} 8 \\ +4 \\ \hline \end{array}$$
$$\begin{array}{r} 14 \\ -6 \\ \hline \end{array}$$

2.
$$\begin{array}{r} 15 \\ -7 \\ \hline \end{array}$$
$$\begin{array}{r} 5 \\ +8 \\ \hline \end{array}$$
$$\begin{array}{r} 17 \\ -8 \\ \hline \end{array}$$
$$\begin{array}{r} 5 \\ +7 \\ \hline \end{array}$$
$$\begin{array}{r} 7 \\ +9 \\ \hline \end{array}$$
$$\begin{array}{r} 13 \\ -8 \\ \hline \end{array}$$

3.
$$\begin{array}{r} 2 \\ +9 \\ \hline \end{array}$$
$$\begin{array}{r} 13 \\ -9 \\ \hline \end{array}$$
$$\begin{array}{r} 16 \\ -7 \\ \hline \end{array}$$
$$\begin{array}{r} 9 \\ +4 \\ \hline \end{array}$$
$$\begin{array}{r} 18 \\ -9 \\ \hline \end{array}$$
$$\begin{array}{r} 7 \\ +4 \\ \hline \end{array}$$

4.
$$\begin{array}{r} 15 \\ -6 \\ \hline \end{array}$$
$$\begin{array}{r} 7 \\ +7 \\ \hline \end{array}$$
$$\begin{array}{r} 14 \\ -7 \\ \hline \end{array}$$
$$\begin{array}{r} 9 \\ +8 \\ \hline \end{array}$$
$$\begin{array}{r} 14 \\ -5 \\ \hline \end{array}$$
$$\begin{array}{r} 7 \\ +8 \\ \hline \end{array}$$

5.
$$\begin{array}{r} 8 \\ +8 \\ \hline \end{array}$$
$$\begin{array}{r} 14 \\ -8 \\ \hline \end{array}$$
$$\begin{array}{r} 7 \\ +6 \\ \hline \end{array}$$
$$\begin{array}{r} 9 \\ +5 \\ \hline \end{array}$$
$$\begin{array}{r} 15 \\ -8 \\ \hline \end{array}$$
$$\begin{array}{r} 12 \\ -7 \\ \hline \end{array}$$

## THINK MATH

Tim used 5 of the eggs for breakfast.
Then he broke 2.
How many does he have left?

_____ eggs

Practice the facts

(one hundred nineteen) 119

## Problem-Solving Strategy

2 pins were knocked down.
8 points were scored.
Which pins were
knocked down?

**Guess**

**Check**

Try

$$3 \atop {+6 \over 9}$$ Wrong!

Try again

$$2 \atop {+6 \over 8}$$ Right!

---

1. 2 pins were knocked down.
11 points were scored.
Which pins were
knocked down? _____ and _____

2. 2 pins were knocked down.
8 points were scored.
Which pins were
knocked down? _____ and _____

Problem solving strategy—guess and check

# CHAPTER REVIEW/TEST

Subtract.

1.  $\begin{array}{r} 8 \\ -5 \\ \hline \end{array}$   $\begin{array}{r} 9 \\ -6 \\ \hline \end{array}$   $\begin{array}{r} 6 \\ -4 \\ \hline \end{array}$   $\begin{array}{r} 10 \\ -6 \\ \hline \end{array}$   $\begin{array}{r} 7 \\ -7 \\ \hline \end{array}$   $\begin{array}{r} 6 \\ -5 \\ \hline \end{array}$

2.  $\begin{array}{r} 10 \\ -5 \\ \hline \end{array}$   $\begin{array}{r} 7 \\ -4 \\ \hline \end{array}$   $\begin{array}{r} 9 \\ -8 \\ \hline \end{array}$   $\begin{array}{r} 8 \\ -6 \\ \hline \end{array}$   $\begin{array}{r} 9 \\ -7 \\ \hline \end{array}$   $\begin{array}{r} 10 \\ -9 \\ \hline \end{array}$

3.  $\begin{array}{r} 11 \\ -5 \\ \hline \end{array}$   $\begin{array}{r} 13 \\ -8 \\ \hline \end{array}$   $\begin{array}{r} 14 \\ -9 \\ \hline \end{array}$   $\begin{array}{r} 12 \\ -6 \\ \hline \end{array}$   $\begin{array}{r} 11 \\ -7 \\ \hline \end{array}$   $\begin{array}{r} 13 \\ -9 \\ \hline \end{array}$

4.  $\begin{array}{r} 12 \\ -3 \\ \hline \end{array}$   $\begin{array}{r} 14 \\ -7 \\ \hline \end{array}$   $\begin{array}{r} 12 \\ -5 \\ \hline \end{array}$   $\begin{array}{r} 13 \\ -7 \\ \hline \end{array}$   $\begin{array}{r} 11 \\ -8 \\ \hline \end{array}$   $\begin{array}{r} 12 \\ -4 \\ \hline \end{array}$

5.  $\begin{array}{r} 17 \\ -8 \\ \hline \end{array}$   $\begin{array}{r} 15 \\ -9 \\ \hline \end{array}$   $\begin{array}{r} 18 \\ -9 \\ \hline \end{array}$   $\begin{array}{r} 16 \\ -8 \\ \hline \end{array}$   $\begin{array}{r} 15 \\ -7 \\ \hline \end{array}$   $\begin{array}{r} 16 \\ -7 \\ \hline \end{array}$

Solve.

6. How many more birds
   than rabbits are there?

_____ more

7. Joan had 14 apples.
   She gave away 9 apples.
   How many apples does
   she have left?

apple   _____ apples

# CUMULATIVE REVIEW

How many are there?

1.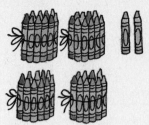
   - ○ 53
   - ○ 42
   - ○ 24

2.
   - ○ 20
   - ○ 27
   - ○ 17

3. What number is next?

   2, 4, 6, __?__
   - ○ 7
   - ○ 8
   - ○ 9

4. Which are the even numbers?
   - ○ 5, 7, 9
   - ○ 4, 6, 8
   - ○ 3, 5, 7

Add.

5.
$$7$$
$$+7$$
   - ○ 12
   - ○ 16
   - ○ 14

6.
$$5$$
$$+4$$
   - ○ 10
   - ○ 11
   - ○ 9

7.
$$6$$
$$+7$$
   - ○ 12
   - ○ 13
   - ○ 14

8.
$$5$$
$$3$$
$$+4$$
   - ○ 9
   - ○ 12
   - ○ 10

9. Solve.

   Craig found 6 shells.

   2 shells broke.

   How many shells does he have now?

   - ○ 4
   - ○ 8
   - ○ 2

# ANOTHER LOOK

| 11 | 12 |
|---|---|
| 6 + 5 | 6 + 6 |
| 7 + 4 | 7 + 5 |
| 8 + 3 | 8 + 4 |
| 9 + 2 | 9 + 3 |

| 13 | 14 |
|---|---|
| 7 + 6 | 7 + 7 |
| 8 + 5 | 8 + 6 |
| 9 + 4 | 9 + 5 |

| 15 | 16 |
|---|---|
| 8 + 7 | 8 + 8 |
| 9 + 6 | 9 + 7 |

| 17 | 18 |
|---|---|
| 9 + 8 | 9 + 9 |

Subtract.

1.
$$\begin{array}{r} 14 \\ -\ 5 \\ \hline \end{array} \qquad \begin{array}{r} 12 \\ -\ 4 \\ \hline \end{array} \qquad \begin{array}{r} 16 \\ -\ 9 \\ \hline \end{array}$$

2.
$$\begin{array}{r} 17 \\ -\ 9 \\ \hline \end{array} \qquad \begin{array}{r} 11 \\ -\ 4 \\ \hline \end{array} \qquad \begin{array}{r} 14 \\ -\ 8 \\ \hline \end{array}$$

3.
$$\begin{array}{r} 12 \\ -\ 7 \\ \hline \end{array} \qquad \begin{array}{r} 13 \\ -\ 6 \\ \hline \end{array} \qquad \begin{array}{r} 11 \\ -\ 8 \\ \hline \end{array}$$

4.
$$\begin{array}{r} 12 \\ -\ 6 \\ \hline \end{array} \qquad \begin{array}{r} 14 \\ -\ 8 \\ \hline \end{array} \qquad \begin{array}{r} 16 \\ -\ 7 \\ \hline \end{array}$$

5.
$$\begin{array}{r} 11 \\ -\ 2 \\ \hline \end{array} \qquad \begin{array}{r} 15 \\ -\ 6 \\ \hline \end{array} \qquad \begin{array}{r} 13 \\ -\ 5 \\ \hline \end{array}$$

6.
$$\begin{array}{r} 12 \\ -\ 9 \\ \hline \end{array} \qquad \begin{array}{r} 13 \\ -\ 4 \\ \hline \end{array} \qquad \begin{array}{r} 15 \\ -\ 8 \\ \hline \end{array}$$

7.
$$\begin{array}{r} 16 \\ -\ 8 \\ \hline \end{array} \qquad \begin{array}{r} 14 \\ -\ 7 \\ \hline \end{array} \qquad \begin{array}{r} 15 \\ -\ 7 \\ \hline \end{array}$$

# ENRICHMENT

Find the secret numbers.

1. Add 7 to me.
   You should
   get 15.
   Who am I? _____

2. First take away 3.
   Then add 1.
   You should have 8.
   Who am I? _____

3. Add 5 to me.
   Then take away 2.
   You should have 6.
   Who am I? _____

4. Add me to myself.
   Then take away 5.
   You should get 7.
   Who am I? _____

5. Add 4 to me.
   Then add 6 more.
   You should get 12.
   Who am I? _____

6. Add me to myself.
   Then add 2 more.
   You should have 10.
   Who am I? _____

# TIME AND MONEY

The hour hand is at __9__.

__9__ o'clock

__9__ :00

Write the times.

1. The hour hand

is at __7__.

__7__ o'clock

__7__ :00

2. The hour hand

is at _____.

_____ o'clock

_____ : 00

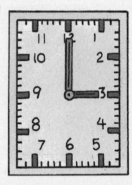

3. The hour hand

is at _____.

_____ o'clock

_____ :00

4. The hour hand

is at _____.

_____ o'clock

_____ :00

5. The hour hand

is at _____.

_____ o'clock

_____ :00

6. The hour hand

is at _____.

_____ o'clock

_____ :00

**7:00**
7 o'clock

Draw the hands. Write the times.

**1.**

**3:00**
3 o'clock

8 o'clock

4 o'clock

**2.**

11 o'clock

5 o'clock

12 o'clock

**3.**

6 o'clock

2 o'clock

9 o'clock

Telling time—hours

Name _____

___5___ minutes after ___8___ o'clock

8:05

**1.**

From the 12 to the 2 is 10 minutes.

__10__ minutes after ___8___ o'clock

8:10

**2.**

From the 12 to the 3 is 15 minutes.

_____ minutes after _____ o'clock

_____

**3.**

_____ minutes after _____ o'clock

_____

**4.**

_____ minutes after _____ o'clock

_____

**5.**

_____ minutes after _____ o'clock

_____

**6.**

_____ minutes after _____ o'clock

_____

**1.** Write the time in two ways.

_____ minutes after _____ o'clock

_____

**2.**

_____ minutes after _____ o'clock

_____

**3.**

_____ minutes after _____ o'clock

_____

**4.**

_____ minutes after _____ o'clock

_____

## THINK MATH

Ring all the clocks that show a time
between 3 o'clock and 4 o'clock.

15 minutes after 1 o'clock

1:15

## Write the time in two ways.

**1.**

_____ minutes after _____ o'clock

_____

**2.**

_____ minutes after _____ o'clock

_____

**3.**

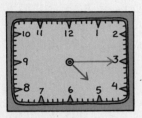

_____ minutes after _____ o'clock

_____

**4.**

_____ minutes after _____ o'clock

_____

**5.**

_____ minutes after _____ o'clock

_____

**6.**

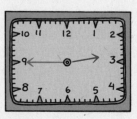

_____ minutes after _____ o'clock

_____

Telling time—15, 30, and 45 minutes after the hour

Ring the time that matches the clock.

**1.**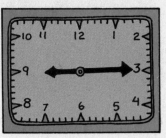

10:15  (9:15)  9:10       12:00  12:05  1:00       7:30  6:35  7:35

**2.**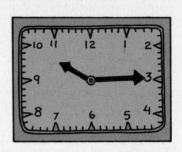

9:55  11:50  11:45      11:15  10:15  3:50      6:25  6:30  5:30

**3.**

12:45  1:45  9:05      12:45  9:00  9:45      3:20  4:15  4:10

## SKILLKEEPER

Add or subtract.

$$\begin{array}{r} 8 \\ +8 \\ \hline \end{array} \qquad \begin{array}{r} 13 \\ -6 \\ \hline \end{array} \qquad \begin{array}{r} 5 \\ +5 \\ \hline \end{array} \qquad \begin{array}{r} 14 \\ -7 \\ \hline \end{array} \qquad \begin{array}{r} 7 \\ +7 \\ \hline \end{array} \qquad \begin{array}{r} 11 \\ -2 \\ \hline \end{array}$$

These clocks show the same time.

## Match the clocks that show the same time.

**1.**

1:55    11:10    5:05    1:25

**2.**

8:40    9:45    8:25    5:40

Write the times.

1.

_____ _____ _____

2.

_____ _____ _____

3.

_____ _____ _____

4.

_____ _____ _____

5. **DATA BANK** What time was music? _____
(See page 341.)

## THINK MATH

You say Ray's age when you count by 3s.
He is between 10 and 17. The number
is even. How old is Ray?

_____ years old

Telling time—practice

Name _____

**1 hour later**

## Ring the correct clock.

**1.**

**1 hour later**

**2.**

**2 hours later**

**3.**

**3 hours later**

**4.**

**5 hours later**

## Problem Solving

Solve.

**1.**

Pam played ball from

 to

How long did she play? _____ hour

**2.**

Sam rode his bike from

 to

How long did he ride? _____ hours

**3.**

Steve flew his kite from

 to

How long did he fly his kite? _____ hours

## THINK MATH

Estimate how much time. Ring it.

15 minutes or 2 hours

6 days or 6 months

Problem solving—elapsed time

Name _____

Write the name of this month.
Write the numbers
for the days in this month.

Month _____

| Sunday | Monday | Tuesday | Wednesday | Thursday | Friday | Saturday |
|--------|--------|---------|-----------|----------|--------|----------|
|        |        |         |           |          |        |          |
|        |        |         |           |          |        |          |
|        |        |         |           |          |        |          |
|        |        |         |           |          |        |          |
|        |        |         |           |          |        |          |

1. How many days are in this month? _____

2. How many

Wednesdays? _____   Saturdays? _____

Tuesdays?   _____   Sundays?   _____

3. Write the day of the week for each.

tenth _____   thirteenth _____

twenty-fifth _____   thirtieth _____

4. **DATA BANK** May fourth, year 2000 _____
   (See page 341.)

There are 12 months in a year.

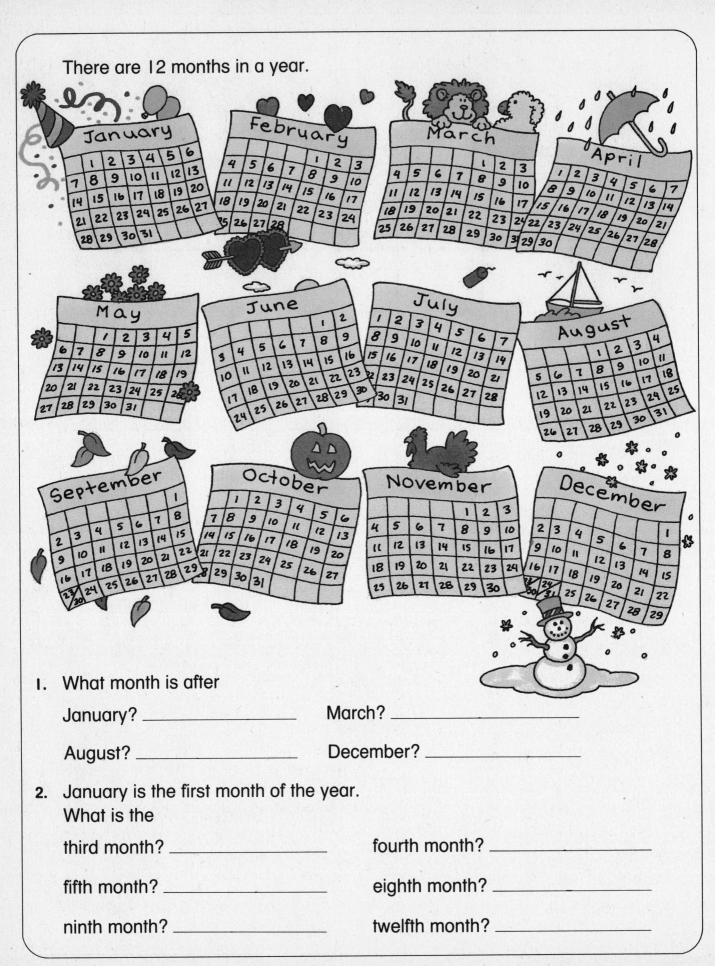

1. What month is after

   January? _____    March? _____

   August? _____    December? _____

2. January is the first month of the year.
   What is the

   third month? _____    fourth month? _____

   fifth month? _____    eighth month? _____

   ninth month? _____    twelfth month? _____

Calendar—order of months

Name _____

| penny | nickel | dime |
|---|---|---|
|  |  |  |
| 1 cent | 5 cents | 10 cents |
| 1¢ | 5¢ | 10¢ |

**1. Count the money. Write the price.**

5    6    7    8    9
___  ___  ___  ___  ___

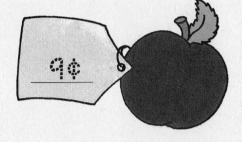
9¢

**2.**

_____

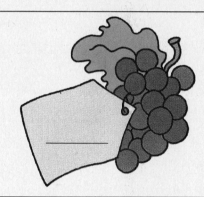

**3.**

_____

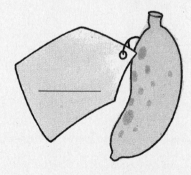

**4.**

_____

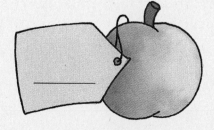

Count the money. Write the price.

10   20   30   35   36

36¢

**1.**

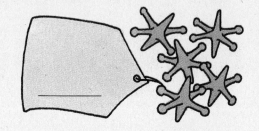

_____

**2.**

_____

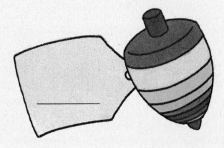

**3.**

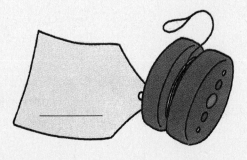

_____

—— **SKILLKEEPER** ——

Subtract.

$$15 - 9$$    $$14 - 7$$    $$12 - 8$$    $$13 - 6$$    $$16 - 7$$    $$18 - 9$$

Counting money—pennies, nickels, and dimes

Name _____

# How much does it cost? Ring the one that costs more.

**1.**
   →

   →

**2.**
      →

     →

**3.**
    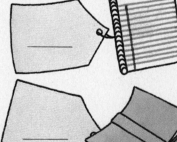 →

     →

**4.**
      →

      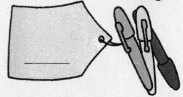 →

Counting and comparing money using pennies, nickels, and dimes

This one has the better price.

22¢    25¢

---

1. How much does it cost? Ring the one with the better price.

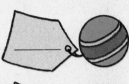

---

2.

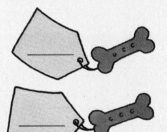

---

3.

---

## SKILLKEEPER

Ring tens and ones to show the number.

23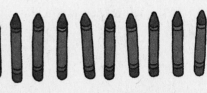

35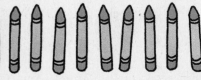

Name _____

Count the money in each bank.
Color the banks that have exact change for a quarter.

1. __30¢__

2. _____

3. _____

4. _____

Is there enough money to buy this?

45¢    25   35   45   46    46¢    (Yes)   No

1.   26¢     Yes   No

2.   35¢     Yes   No

3.   47¢     Yes   No

4.   42¢     Yes   No

## THINK MATH

Pam's money    Jack's money    Pam can buy the

Jack cannot.

How much is the   ?

    Counting money—pennies, nickels, dimes, and quarters

Name _____

A half dollar is 50¢.

Count the money in each jar.
Color the jars that have exact change for a half-dollar.

1. _____

2. _____

3. _____

4. _____

Counting money—half dollar

Is there enough money to buy this?

 **68¢**

**70¢** (**Yes**)

50    60    70

No

**1.**  **49¢**

Yes

_____

No

_____

**2.**  **65¢**

Yes

_____

No

_____

**3.**  **60¢**

Yes

_____

No

_____

**4.**  **79¢**

Yes

_____

No

_____  _____  _____

# SKILLKEEPER

Subtract.

$$\begin{array}{r} 11 \\ -\ 4 \\ \hline \end{array} \qquad \begin{array}{r} 12 \\ -\ 7 \\ \hline \end{array} \qquad \begin{array}{r} 11 \\ -\ 8 \\ \hline \end{array} \qquad \begin{array}{r} 12 \\ -\ 5 \\ \hline \end{array} \qquad \begin{array}{r} 11 \\ -\ 9 \\ \hline \end{array} \qquad \begin{array}{r} 12 \\ -\ 6 \\ \hline \end{array}$$

Counting money—all coins

Name _____

Mark the coins needed to pay the exact amount.

**1.**

**2.**

**3.**

**4.**

**5.**

Mark the coins needed. Is there any change?

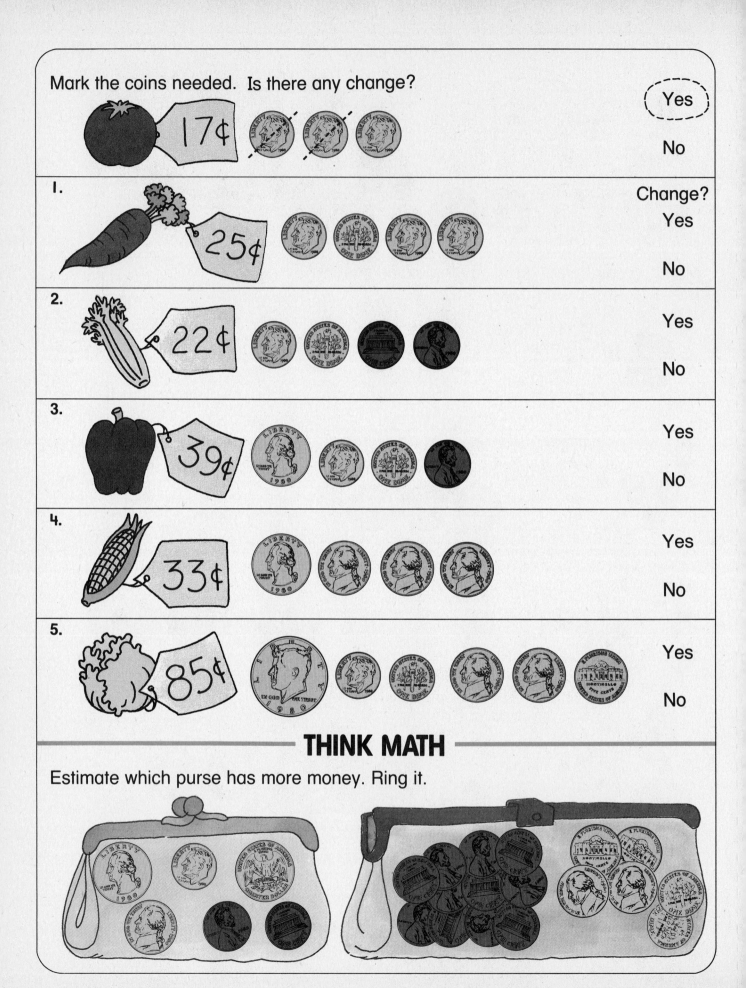

17¢

( Yes )

No

1.

25¢

Change?

Yes

No

2.

22¢

Yes

No

3.

39¢

Yes

No

4.

33¢

Yes

No

5.

85¢

Yes

No

## THINK MATH

Estimate which purse has more money. Ring it.

Change

Solve.

1. Meg had

   She earned 7¢ more.

   How much money does she have now?

$$
\begin{array}{r}
8¢ \\
+\ 7¢ \\
\hline
15¢
\end{array}
$$

2. Cliff had

   He spent 8¢.

   How much money does he have now?

3. Henry has

   Sue has 9¢.

   How much more money does Henry have?

4. Rosa has

   Dave has 9¢.

   How much do they have in all?

Problem solving—counting money

## Problem Solving

Solve.

**1.** Buy a ◯ .

Buy a 🎺 .

How much is it for both?

```
    4 ¢
  + 7 ¢
 -------
   11 ¢
```

**2.** Buy a 🚗 .

Buy a ✈ .

How much more for the 🚗 ?

**3.** Buy a 🐷 .

Buy a ◯ .

How much more for the  ?

**4.** Buy a 🎺 .

Buy a ✈ .

How much is it for both?

**5.** Buy a ⚾ .

Buy a 🎺 .

How much is it for both?

**6.** DATA BANK

Buy a  .

Buy a  .

How much is it for both?
(See page 341.)

Problem solving—using data from a price tag

Name _____

## CHAPTER REVIEW/TEST

Give the times.

1.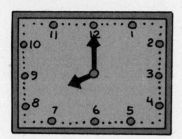

_____

2.

_____

3.

_____

4.

_____

5.

_____

6.

_____

Count the money.

7.

_____

8.

_____

9.

_____

10.

_____

Solve.

11. Kim rode the bus from

 to

How long was her bus ride? _____ hours

12.

Buy a 9¢.

Buy a 6¢.

How much is it for both? _____

# CUMULATIVE REVIEW

Add.

1.  $\begin{array}{r} 4 \\ +4 \\ \hline \end{array}$
    ○ 0
    ○ 7
    ○ 8

2.  $\begin{array}{r} 9 \\ +9 \\ \hline \end{array}$
    ○ 18
    ○ 16
    ○ 0

3.  $\begin{array}{r} 9 \\ +4 \\ \hline \end{array}$
    ○ 13
    ○ 14
    ○ 5

4.  $\begin{array}{r} 6 \\ 2 \\ +4 \\ \hline \end{array}$
    ○ 16
    ○ 12
    ○ 14

Subtract.

5.  $\begin{array}{r} 8 \\ -2 \\ \hline \end{array}$
    ○ 4
    ○ 10
    ○ 6

6.  $\begin{array}{r} 11 \\ -7 \\ \hline \end{array}$
    ○ 15
    ○ 4
    ○ 8

7.  $\begin{array}{r} 15 \\ -8 \\ \hline \end{array}$
    ○ 7
    ○ 8
    ○ 18

8.  $\begin{array}{r} 17 \\ -9 \\ \hline \end{array}$
    ○ 15
    ○ 7
    ○ 8

9.  Solve.

18 bears

9 birds

How many more bears than birds are there?

○ 10 more

○ 9 more

○ 8 more

# ANOTHER LOOK

25 minutes after 1 o'clock.

1:25

## What time is it?

**1.**

_____ minutes after _____ o'clock.

_____

**2.**

_____ minutes after _____ o'clock.

_____

## Count the money.

**3.**

25 _____ _____ _____

**4.**

_____

**5.**

_____

25  and 10  and 5  and 5
25    35    40    45

50  and 10  and 1  and 1
50    60    61    62

Another look

(one hundred fifty-one)  **151**

# ENRICHMENT

Color the last four strings
to match the pattern.

Count the beads.

| | 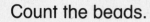 | | Total |
|---|---|---|---|
| | 2 | 1 | 3 |
| | | | |
| | | | |
| | | | |
| | | | |
| | | | |
| | | | |

How many green beads will you
need for a string with 24 beads?

_____ green beads

Enrichment—patterns

# 6 ADDITION—2 DIGIT NUMBERS

Name _____

__1__ __4__ ones ⟶ __1__ ten __4__ ones

---

## Count the sticks. Ring ten. Write the numbers.

**1.**

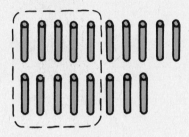

Trade 10 ones for 1 ten.

_____ ones ⟶ _____ ten _____ ones

---

**2.**

_____ ones ⟶ _____ ten _____ ones

---

**3.**

_____ ones ⟶ _____ ten _____ ones

---

Trading 10 ones for 1 ten

Count the pennies.
Ring ten. Write the numbers.

**1.**

Trade 10 pennies for 1 dime.

__12__ pennies ⟶ __1__ dime __2__ pennies

**2.**

____ pennies ⟶ ____ dime ____ pennies

**3.**

____ pennies ⟶ ____ dime ____ pennies

## SKILLKEEPER

Add or subtract.

$$\begin{array}{cccccc} 8 & 10 & 7 & 15 & 9 & 14 \\ +3 & -3 & +4 & -9 & +6 & -7 \end{array}$$

Name _____

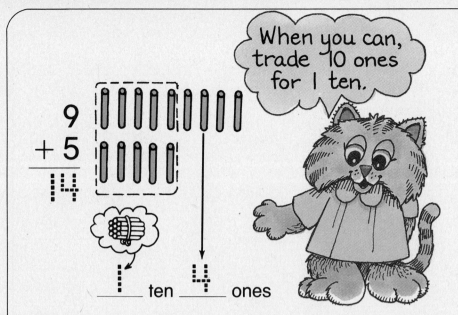

When you can, trade 10 ones for 1 ten.

9
+5
14

__1__ ten __4__ ones

4
+5
9

_____ ten __9__ ones

Add.
Ring 10 ones when you can.
Write the numbers.

**1.**

9
+3
12

__1__ ten __2__ ones

**2.**

6
+2
8

_____ ten __8__ ones

**3.**

8
+5
___

_____ ten _____ ones

**4.**

3
+4
___

_____ ten _____ ones

Add. Trade when you can.
Write the numbers.

1.
$$\begin{array}{r} 5 \\ +7 \\ \hline 12 \end{array}$$
→ __1__ ten __2__ ones

2.
$$\begin{array}{r} 2 \\ +5 \\ \hline 7 \end{array}$$
→ ____ ten __7__ ones

3.
$$\begin{array}{r} 6 \\ +7 \\ \hline \end{array}$$
→ ____ ten ____ ones

4.
$$\begin{array}{r} 4 \\ +4 \\ \hline \end{array}$$
→ ____ ten ____ ones

5.
$$\begin{array}{r} 8 \\ +8 \\ \hline \end{array}$$
→ ____ ten ____ ones

6.
$$\begin{array}{r} 9 \\ +5 \\ \hline \end{array}$$
→ ____ ten ____ ones

7.
$$\begin{array}{r} 6 \\ +3 \\ \hline \end{array}$$
→ ____ ten ____ ones

8.
$$\begin{array}{r} 8 \\ +5 \\ \hline \end{array}$$
→ ____ ten ____ ones

## SKILLKEEPER

Match .

Readiness for adding with trading

Name _____

▶ Add the ones first.

▶ Trade if you need to.

▶ Add the tens.

Use these steps when you add 2-digit numbers.

What is the total score?

Trade

| Tens | Ones |
|------|------|
| 2 | 7 |
| + | 5 |
| 3 | 2 |

The score is 32.

Trade

27 →
5 →

No trade

| Tens | Ones |
|------|------|
| 4 | 3 |
| + | 5 |
| 4 | 8 |

The score is 48.

No trade

43 →
5 →

Adding with and without trading—2-digit plus 1-digit.

**No trade**

| Tens | Ones |
|------|------|
| 4 | 1 |
| + | 6 |
| 4 | 7 |

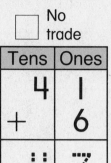

**Trade** | 1

| Tens | Ones |
|------|------|
| 3 | 7 |
| + | 8 |
| 4 | 5 |

15

Add.

1. **Trade** | 1

| Tens | Ones |
|------|------|
| 2 | 8 |
| + | 6 |
| | |

14

**No trade**

| Tens | Ones |
|------|------|
| 3 | 2 |
| + | 6 |
| | |

8

**Trade** | 1

| Tens | Ones |
|------|------|
| | 6 |
| +3 | 7 |
| | |

13

2. **No trade**

| Tens | Ones |
|------|------|
| 5 | 4 |
| + | 2 |
| | |

**Trade**

| Tens | Ones |
|------|------|
| 4 | 9 |
| + | 6 |
| | |

**No trade**

| Tens | Ones |
|------|------|
| | 7 |
| +3 | 2 |
| | |

## THINK MATH

| | 1st inning |
|------|------|
| **Birds** | 2 |
| **Eagles** | 4 |

Which team won? _____

How do you know?

**Final score:** 5 to 3

Adding with and without trading—2-digit plus 1-digit

How many pets
are for sale?

36 hamsters

| Tens | Ones |
|------|------|
| 3 | 6 |
| + | 7 |
| 4 | 3 |

 13

 7 guinea pigs

There are 43 pets for sale.

Add.

**1.**

| Tens | Ones |
|------|------|
| 3 | 4 |
| + | 3 |
| | |

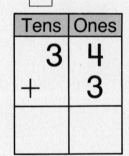

| Tens | Ones |
|------|------|
| 3 | 4 |
| + | 8 |
| | |

| Tens | Ones |
|------|------|
| 6 | 2 |
| + | 5 |
| | |

**2.**

| Tens | Ones |
|------|------|
| 5 | 6 |
| + | 7 |
| | |

| Tens | Ones |
|------|------|
| | 5 |
| +8 | 3 |
| | |

| Tens | Ones |
|------|------|
| | 8 |
| +6 | 7 |
| | |

**3.**

| Tens | Ones |
|------|------|
| | 4 |
| +4 | 6 |
| | |

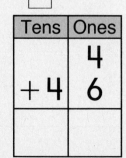

| Tens | Ones |
|------|------|
| 5 | 0 |
| + | 7 |
| | |

| Tens | Ones |
|------|------|
| | 9 |
| +3 | 8 |
| | |

Adding with and without trading—2-digit plus 1-digit

(one hundred fifty-nine) **159**

|   | Trade | No Trade | |
|---|-------|----------|---|

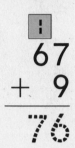
```
   67
 +  9
 ───
   76
```

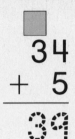
```
   34
 +  5
 ───
   39
```

When you have ten or more ones, trade

Add.

**1.**
```
  45        63        86        43        58        32
 + 6       + 5       + 4       + 6       + 5       + 4
 ───       ───       ───       ───       ───       ───
```

**2.**
```
  27         5        48        36        74         4
 + 6       +13       + 8       + 6       + 9       +14
 ───       ───       ───       ───       ───       ───
```

**3.**
```
  66        34        50        63        51        48
 + 4       + 9       + 8       + 9       + 7       + 4
 ───       ───       ───       ───       ───       ───
```

## SKILLKEEPER

Add or subtract.

```
  12         8         9         8        12         5
 - 7       + 6       - 5       + 9       - 8       + 9
 ───       ───       ───       ───       ───       ───
```

Adding with and without trading—2-digit plus 1-digit

Name _____

Do you trade? Ring **yes** or **no**. Then add.

1.
| 44 Yes | 25 Yes | 62 Yes | 59 Yes |
| + 8 No | + 5 No | + 4 No | + 3 No |

2.
| 55 Yes | 8 Yes | 36 Yes | 9 Yes |
| + 2 No | +47 No | + 9 No | +37 No |

3.
| 15 Yes | 17 Yes | 34 Yes | 45 Yes |
| + 8 No | + 2 No | + 8 No | + 4 No |

4.
| 27 Yes | 3 Yes | 22 Yes | 68 Yes |
| + 6 No | +16 No | + 7 No | + 5 No |

5.
| 46 Yes | 65 Yes | 3 Yes | 16 Yes |
| + 3 No | + 9 No | +27 No | + 8 No |

Practice deciding when to trade

## Problem Solving

Solve.

1.  17 brown cows are in the barn.
    4 black cows are in the barn.
    Altogether, how many brown and
    black cows are in the barn?

    _____ cows

$$\begin{array}{r} 17 \\ +\phantom{0}4 \\ \hline 21 \end{array}$$

2.

    10 horses are in the barn.
    5 horses are in the field.
    Altogether, how many horses
    are in the barn and field?

    _____ horses

3.

    14 chickens were in the yard.
    8 ran away.
    How many chickens stayed in
    the yard?

    _____ chickens

4.

    8 big pigs are playing in the mud.
    32 baby pigs are playing in the mud.
    How many pigs are playing in
    the mud?

    _____ pigs

Problem solving—short sentence

Name _____

How many fish were caught
at each lake?

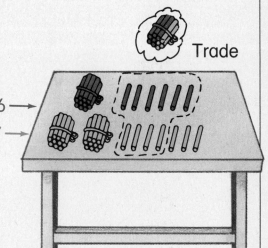

Trade

| | Tens | Ones |
|---|---|---|
| | 1 | 6 |
| + | 2 | 7 |
| | 4 | 3 |

Trade: 1    13

16 →
27 →

43 fish were caught at Lake Lemon.

No trade

| | Tens | Ones |
|---|---|---|
| | 2 | 6 |
| + | 3 | 2 |
| | 5 | 8 |

No trade    8

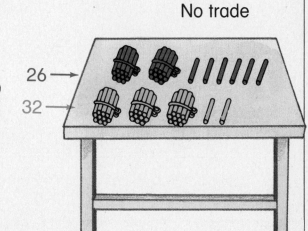

26 →
32 →

58 fish were caught at Blue Lake.

Do you trade? Ring **yes** or **no**. Then add.

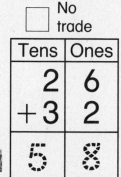

$$56 \quad \text{Yes}$$
$$+21 \quad \text{No}$$

$$48 \quad \text{Yes}$$
$$+17 \quad \text{No}$$

$$32 \quad \text{Yes}$$
$$+17 \quad \text{No}$$

$$16 \quad \text{Yes}$$
$$+48 \quad \text{No}$$

2-digit addition with and without trading

Add. Trade if you need to.

1.
$$58 + 25$$    $$49 + 36$$    $$34 + 24$$    $$17 + 15$$    $$56 + 24$$    $$27 + 34$$

2.
$$24 + 39$$    $$68 + 15$$    $$45 + 36$$    $$18 + 37$$    $$43 + 5$$    $$58 + 37$$

3.
$$63 + 14$$    $$6 + 17$$    $$29 + 18$$    $$33 + 37$$    $$62 + 24$$    $$46 + 15$$

4.
$$25 + 15$$    $$41 + 26$$    $$38 + 6$$    $$53 + 37$$    $$28 + 28$$    $$63 + 28$$

5.
$$36 + 12$$    $$53 + 19$$    $$20 + 59$$    $$48 + 19$$    $$27 + 36$$    $$52 + 18$$

## THINK MATH

Pretend you tossed a coin 20 times.
How may times do you think
it would land heads up? _____

Now try it.
How many times did it
land heads up? _____

2-digit addition with and without trading

Name _____

How many pencils
are there?

12 pencils

24 pencils

$$\begin{array}{r} 12 \\ + 24 \\ \hline 36 \end{array}$$

Altogether there are
36 pencils.

Copy and add.

**1.**

42 + 36          38 + 14          27 + 39

**2.**

4 + 33          27 + 25          52 + 36

**3.**

16 + 39          58 + 6          26 + 70

**4.**

35 + 22          42 + 39          28 + 45

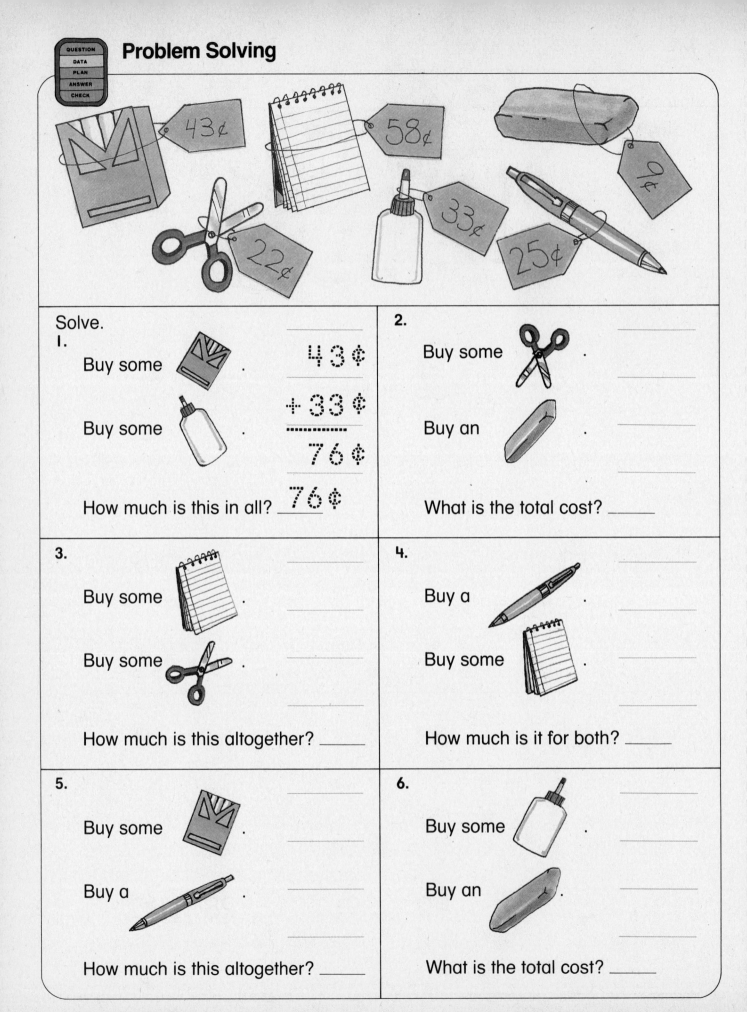

## Problem Solving

QUESTION
DATA
PLAN
ANSWER
CHECK

Solve.

**1.**

Buy some ▨.     4 3 ¢

Buy some 🫗.    + 3 3 ¢
                   ----------
                   7 6 ¢

How much is this in all? __76¢__

**2.**

Buy some ✂. _____

Buy an ▱. _____

What is the total cost? _____

**3.**

Buy some 📓. _____

Buy some ✂. _____

How much is this altogether? _____

**4.**

Buy a 🖊. _____

Buy some 📓. _____

How much is it for both? _____

**5.**

Buy some ▨. _____

Buy a 🖊. _____

How much is this altogether? _____

**6.**

Buy some 🫗. _____

Buy an ▱. _____

What is the total cost? _____

         Problem solving—using data from a price tag

Name _____

Add to fill in the boxes.

## Down

1. $23 + 14$

$$\begin{array}{r} 23 \\ + 14 \\ \hline 37 \end{array}$$

2. $18 + 19$

3. $55 + 27$

4. $26 + 5$

7. $23 + 23$

8. $31 + 29$

9. $27 + 16$

10. $20 + 19$

Check your answers with these.

## Across

1. $\begin{array}{r} 17 \\ + 16 \\ \hline \end{array}$

3. $\begin{array}{r} 75 \\ + 8 \\ \hline \end{array}$

5. $\begin{array}{r} 38 \\ + 39 \\ \hline \end{array}$

6. $\begin{array}{r} 5 \\ + 16 \\ \hline \end{array}$

7. $\begin{array}{r} 18 \\ + 28 \\ \hline \end{array}$

9. $\begin{array}{r} 36 \\ + 7 \\ \hline \end{array}$

11. $\begin{array}{r} 43 \\ + 17 \\ \hline \end{array}$

12. $\begin{array}{r} 15 \\ + 24 \\ \hline \end{array}$

## Crossnumber Puzzle

Addition practice

(one hundred sixty-seven)   167

Add. Trade if necessary.

1.
```
  17      13      43      69      53      32
+ 38    + 28    + 26    + 23    + 19    + 42
```

2.
```
  46      34      18      25      63      58
+ 42    + 47    + 48    + 25    + 36    + 24
```

3.
```
  77      45      37      66      16      21
+ 18    + 19    + 53    + 12    + 18    + 17
```

4.
```
  23      41      36      36      68      13
+ 33    + 19    + 51    + 20    + 29    + 44
```

## THINK MATH

Add "in your head." Write answers only.

5 + 3    20 + 8    4 + 2    30 + 6    2 + 7    50 + 9

1. 25 + 3 = ____   2. 34 + 2 = ____   3. 52 + 7 = ____

4. 43 + 4 = ____   5. 62 + 4 = ____   6. 71 + 8 = ____

7. 56 + 3 = ____   8. 24 + 4 = ____   9. 35 + 2 = ____

Addition practice

Name _____

Add. Ring the problems where you had to trade.

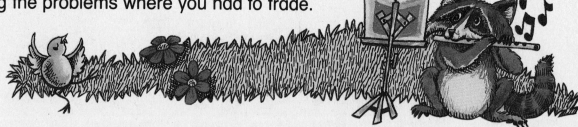

1.
$$
\begin{array}{r} 39 \\ +16 \\ \hline \end{array}
\qquad
\begin{array}{r} 45 \\ +\ 9 \\ \hline \end{array}
\qquad
\begin{array}{r} 23 \\ +18 \\ \hline \end{array}
\qquad
\begin{array}{r} 67 \\ +21 \\ \hline \end{array}
\qquad
\begin{array}{r} 52 \\ +\ 7 \\ \hline \end{array}
\qquad
\begin{array}{r} 18 \\ +35 \\ \hline \end{array}
$$

2.
$$
\begin{array}{r} 66 \\ +19 \\ \hline \end{array}
\qquad
\begin{array}{r} 5 \\ +28 \\ \hline \end{array}
\qquad
\begin{array}{r} 8 \\ +37 \\ \hline \end{array}
\qquad
\begin{array}{r} 77 \\ +21 \\ \hline \end{array}
\qquad
\begin{array}{r} 49 \\ +41 \\ \hline \end{array}
\qquad
\begin{array}{r} 36 \\ +10 \\ \hline \end{array}
$$

3.
$$
\begin{array}{r} 22 \\ +13 \\ \hline \end{array}
\qquad
\begin{array}{r} 38 \\ +56 \\ \hline \end{array}
\qquad
\begin{array}{r} 35 \\ +14 \\ \hline \end{array}
\qquad
\begin{array}{r} 8 \\ +12 \\ \hline \end{array}
\qquad
\begin{array}{r} 67 \\ +25 \\ \hline \end{array}
\qquad
\begin{array}{r} 43 \\ +38 \\ \hline \end{array}
$$

4.
$$
\begin{array}{r} 44 \\ +55 \\ \hline \end{array}
\qquad
\begin{array}{r} 63 \\ +27 \\ \hline \end{array}
\qquad
\begin{array}{r} 57 \\ +\ 8 \\ \hline \end{array}
\qquad
\begin{array}{r} 25 \\ +77 \\ \hline \end{array}
\qquad
\begin{array}{r} 36 \\ +49 \\ \hline \end{array}
\qquad
\begin{array}{r} 72 \\ +12 \\ \hline \end{array}
$$

5.
$$
\begin{array}{r} 34 \\ +14 \\ \hline \end{array}
\qquad
\begin{array}{r} 58 \\ +25 \\ \hline \end{array}
\qquad
\begin{array}{r} 13 \\ +20 \\ \hline \end{array}
\qquad
\begin{array}{r} 7 \\ +18 \\ \hline \end{array}
\qquad
\begin{array}{r} 25 \\ +16 \\ \hline \end{array}
\qquad
\begin{array}{r} 38 \\ +\ 6 \\ \hline \end{array}
$$

Addition practice

Add. Write the letter of the problem above the answer.

| L 55 +28 | I 24 +17 | S 36 +32 | U 26 +24 | O 27 +35 |
|---|---|---|---|---|
| T 48 + 6 | N 41 +54 | E 16 +26 | D 64 +27 | C 35 +16 |

L __ __ __ __ __ __ __ __ __ .
83 42 54 54 50 51 42  41 95

__ __ __ __ __ __ __ __
41 54  41 68  51 62 83 91

__ __ __ __ __ __ __ .
62 50 54 68 41 91 42

Addition practice

How many children are at camp?

Camp Timberland

| Tent 1 | 24 girls |
| Tent 2 | 22 boys |
| Tent 3 | 15 girls |

Add the ones. Trade if you need to.

Then add the tens.

$$\begin{array}{r} 24 \\ 22 \\ +15 \\ \hline \end{array}$$

$$\begin{array}{r} 4 \\ 2 \\ +5 \\ \hline 11 \end{array}$$ Trade.

$$\begin{array}{r} 24 \\ 22 \\ +15 \\ \hline 61 \end{array}$$

There are 61 children at camp.

Add. Trade if necessary.

**1.**

$$\begin{array}{r} 22 \\ 16 \\ +33 \\ \hline \end{array} \quad \begin{array}{r} 41 \\ 16 \\ +22 \\ \hline \end{array} \quad \begin{array}{r} 33 \\ 3 \\ +14 \\ \hline \end{array} \quad \begin{array}{r} 11 \\ 6 \\ +3 \\ \hline \end{array} \quad \begin{array}{r} 51 \\ 7 \\ +2 \\ \hline \end{array} \quad \begin{array}{r} 32 \\ 19 \\ +20 \\ \hline \end{array}$$

**2.**

$$\begin{array}{r} 50 \\ 35 \\ +14 \\ \hline \end{array} \quad \begin{array}{r} 28 \\ 11 \\ +4 \\ \hline \end{array} \quad \begin{array}{r} 6 \\ 13 \\ +21 \\ \hline \end{array} \quad \begin{array}{r} 43 \\ 12 \\ +21 \\ \hline \end{array} \quad \begin{array}{r} 32 \\ 47 \\ +2 \\ \hline \end{array} \quad \begin{array}{r} 50 \\ 20 \\ +19 \\ \hline \end{array}$$

**3.**

$$\begin{array}{r} 25 \\ 45 \\ +15 \\ \hline \end{array} \quad \begin{array}{r} 62 \\ 4 \\ +3 \\ \hline \end{array} \quad \begin{array}{r} 35 \\ 23 \\ +26 \\ \hline \end{array} \quad \begin{array}{r} 26 \\ 2 \\ +31 \\ \hline \end{array} \quad \begin{array}{r} 42 \\ 25 \\ +14 \\ \hline \end{array} \quad \begin{array}{r} 10 \\ 12 \\ +45 \\ \hline \end{array}$$

Column addition—2-digit

QUESTION
DATA
PLAN
ANSWER
CHECK

Solve.

1.

25 in the space ship
65 on the playground

How many Gorkeys is this in all? _____ Gorkeys

$$\begin{array}{r} 25 \\ +65 \\ \hline 90 \end{array}$$

2.

48 played kickball
35 played tag

How many were playing in all? _____ Gorkeys

3.

17 on the monkey bars
8 climbing trees

How many more Gorkeys on the monkey bars? _____ more

4.

12 on the big slide
28 on the small slide

How many Gorkeys on slides? _____ on slides

5. **DATA BANK** How many Gorkeys on swings?
(See page 342.)

_____ on swings

Problem solving—data card

I have to trade.
The answer is 20 or more.

$$15 \\ + \ 7$$

( 20 or more )

less than 20

I do not have to trade.
The answer is less than 20.

$$15 \\ + \ 3$$

20 or more

( less than 20 )

Ring the better estimate.

**1.**

$$16 \\ + \ 5$$

20 or more

less than 20

$$14 \\ + \ 4$$

20 or more

less than 20

$$18 \\ + \ 4$$

20 or more

less than 20

$$13 \\ + \ 6$$

20 or more

less than 20

**2.**

$$25 \\ + \ 3$$

30 or more

less than 30

$$24 \\ + \ 7$$

30 or more

less than 30

$$26 \\ + \ 3$$

30 or more

less than 30

$$27 \\ + \ 6$$

30 or more

less than 30

**3.**

$$14 \\ + 14$$

30 or more

less than 30

$$17 \\ + 14$$

30 or more

less than 30

$$12 \\ + 17$$

30 or more

less than 30

$$15 \\ + 17$$

30 or more

less than 30

**4.**

$$24 \\ + 18$$

40 or more

less than 40

$$27 \\ + 15$$

40 or more

less than 40

$$26 \\ + 13$$

40 or more

less than 40

$$26 \\ + 17$$

40 or more

less than 40

What are the missing house numbers on Royal Street?
Look for a pattern.

Royal Street

I see a pattern!

Each number is 2 more.

The missing house numbers are 10 and 12.

1. Write the missing numbers on the elevator buttons.

2. Write the room numbers for grades 2 and 3.

Name _____

## CHAPTER REVIEW/TEST

Add.

1.
$$\begin{array}{r} 34 \\ +23 \\ \hline \end{array}\qquad \begin{array}{r} 42 \\ +15 \\ \hline \end{array}\qquad \begin{array}{r} 26 \\ +\ 3 \\ \hline \end{array}\qquad \begin{array}{r} 14 \\ +14 \\ \hline \end{array}\qquad \begin{array}{r} 55 \\ +34 \\ \hline \end{array}\qquad \begin{array}{r} 22 \\ +\ 6 \\ \hline \end{array}$$

2.
$$\begin{array}{r} 53 \\ +\ 9 \\ \hline \end{array}\qquad \begin{array}{r} 35 \\ +\ 8 \\ \hline \end{array}\qquad \begin{array}{r} 17 \\ +\ 8 \\ \hline \end{array}\qquad \begin{array}{r} 68 \\ +\ 5 \\ \hline \end{array}\qquad \begin{array}{r} 24 \\ +\ 7 \\ \hline \end{array}\qquad \begin{array}{r} 46 \\ +\ 8 \\ \hline \end{array}$$

3.
$$\begin{array}{r} 42 \\ +27 \\ \hline \end{array}\qquad \begin{array}{r} 30 \\ +64 \\ \hline \end{array}\qquad \begin{array}{r} 26 \\ +17 \\ \hline \end{array}\qquad \begin{array}{r} 34 \\ +28 \\ \hline \end{array}\qquad \begin{array}{r} 56 \\ +26 \\ \hline \end{array}\qquad \begin{array}{r} 74 \\ +16 \\ \hline \end{array}$$

4.
$$\begin{array}{r} 18 \\ 46 \\ +10 \\ \hline \end{array}\qquad \begin{array}{r} 53 \\ 19 \\ +20 \\ \hline \end{array}\qquad \begin{array}{r} 23 \\ 2 \\ +13 \\ \hline \end{array}\qquad \begin{array}{r} 5 \\ 12 \\ +14 \\ \hline \end{array}\qquad \begin{array}{r} 22 \\ 16 \\ +32 \\ \hline \end{array}\qquad \begin{array}{r} 36 \\ 1 \\ +15 \\ \hline \end{array}$$

Solve.

5. Mrs. Swartz's class rode a bus to a baseball game. 28 girls and 15 boys rode on the bus. How many children rode the bus?

_____ children

6. Sandra bought an old baseball and an old bat. How much did she spend altogether?

_____ altogether

# CUMULATIVE REVIEW

Subtract.

1.
$$\begin{array}{r} 1\ 1 \\ -\ \ 8 \\ \hline \end{array}$$
○ 7
○ 5
○ 3

2.
$$\begin{array}{r} 1\ 4 \\ -\ \ 5 \\ \hline \end{array}$$
○ 7
○ 16
○ 9

3.
$$\begin{array}{r} 1\ 5 \\ -\ \ 7 \\ \hline \end{array}$$
○ 8
○ 9
○ 18

4.
$$\begin{array}{r} 1\ 8 \\ -\ \ 9 \\ \hline \end{array}$$
○ 9
○ 1
○ 8

Give the time.

5.
○ 12 o'clock
○ 4 o'clock
○ 5 o'clock

6.
○ 3:20
○ 2:20
○ 4:10

Count the money.

7.
○ 30¢
○ 21¢
○ 25¢

8.
○ 75¢
○ 65¢
○ 85¢

9. Solve.

Kevin had 11 kittens.
9 kittens were asleep.
How many kittens were
awake?

○ 2
○ 3
○ 5

Name _____

# ANOTHER LOOK

Add the ones.

$\begin{array}{r}33\\+24\\\hline 7\end{array}$

Then add the tens.

$\begin{array}{r}33\\+24\\\hline 57\end{array}$

Add.

1.
$\begin{array}{r}26\\+13\\\hline\end{array}$
$\begin{array}{r}71\\+4\\\hline\end{array}$
$\begin{array}{r}33\\+25\\\hline\end{array}$

2.
$\begin{array}{r}16\\+12\\\hline\end{array}$
$\begin{array}{r}4\\+21\\\hline\end{array}$
$\begin{array}{r}44\\+33\\\hline\end{array}$

Add the ones. Trade.

$\begin{array}{r}1\\26\\+18\\\hline 4\end{array}$

Then add the tens.

$\begin{array}{r}1\\26\\+18\\\hline 44\end{array}$

Add. Trade 10 ones for 1 ten.

3.
$\begin{array}{r}45\\+7\\\hline\end{array}$
$\begin{array}{r}26\\+25\\\hline\end{array}$
$\begin{array}{r}34\\+46\\\hline\end{array}$

4.
$\begin{array}{r}52\\+19\\\hline\end{array}$
$\begin{array}{r}8\\+24\\\hline\end{array}$
$\begin{array}{r}15\\+38\\\hline\end{array}$

Add. Trade if you need to.

5.
$\begin{array}{r}32\\+26\\\hline\end{array}$
$\begin{array}{r}75\\+15\\\hline\end{array}$
$\begin{array}{r}43\\+9\\\hline\end{array}$
$\begin{array}{r}57\\+17\\\hline\end{array}$
$\begin{array}{r}62\\+8\\\hline\end{array}$
$\begin{array}{r}70\\+24\\\hline\end{array}$

6.
$\begin{array}{r}18\\+11\\\hline\end{array}$
$\begin{array}{r}7\\+29\\\hline\end{array}$
$\begin{array}{r}20\\+62\\\hline\end{array}$
$\begin{array}{r}38\\+47\\\hline\end{array}$
$\begin{array}{r}46\\+4\\\hline\end{array}$
$\begin{array}{r}9\\+77\\\hline\end{array}$

# ENRICHMENT

This is a fence.
The animals cannot cross the fence.
Ring the animals that cannot get out.

Enrichment—simple closed curves

# GEOMETRY AND GRAPHING

Match.

sphere

cube

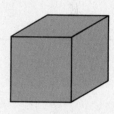

cylinder

cone

Ring the figure that was made by
tracing around the shape.

1.

2.

3.

4.

## SKILLKEEPER

Add.

$$\begin{array}{r} 22 \\ +14 \\ \hline \end{array} \qquad \begin{array}{r} 45 \\ +14 \\ \hline \end{array} \qquad \begin{array}{r} 26 \\ +5 \\ \hline \end{array} \qquad \begin{array}{r} 68 \\ +4 \\ \hline \end{array} \qquad \begin{array}{r} 40 \\ +24 \\ \hline \end{array} \qquad \begin{array}{r} 24 \\ +36 \\ \hline \end{array}$$

Space figures

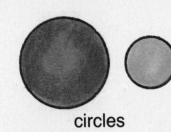     

| circles | squares | triangles | rectangles |

Ring the name for the shape.

**1.**

(circle)

square

triangle

square

triangle

rectangle

rectangle

triangle

circle

**2.**

circle

square

triangle

square

rectangle

circle

rectangle

triangle

square

**3.**

triangle

square

rectangle

triangle

square

circle

triangle

circle

square

**4.**

rectangle

triangle

square

square

circle

triangle

circle

square

triangle

Plane shapes

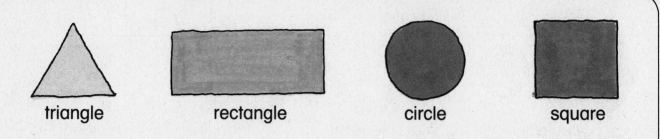

| triangle | rectangle | circle | square |

Color to match.

## — THINK MATH —

Ring one. Today is Wednesday.        Tuesday
In six days it will be
                                     Wednesday

                                     Thursday

Name _____

Mark each side with an ✗.
Mark each corner with a ◯.

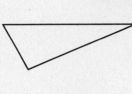

**4** sides

**4** corners

Give the number of sides and corners for each.

**1.**

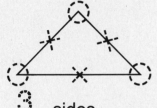

**3** _____ sides

**3** _____ corners

_____ sides

_____ corners

_____ sides

_____ corners

**2.**

_____ sides

_____ corners

_____ sides

_____ corners

_____ sides

_____ corners

**3.**

_____ sides

_____ corners

_____ sides

_____ corners

_____ sides

_____ corners

**4.**

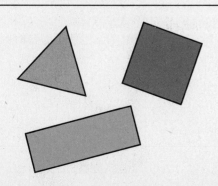

Triangles have _____ sides and _____ corners.

Rectangles have _____ sides and _____ corners.

Squares have _____ sides and _____ corners.

Plane shapes—sides and corners

Find the piece that fits. Color to match.

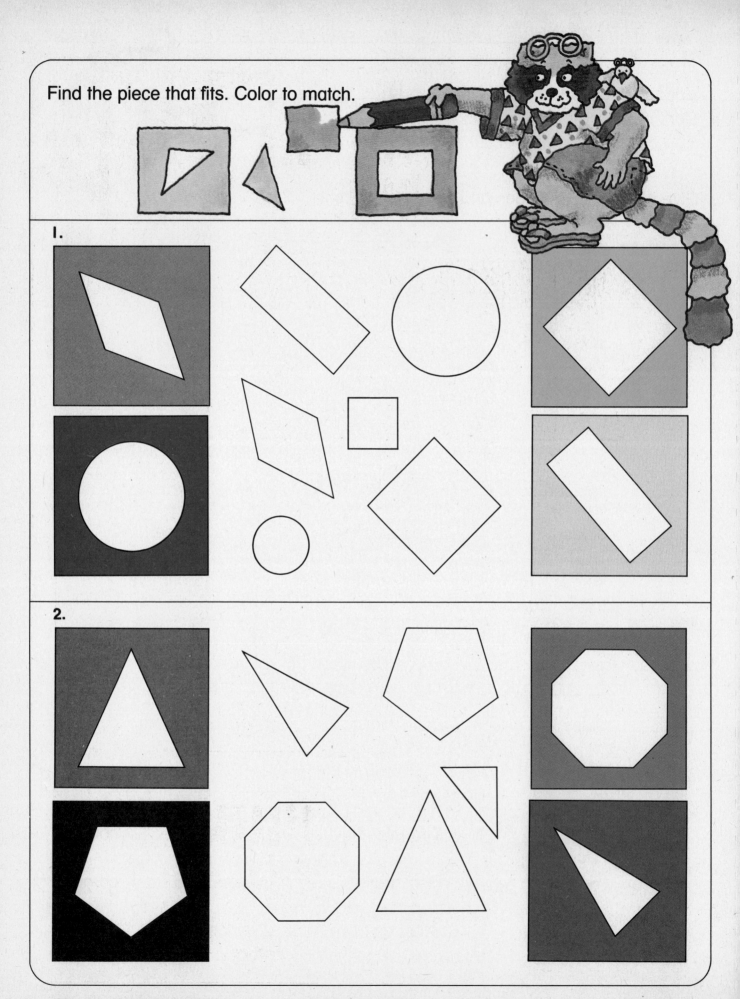

**1.**

**2.**

Congruence

Name _____

# Ring the pictures with two matching parts.

**1.**

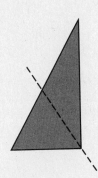 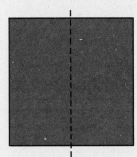 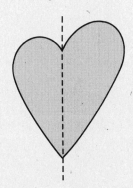

**2.**

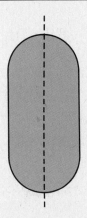 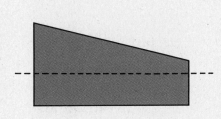 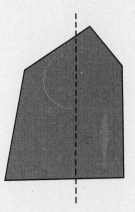

**3.**

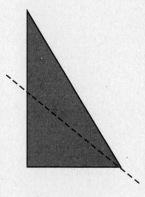 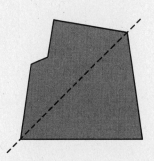 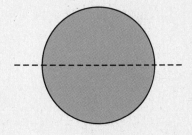

**4.**

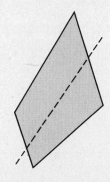 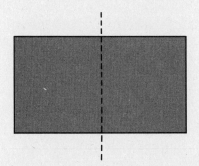 

Symmetry

Ring the figure that shows the fold in the correct place.

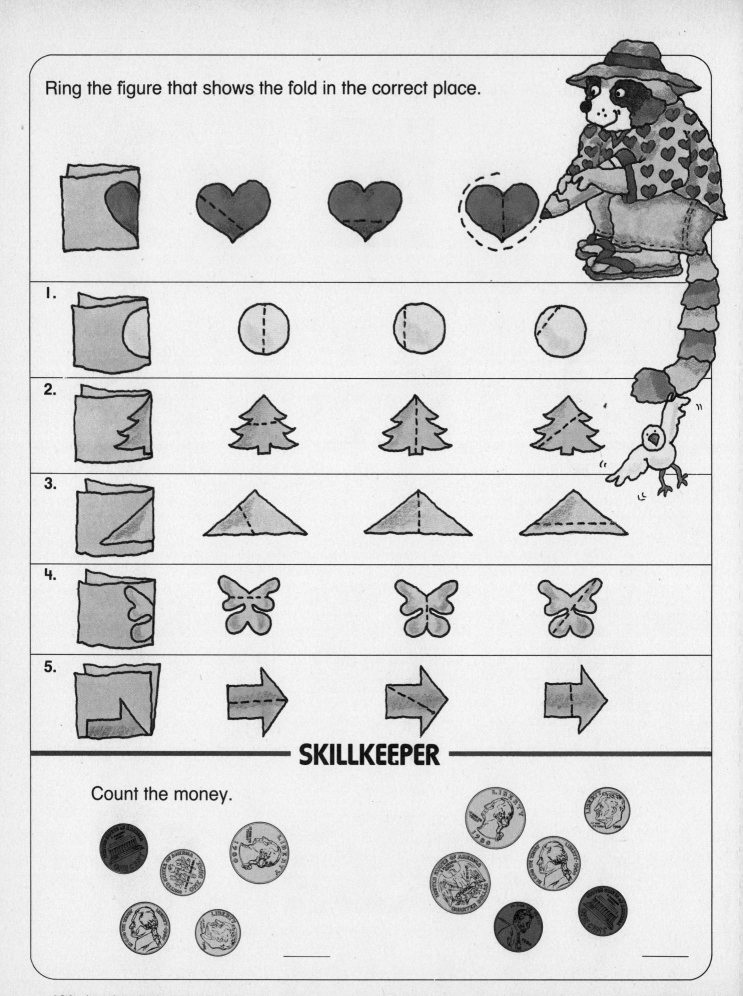

1.

2.

3.

4.

5.

## SKILLKEEPER

Count the money.

_____                    _____

Symmetry

Name _____

Look at the **bar graph.**

1. Finish coloring the bar graph
   to show how many
   chose each type of fruit.

## Favorite Fruit Snacks

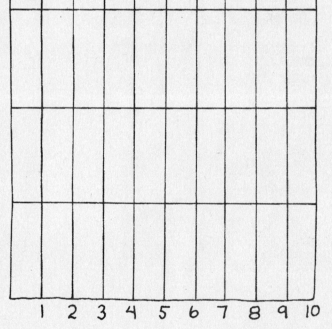

1  2  3  4  5  6  7  8  9  10

2. Ring the fruit more animals chose.

  or

  or

  or

  or

  or

  or

Bar graphs                                    (one hundred eighty-seven)  **187**

1. Finish coloring the bar graph to show the number of each kind of shirt.

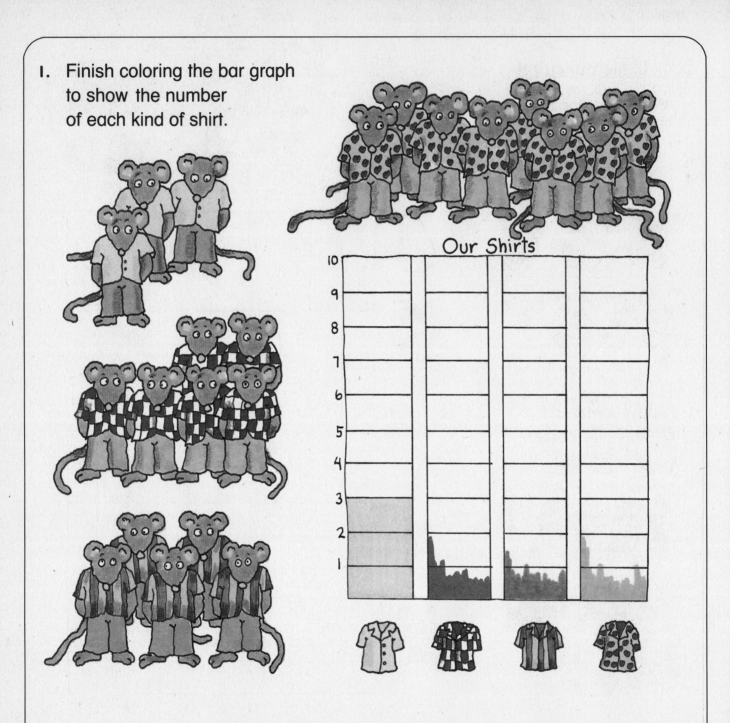

Our Shirts

2. Which is more?

3. Which is less?

4. How many 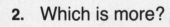 and 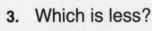 shirts are there in all? _____

5. How many  and  shirts are there in all? _____

Bar graphs

Name _____

Some children voted on which
game to play.
They made **tally marks**
for the votes.

| means 1 vote    ||||  means 5 votes

1. Count the tally marks and then
   color the graph to match.

Game Votes

Soccer        ||||  |||     Total: 8 ____

Kickball      ||||  ||||    Total: ____

Relay Races   ||||          Total: ____

Horseshoes    ||||          Total: ____

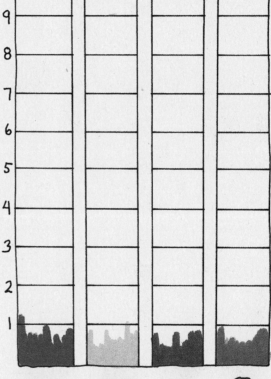

2. How many more votes for  than  are there? _____

3. How many fewer votes for  than  are there? _____

4. How many votes are there in all? _____

Bar graphs and tally marks

1. Finish making the tally marks.
   Cross out a shell for each mark.
   Write the total for each kind of shell.

Tally marks    Total

| | _____

| | _____

_____    _____

_____    _____

_____    _____

2. Use the tally marks. Color the graph.

Kinds of Shells

3. How many more [img] than [img] ? _____

4. How many fewer [img] than [img] ? _____

5. How many [img] and [img] in all? _____

6. How many [img] and [img] in all? _____

1  2  3  4  5  6  7  8  9  10

## SKILLKEEPER

Add.

$$\begin{array}{r} 45 \\ +37 \\ \hline \end{array} \qquad \begin{array}{r} 16 \\ +29 \\ \hline \end{array} \qquad \begin{array}{r} 38 \\ +33 \\ \hline \end{array} \qquad \begin{array}{r} 57 \\ +15 \\ \hline \end{array} \qquad \begin{array}{r} 19 \\ +78 \\ \hline \end{array} \qquad \begin{array}{r} 68 \\ +24 \\ \hline \end{array}$$

Bar graphs and tally marks

Emily's class made a **picture graph** of the
tickets they sold for the talent show.

Each  means I ticket.

Tickets Sold

| | |
|---|---|
| Monday | 🎟 🎟 🎟 🎟 🎟 🎟 🎟 🎟 |
| Tuesday | 🎟 🎟 🎟 🎟 🎟 |
| Wednesday | 🎟 🎟 🎟 🎟 🎟 🎟 🎟 |
| Thursday | 🎟 🎟 🎟 🎟 🎟 🎟 🎟 🎟 🎟 |
| Friday | 🎟 🎟 🎟 🎟 |

1. How many tickets were sold

   on Monday? _____     on Wednesday? _____     on Friday? _____

   on Tuesday? _____     on Thursday? _____

2. On what day were the most tickets sold? _____

3. On what day were the fewest tickets sold? _____

Picture graphs                                            (one hundred ninety-one) **191**

Ricky's class had a pencil sale.
They are making a graph to show the number
of pencils they sold.

Each colored box means 5 pencils sold.

On Monday they sold __25__ pencils.

Pencils Sold

| Monday | | | | | | | | | | |
|---|---|---|---|---|---|---|---|---|---|---|
| Tuesday | | | | | | | | | | |
| Wednesday | | | | | | | | | | |
| Thursday | | | | | | | | | | |
| Friday | | | | | | | | | | |

1. Color 4 boxes for Tuesday.    Number of pencils __20__

2. Color 7 boxes for Wednesday.    Number of pencils _____

3. Color 5 boxes for Thursday.    Number of pencils _____

4. Color 8 boxes for Friday.    Number of pencils _____

5. On what two days did they sell the same number of pencils?

_____

6. **DATA BANK**  How many pencils were sold on
Saturday and Sunday together? (See page 342.)    _____

Picture graphs

Name _____

**I.** Give the number of sides and corners and ring the correct name.

_____ sides

_____ corners

triangle

square

_____ sides

_____ corners

circle

square

_____ sides

_____ corners

triangle

rectangle

**2.** Find a figure to match each of these in size and shape. Color to match.

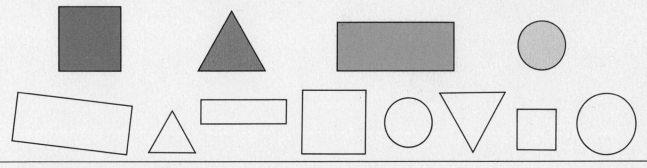

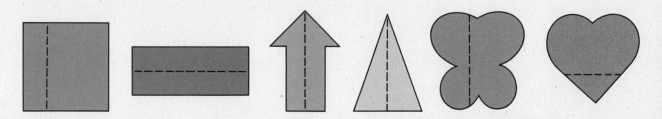

**3.** Ring the figures that match on both sides of the fold.

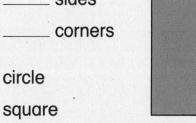

**4.** Color the graph.

Spaghetti Graph

Like Spaghetti

Don't like Spaghetti

1  2  3  4  5  6  7  8  9  10

# CUMULATIVE REVIEW

Give the time.

1.

○ 6:45
○ 9:30
○ 8:30

Count the money.

2.

○ 15¢
○ 25¢
○ 17¢

3.

○ 60¢
○ 40¢
○ 55¢

How much for both toys?

4.

○ 14¢
○ 15¢
○ 4¢

Add.

5.
$$\begin{array}{r} 25 \\ +\ 3 \\ \hline \end{array}$$

○ 22
○ 28
○ 10

6.
$$\begin{array}{r} 32 \\ +28 \\ \hline \end{array}$$

○ 60
○ 50
○ 70

7.
$$\begin{array}{r} 45 \\ +26 \\ \hline \end{array}$$

○ 71
○ 61
○ 70

8.
$$\begin{array}{r} 8 \\ 11 \\ +17 \\ \hline \end{array}$$

○ 56
○ 36
○ 46

9. Solve.

How many letters are there altogether?

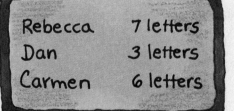

Rebecca    7 letters
Dan        3 letters
Carmen     6 letters

○ 16

○ 15

○ 14

Name _____

# ANOTHER LOOK

**Same shape, different size**

**Same shape, same size**

**1.** Ring **same shape** if the figures have the same shape.

Ring **same size** if the figures have the same size.

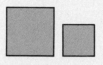

same shape
same size

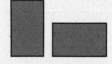

same shape
same size

same shape
same size

same shape
same size

Each ☐ means 1.

| 1 | 2 | 3 | 4 | 5 | 6 | 7 | 8 | 9 | 10 |

This means 8.

| 1 | 2 | 3 | 4 | 5 | 6 | 7 | 8 | 9 | 10 |

This means 5.

## Our Favorite Drinks

 Juice

 Juice

Juice

  1   2   3   4   5   6   7   8

**2.** How many children picked

 Juice? _____

Juice? _____

Juice? _____

# ENRICHMENT

Where is the 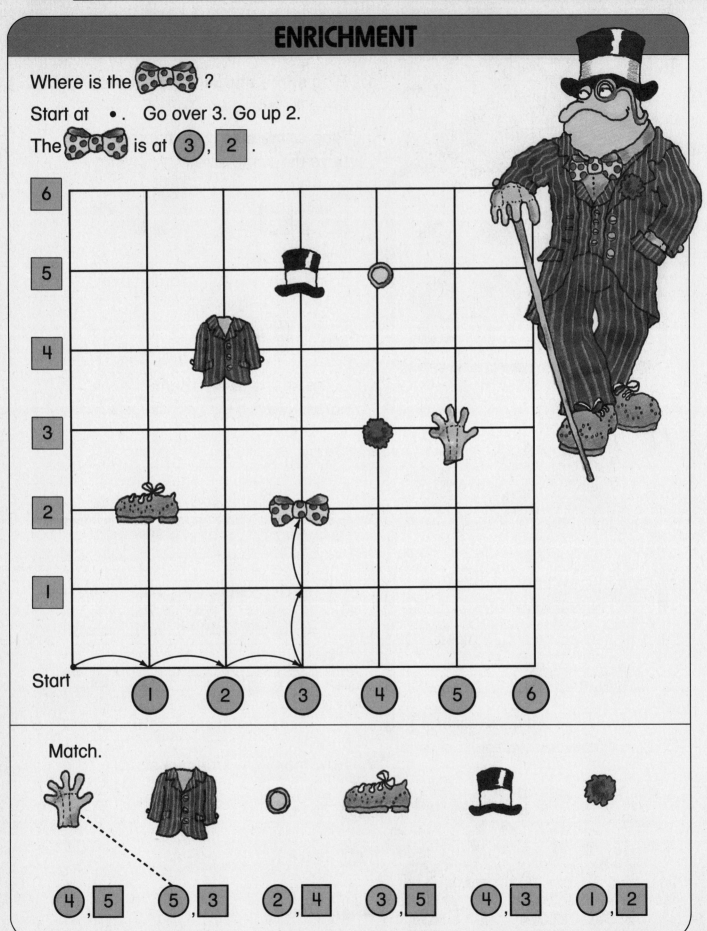 ?

Start at • . Go over 3. Go up 2.

The ⬡ is at (3), 2 .

Match.

Enrichment—coordinate graphing

# SUBTRACTION: 2-DIGIT NUMBERS

I ten makes 10 ones.

__1__ ten __2__ ones ⟶ __12__ ones

**Write the numbers.**

Trade 1 ten for 10 ones.

**1.**

_____ ten _____ ones ⟶ _____ ones

**2.**

_____ ten _____ ones ⟶ _____ ones

**3.**

_____ ten _____ ones ⟶ _____ ones

Trading 1 ten for 10 ones

Write the numbers.

**1.**

Trade 1 dime
for 10 pennies.

___1___ dime ___3___ pennies ⟶ ___13___ pennies

**2.**

_____ dime _____ pennies ⟶ _____ pennies

**3.**

_____ dime _____ pennies ⟶ _____ pennies

## THINK MATH

penny      nickel      dime

2 coins → 10¢      What are the coins? _____

6 coins → 10¢      What are the coins? _____

4 coins → 8¢       What are the coins? _____

Name _____

Trade 1 ten for 10 ones.

Trade 1 ten for 10 ones. Write the numbers.

**1.**

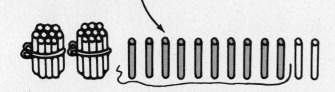

___3___ tens  ___2___ ones

⬇

___2___ tens  __12__ ones

**2.**

___4___ tens  ___3___ ones

⬇

___3___ tens  _____ ones

**3.**

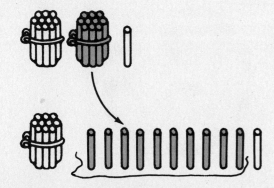

___2___ tens  ___1___ one

⬇

_____ ten  _____ ones

Trading 1 ten for 10 ones

Trade 1 ten for 10 ones. Write the numbers.

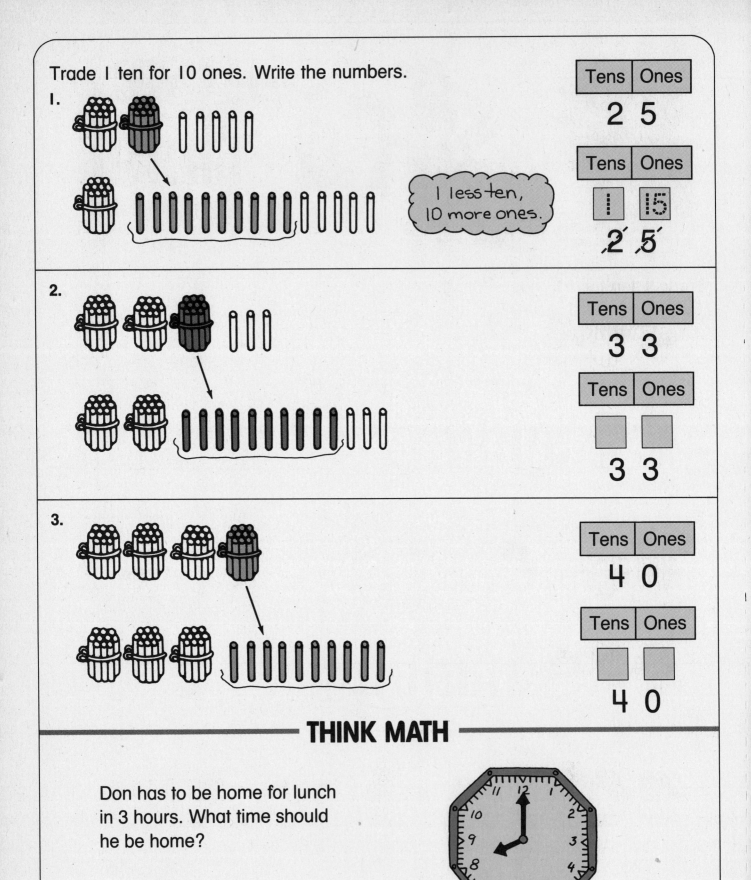

1.

| Tens | Ones |
|------|------|
| 2 | 5 |

| Tens | Ones |
|------|------|
| 1 | 15 |

*I less ten, 10 more ones.*

2́ 5́

2.

| Tens | Ones |
|------|------|
| 3 | 3 |

| Tens | Ones |
|------|------|
|  |  |

3 3

3.

| Tens | Ones |
|------|------|
| 4 | 0 |

| Tens | Ones |
|------|------|
|  |  |

4 0

## THINK MATH

Don has to be home for lunch in 3 hours. What time should he be home?

_____

Trade 1 ten for 10 ones. Write the numbers.

Remember
1 less 10,
10 more ones.

**1.**

3 tens    4 ones   →   __2__ tens    __14__ ones

| 2 | 14 |

**34**   →   ~~34~~

**2.**

4 tens    2 ones   →   __3__ tens    __12__ ones

| | |

**42**   →   **42**

**3.**

3 tens    5 ones   →   _____ tens    _____ ones

| | |

**35**   →   **35**

**4.**

2 tens    4 ones   →   _____ ten    _____ ones

| | |

**24**   →   **24**

Readiness for trading       

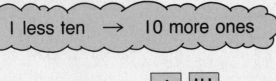

1 less ten → 10 more ones

1 14

24 —→ 2 4

---

Trade 1 ten for 10 ones. Write the numbers.

1.
| 4 | 14 |
~~5~~ ~~4~~

| 1 | |
~~2~~ ~~3~~

| | 17 |
~~3~~ ~~7~~

| 3 | |
~~4~~ ~~0~~

2.
6 2

5 5

4 1

2 8

3.
2 0

3 1

7 3

9 1

4.
3 2

6 7

2 5

6 0

---

## SKILLKEEPER

Subtract.

$$16 - 9$$   $$14 - 7$$   $$12 - 4$$   $$17 - 9$$   $$13 - 6$$   $$11 - 3$$

---

Readiness for trading

Use these steps to subtract 2-digit numbers.

- See if you need more ones.
- Trade if you need to.
- Subtract the ones.
- Subtract the tens.

How many apples were left in each tree?

42 red apples were in the tree.

| Tens | Ones |
|------|------|
| 3    | 12   |

Trade

$$\begin{array}{r} \!4\,2 \\ -\,1\,5 \\ \hline 2\,7 \end{array}$$

Trade

42 → take away 15

Benny picked 15.

There were 27 red apples left.

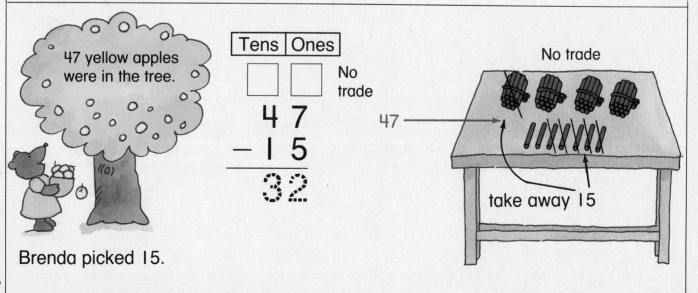

47 yellow apples were in the tree.

| Tens | Ones |
|------|------|
|      |      |

No trade

$$\begin{array}{r} 4\,7 \\ -\,1\,5 \\ \hline 3\,2 \end{array}$$

No trade

47 → take away 15

Brenda picked 15.

There were 32 yellow apples left.

2-digit subtraction with and without trading

| Tens | Ones |
|------|------|
| 4 | 13 | Trade
| 5̶ | 3̶ |
| − 1 | 8 |
| 3 | 5 |

| Tens | Ones |
|------|------|
| ☐ | ☐ | No trade
| 5 | 9 |
| − 1 | 8 |
| 4 | 1 |

Subtract.

1.

| Tens | Ones |
|------|------|
| ☐ | ☐ | No trade
| 3 | 7 |
| − 1 | 4 |
| 2 | 3 |

| Tens | Ones |
|------|------|
| 3 | 12 | Trade
| 4̶ | 2̶ |
| − 1 | 8 |
| 2 | 4 |

| Tens | Ones |
|------|------|
| 4 | 15 | Trade
| 5̶ | 5̶ |
| − 1 | 7 |

2.

| Tens | Ones |
|------|------|
| ☐ | ☐ | No trade
| 6 | 7 |
| − 2 | 4 |

| Tens | Ones |
|------|------|
| ☐ | ☐ | Trade
| 4 | 3 |
| − 1 | 5 |

| Tens | Ones |
|------|------|
| ☐ | ☐ | No trade
| 7 | 8 |
| − 2 | 5 |

3.

| Tens | Ones |
|------|------|
| ☐ | ☐ | Trade
| 6 | 0 |
| − 3 | 7 |

| Tens | Ones |
|------|------|
| ☐ | ☐ | No trade
| 5 | 9 |
| − 2 | 9 |

| Tens | Ones |
|------|------|
| ☐ | ☐ | Trade
| 6 | 4 |
| − 1 | 9 |

2-digit subtraction with and without trading

Name _____

64 carrots were in a field.
6 carrots were eaten.
How many carrots
were left?

58 carrots were left.

| Tens | Ones |
|------|------|
| 5 | 14 |

$$\begin{array}{r} 6\,4 \\ -\ \ 6 \\ \hline 5\,8 \end{array}$$

Do you trade?
Ring **yes** or **no.** Then subtract.

**1.**

| Tens | Ones |
|------|------|
| 6 | 12 |

$$\begin{array}{r} 7\,2 \\ -\ \ 5 \\ \hline 6\,7 \end{array}$$  (yes)  no

| Tens | Ones |
|------|------|
|  |  |

$$\begin{array}{r} 6\,9 \\ -\,2\,7 \\ \hline \end{array}$$  yes  no

| Tens | Ones |
|------|------|
|  |  |

$$\begin{array}{r} 8\,1 \\ -\ \ 6 \\ \hline \end{array}$$  yes  no

| Tens | Ones |
|------|------|
|  |  |

$$\begin{array}{r} 3\,5 \\ -\,1\,3 \\ \hline \end{array}$$  yes  no

**2.**

| Tens | Ones |
|------|------|
|  |  |

$$\begin{array}{r} 7\,8 \\ -\ \ 4 \\ \hline \end{array}$$  yes  no

| Tens | Ones |
|------|------|
|  |  |

$$\begin{array}{r} 6\,0 \\ -\,1\,3 \\ \hline \end{array}$$  yes  no

| Tens | Ones |
|------|------|
|  |  |

$$\begin{array}{r} 9\,2 \\ -\,4\,6 \\ \hline \end{array}$$  yes  no

| Tens | Ones |
|------|------|
|  |  |

$$\begin{array}{r} 8\,5 \\ -\,4\,7 \\ \hline \end{array}$$  yes  no

**3.**

| Tens | Ones |
|------|------|
|  |  |

$$\begin{array}{r} 5\,7 \\ -\,2\,7 \\ \hline \end{array}$$  yes  no

| Tens | Ones |
|------|------|
|  |  |

$$\begin{array}{r} 7\,0 \\ -\,2\,3 \\ \hline \end{array}$$  yes  no

| Tens | Ones |
|------|------|
|  |  |

$$\begin{array}{r} 9\,5 \\ -\ \ 8 \\ \hline \end{array}$$  yes  no

| Tens | Ones |
|------|------|
|  |  |

$$\begin{array}{r} 8\,9 \\ -\,1\,7 \\ \hline \end{array}$$  yes  no

2-digit subtraction with and without trading

Subtract.

1.
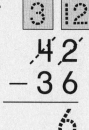

$$\begin{array}{r} ^{3}\!\!\!/\!4 \;^{12}\!\!\!\!/\!2 \\ -3\,6 \\ \hline 6 \end{array}$$

$$\begin{array}{r} 3\,7 \\ -2\,9 \\ \hline \end{array}$$

$$\begin{array}{r} 4\,1 \\ -\ \ 4 \\ \hline \end{array}$$

2.
$$\begin{array}{r} 6\,4 \\ -1\,8 \\ \hline \end{array}$$

$$\begin{array}{r} 5\,1 \\ -4\,8 \\ \hline \end{array}$$

$$\begin{array}{r} 7\,8 \\ -1\,6 \\ \hline \end{array}$$

$$\begin{array}{r} 8\,3 \\ -\ \ 9 \\ \hline \end{array}$$

3.
$$\begin{array}{r} 4\,1 \\ -3\,6 \\ \hline \end{array}$$

$$\begin{array}{r} 9\,7 \\ -7\,3 \\ \hline \end{array}$$

$$\begin{array}{r} 8\,0 \\ -1\,9 \\ \hline \end{array}$$

$$\begin{array}{r} 3\,9 \\ -2\,9 \\ \hline \end{array}$$

4.
$$\begin{array}{r} 3\,0 \\ -1\,3 \\ \hline \end{array}$$

$$\begin{array}{r} 6\,5 \\ -\ \ 9 \\ \hline \end{array}$$

$$\begin{array}{r} 4\,9 \\ -1\,7 \\ \hline \end{array}$$

$$\begin{array}{r} 5\,5 \\ -3\,8 \\ \hline \end{array}$$

## THINK MATH

How many more tickets did
Al sell than Tina?

_____ more

| Tickets Sold | |
|---|---|
| Jay | 15 |
| Al | 27 |
| Sue | 32 |
| Tina | 19 |

2-digit subtraction with and without trading

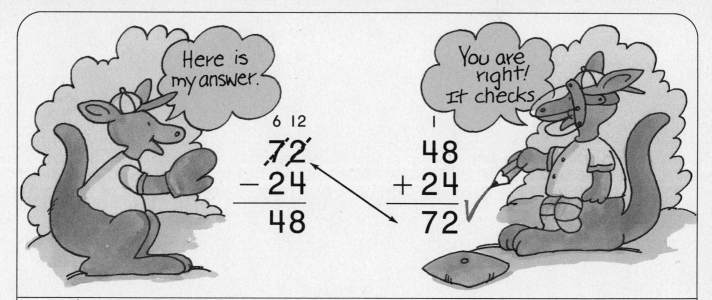

Subtract. Check by adding.

**1.**
$$\begin{array}{r} 35 \\ -14 \\ \hline 21 \end{array}$$
$$\begin{array}{r} 2\,1 \\ +1\,4 \\ \hline 35 \end{array}$$
$$\begin{array}{r} 43 \\ -\ \ 6 \\ \hline 37 \end{array}$$
$$\begin{array}{r} 3\,7 \\ +\ \ 6 \\ \hline 4\,3 \end{array}$$
$$\begin{array}{r} 60 \\ -24 \\ \hline \end{array}$$

**2.**
$$\begin{array}{r} 75 \\ -59 \\ \hline \end{array}$$
$$\begin{array}{r} 23 \\ -\ \ 6 \\ \hline \end{array}$$
$$\begin{array}{r} 82 \\ -30 \\ \hline \end{array}$$

**3.**
$$\begin{array}{r} 59 \\ -38 \\ \hline \end{array}$$
$$\begin{array}{r} 27 \\ -23 \\ \hline \end{array}$$
$$\begin{array}{r} 83 \\ -79 \\ \hline \end{array}$$

**4.**
$$\begin{array}{r} 45 \\ -13 \\ \hline \end{array}$$
$$\begin{array}{r} 36 \\ -\ \ 9 \\ \hline \end{array}$$
$$\begin{array}{r} 78 \\ -21 \\ \hline \end{array}$$

Checking subtraction

Trade if you need to.
Then subtract.

1.
$$\begin{array}{r} 36 \\ -\ 7 \\ \hline \end{array}$$
$$\begin{array}{r} 42 \\ -\ 8 \\ \hline \end{array}$$
$$\begin{array}{r} 54 \\ -23 \\ \hline \end{array}$$
$$\begin{array}{r} 24 \\ -\ 7 \\ \hline \end{array}$$
$$\begin{array}{r} 87 \\ -24 \\ \hline \end{array}$$
$$\begin{array}{r} 32 \\ -12 \\ \hline \end{array}$$

2.
$$\begin{array}{r} 40 \\ -\ 7 \\ \hline \end{array}$$
$$\begin{array}{r} 26 \\ -19 \\ \hline \end{array}$$
$$\begin{array}{r} 47 \\ -\ 3 \\ \hline \end{array}$$
$$\begin{array}{r} 32 \\ -16 \\ \hline \end{array}$$
$$\begin{array}{r} 38 \\ -19 \\ \hline \end{array}$$
$$\begin{array}{r} 81 \\ -26 \\ \hline \end{array}$$

3.
$$\begin{array}{r} 62 \\ -\ 3 \\ \hline \end{array}$$
$$\begin{array}{r} 80 \\ -\ 7 \\ \hline \end{array}$$
$$\begin{array}{r} 43 \\ -24 \\ \hline \end{array}$$
$$\begin{array}{r} 65 \\ -35 \\ \hline \end{array}$$
$$\begin{array}{r} 57 \\ -20 \\ \hline \end{array}$$
$$\begin{array}{r} 51 \\ -\ 6 \\ \hline \end{array}$$

4.
$$\begin{array}{r} 73 \\ -\ 9 \\ \hline \end{array}$$
$$\begin{array}{r} 64 \\ -\ 4 \\ \hline \end{array}$$
$$\begin{array}{r} 60 \\ -13 \\ \hline \end{array}$$
$$\begin{array}{r} 55 \\ -37 \\ \hline \end{array}$$
$$\begin{array}{r} 62 \\ -47 \\ \hline \end{array}$$
$$\begin{array}{r} 44 \\ -15 \\ \hline \end{array}$$

## THINK MATH

How much does Mike weigh?
He weighs 7 pounds less than Nick.
Nick weighs 62 pounds.

_____ pounds

Subtraction practice

How many more are there in the
large box?

$$\begin{array}{r} \overset{3\ \ 10}{\cancel{40}} \\ -\ 25 \\ \hline 15 \end{array}$$

There are 15 more.

| Copy and subtract. Trade if you need to. | 2. |
|---|---|
| **1.** 33 − 14 $\quad\begin{array}{r}\overset{2\ \ 13}{\cancel{33}}\\ -\ 14\\ \hline 19\end{array}$ | 25 − 7 |

| **3.** 43 − 12 | **4.** 62 − 17 |
|---|---|

| **5.** 50 − 3 | **6.** 77 − 54 |
|---|---|

## Problem Solving

QUESTION
DATA
PLAN
ANSWER
CHECK

75¢

49¢

54¢

36¢

52¢

45¢

Solve.

1. Buy a _____ .

Buy some _____ .

How much more does

the _____ cost? __26¢__

```
  6 15
  7̸5̸
— 4 9
────────
  2 6
```

2. Buy _____ .

Buy a _____ .

How much is it for both? _____

3. Buy a _____ .

Buy a _____ .

How much more does

the _____ cost? _____

4. Buy _____ .

Buy a _____ .

How much more does

the _____ cost? _____

5. Buy a _____ .

Buy a _____ .

How much is it for both? _____

6. DATA BANK

Buy a _____ .

Buy a _____ .

How much less does

the _____ cost? _____

(See page 342.)

Problem solving—using data from a price tag

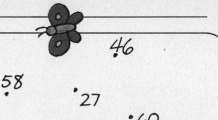

Connect the answers in order.
What animal have you drawn?

1.
$$\begin{array}{r} 32 \\ -14 \\ \hline \end{array}$$
$$\begin{array}{r} 45 \\ -12 \\ \hline \end{array}$$
$$\begin{array}{r} 62 \\ -7 \\ \hline \end{array}$$
$$\begin{array}{r} 14 \\ -8 \\ \hline \end{array}$$
$$\begin{array}{r} 53 \\ -27 \\ \hline \end{array}$$
$$\begin{array}{r} 30 \\ -18 \\ \hline \end{array}$$

2.
$$\begin{array}{r} 42 \\ -2 \\ \hline \end{array}$$
$$\begin{array}{r} 24 \\ -8 \\ \hline \end{array}$$
$$\begin{array}{r} 35 \\ -18 \\ \hline \end{array}$$
$$\begin{array}{r} 64 \\ -27 \\ \hline \end{array}$$
$$\begin{array}{r} 50 \\ -40 \\ \hline \end{array}$$
$$\begin{array}{r} 31 \\ -19 \\ \hline \end{array}$$

3.
$$\begin{array}{r} 47 \\ -32 \\ \hline \end{array}$$
$$\begin{array}{r} 85 \\ -17 \\ \hline \end{array}$$
$$\begin{array}{r} 70 \\ -49 \\ \hline \end{array}$$
$$\begin{array}{r} 56 \\ -21 \\ \hline \end{array}$$
$$\begin{array}{r} 31 \\ -8 \\ \hline \end{array}$$
$$\begin{array}{r} 64 \\ -4 \\ \hline \end{array}$$

4.
$$\begin{array}{r} 93 \\ -47 \\ \hline \end{array}$$
$$\begin{array}{r} 67 \\ -40 \\ \hline \end{array}$$
$$\begin{array}{r} 21 \\ -7 \\ \hline \end{array}$$
$$\begin{array}{r} 83 \\ -25 \\ \hline \end{array}$$
$$\begin{array}{r} 91 \\ -87 \\ \hline \end{array}$$
$$\begin{array}{r} 74 \\ -18 \\ \hline \end{array}$$

Subtraction practice

(two hundred eleven) 211

Solve.

**1.**

There were 35 ponies to ride.
17 were put in a barn.
How many ponies were left to ride?

_____ ponies

**2.**

18 tigers are in the circus.
35 lions are in the circus.
How many more lions than tigers
are in the circus?

_____ more

**3.**

13 clowns had happy faces.
9 clowns had sad faces.
How many clowns were in the circus?

_____ clowns

**4.**

21 elephants were in a field.
9 went into a tent.
How many elephants stayed
in the field?

_____ elephants

Problem solving—story problems

# Problem Solving  Name_____

## Favorite Sports

Number of Students

20 19 18 17 16 15 14 13 12 11 10 9 8 7 6 5 4 3 2 1

Soccer  Kickball  Softball  Swimming

---

Use the graph. Solve the problems.

**1.**
How many more people
like soccer
than kickball?

_____ more

**2.**
What is the total number
who picked kickball
and softball?

_____ in all

**3.**
How many more people
like softball
than swimming?

_____ more

**4. DATA BANK**
Altogether, how
many people picked
tennis, golf, or
football?
(See page 343.)

_____ in all

Problem solving—using data from a graph

Add or subtract.

1.  $\begin{array}{r} 63 \\ -42 \\ \hline \end{array}$  $\begin{array}{r} 24 \\ +17 \\ \hline \end{array}$  $\begin{array}{r} 72 \\ -\phantom{0}5 \\ \hline \end{array}$

2.  $\begin{array}{r} 42 \\ +48 \\ \hline \end{array}$  $\begin{array}{r} 35 \\ +13 \\ \hline \end{array}$  $\begin{array}{r} 92 \\ -56 \\ \hline \end{array}$  $\begin{array}{r} 76 \\ -\phantom{0}6 \\ \hline \end{array}$  $\begin{array}{r} 16 \\ +65 \\ \hline \end{array}$  $\begin{array}{r} 47 \\ -29 \\ \hline \end{array}$

3.  $\begin{array}{r} 53 \\ -38 \\ \hline \end{array}$  $\begin{array}{r} 60 \\ +19 \\ \hline \end{array}$  $\begin{array}{r} 4 \\ +19 \\ \hline \end{array}$  $\begin{array}{r} 38 \\ -10 \\ \hline \end{array}$  $\begin{array}{r} 47 \\ -\phantom{0}8 \\ \hline \end{array}$  $\begin{array}{r} 71 \\ +27 \\ \hline \end{array}$

4.  $\begin{array}{r} 72 \\ +14 \\ \hline \end{array}$  $\begin{array}{r} 7 \\ +33 \\ \hline \end{array}$  $\begin{array}{r} 45 \\ +25 \\ \hline \end{array}$  $\begin{array}{r} 50 \\ -35 \\ \hline \end{array}$  $\begin{array}{r} 75 \\ -48 \\ \hline \end{array}$  $\begin{array}{r} 80 \\ +19 \\ \hline \end{array}$

## SKILLKEEPER

Write the times.

_____   _____   _____   _____

Addition and subtraction practice

Add or subtract.

1.  47    33    55    62    43
   −15   +18   + 8   − 6   −26
   _____ _____ _____ _____ _____

2.  62    81    93    74    58
   +28   +16   −67   − 4   +25
   _____ _____ _____ _____ _____

3.  44    80    16    68    27    31
   −19   +19   +19   −20   − 9   −17
   _____ _____ _____ _____ _____ _____

4.  55     7    24    35    40    62
   − 6   +36   +13   − 9   −12   −50
   _____ _____ _____ _____ _____ _____

5.  61    42    65    53    72    19
   −31   +15   −18   − 6   + 8   +54
   _____ _____ _____ _____ _____ _____

6.  33    49    67    21    54    31
   +48   −31   −39   + 9   +27   − 8
   _____ _____ _____ _____ _____ _____

Addition and subtraction practice

## Across

1. 42 − 5
3. 36 + 55
6. 76 − 25
8. 42 − 17
10. 56, _____, 58
12. 58 + 36
14. 20 + 1
16. 82 − 50
19. before 80
21. 60 − 17

23. 39 + 45
25. after 20
27. 79, _____, 81
28. 3 tens, 6 ones

## Down

2. 28 + 47
4. 50 − 38
5. 26 + 59
7. before 20
9. 5 tens
11. 94 − 22
13. 70 − 27
15. 9 + 8
17. 2 tens, 4 ones
18. 49 + 19

20. 58 + 34
22. 51 − 15
24. 47, _____, 49
26. 7 + 6

Addition and subtraction practice

Copy.
Then add or subtract.

**1.**

$62 - 27$

$$\begin{array}{r} \overset{5}{\cancel{6}}\overset{12}{\cancel{2}} \\ -2\,7 \\ \hline \end{array}$$

**2.**

$28 + 35$

**3.**

$71 - 48$

**4.**

$36 + 49$

**5.**

$58 + 19$

**6.**

$53 - 8$

**7.**

$65 - 47$

**8.**

$38 + 6$

Practice copying and adding or subtracting

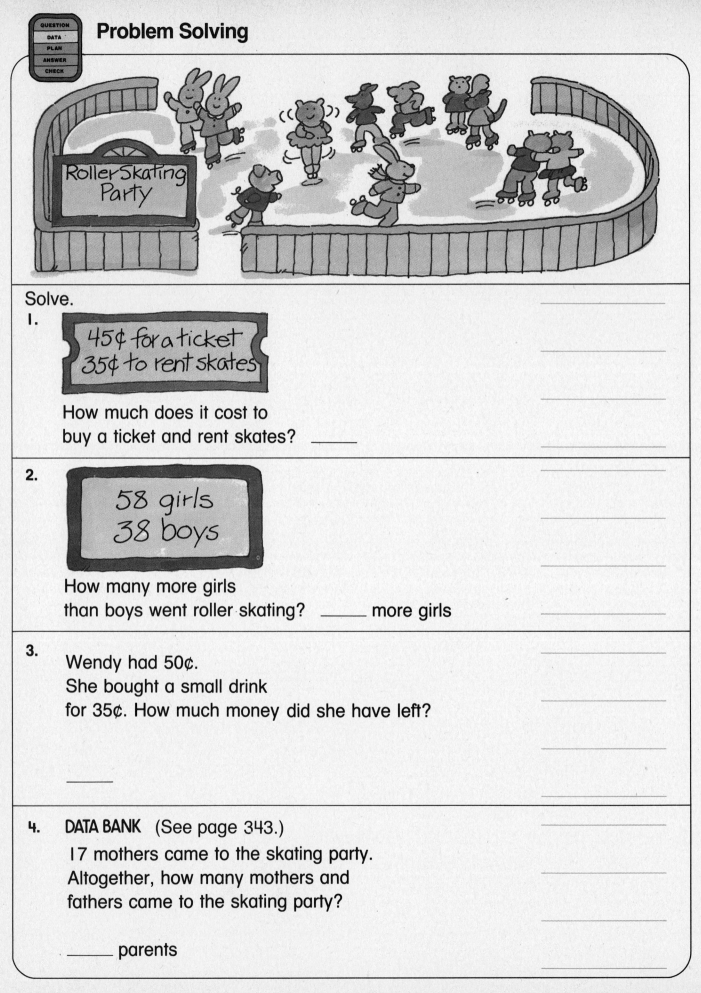

Roller Skating Party

Solve.

**1.**

45¢ for a ticket
35¢ to rent skates

How much does it cost to
buy a ticket and rent skates? _____

**2.**

58 girls
38 boys

How many more girls
than boys went roller skating? _____ more girls

**3.** Wendy had 50¢.
She bought a small drink
for 35¢. How much money did she have left?

_____

**4.** DATA BANK (See page 343.)
17 mothers came to the skating party.
Altogether, how many mothers and
fathers came to the skating party?

_____ parents

I have to trade. The answer is less than 20.

25
− 7

20 or more
*(less than 20)*

I do not trade. The answer is 20 or more.

25
− 3

*(20 or more)*
less than 20

Ring the better estimate.

1.
26
− 4

20 or more

less than 20

24
− 6

20 or more

less than 20

28
− 6

20 or more

less than 20

23
− 4

20 or more

less than 20

2.
35
− 7

30 or more

less than 30

34
− 6

30 or more

less than 30

36
− 5

30 or more

less than 30

37
− 4

30 or more

less than 30

3.
38
− 14

20 or more

less than 20

32
− 14

20 or more

less than 20

35
− 14

20 or more

less than 20

31
− 14

20 or more

less than 20

4.
46
− 15

30 or more

less than 30

43
− 15

30 or more

less than 30

47
− 15

30 or more

less than 30

45
− 15

30 or more

less than 30

Estimation—differences

# Problem-Solving Strategy

**1.** What is the cost of 4 pencils?

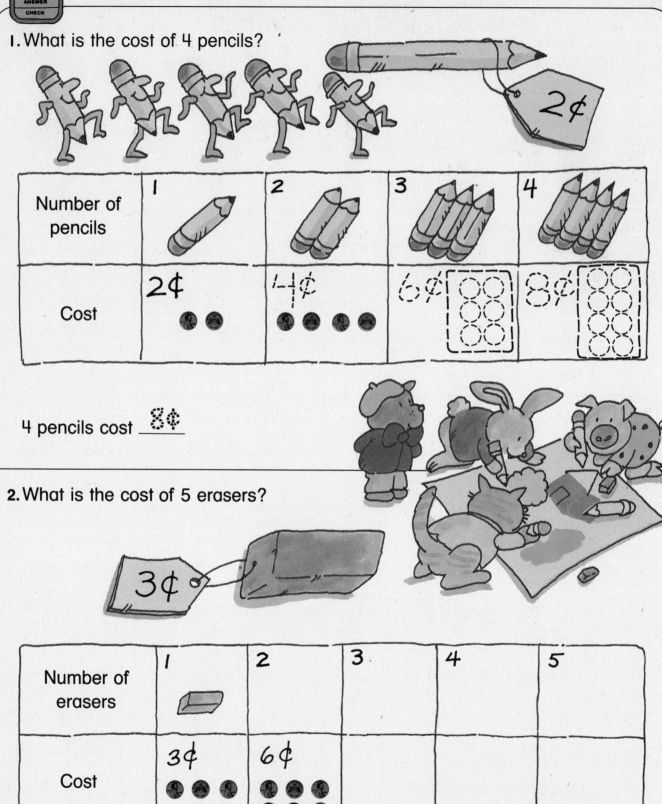

| Number of pencils | 1 | 2 | 3 | 4 |
|---|---|---|---|---|
| Cost | 2¢ | 4¢ | 6¢ | 8¢ |

4 pencils cost ___8¢___

**2.** What is the cost of 5 erasers?

| Number of erasers | 1 | 2 | 3 | 4 | 5 |
|---|---|---|---|---|---|
| Cost | 3¢ | 6¢ | | | |

5 erasers cost _____

# CHAPTER REVIEW/TEST

Subtract.

1.
| 47 | 32 | 58 | 74 | 86 | 56 |
|---|---|---|---|---|---|
| −23 | −11 | − 6 | −50 | −56 | −36 |

2.
| 32 | 41 | 25 | 54 | 62 | 50 |
|---|---|---|---|---|---|
| −14 | −25 | −17 | −27 | −48 | −18 |

3.
| 46 | 26 | 71 | 83 | 70 | 82 |
|---|---|---|---|---|---|
| −38 | − 8 | −24 | −78 | −53 | − 8 |

4.
| 71 | 46 | 40 | 35 | 72 | 53 |
|---|---|---|---|---|---|
| −26 | −29 | −12 | −19 | −18 | −26 |

5. Solve.

Carla had 73 baseball cards.
She sold 55 baseball cards.
How many cards did she have left?

_____ cards

# CUMULATIVE REVIEW

Add.

1.
$$\begin{array}{r} 34 \\ +32 \\ \hline \end{array}$$

○ 66
○ 76
○ 2

2.
$$\begin{array}{r} 44 \\ +\ 8 \\ \hline \end{array}$$

○ 54
○ 52
○ 36

3.
$$\begin{array}{r} 15 \\ 23 \\ +35 \\ \hline \end{array}$$

○ 88
○ 73
○ 63

4.
$$\begin{array}{r} 54 \\ 10 \\ +16 \\ \hline \end{array}$$

○ 80
○ 90
○ 70

Mark the correct name.

5.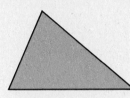

○ triangle
○ circle
○ square

6.

○ triangle
○ rectangle
○ circle

7.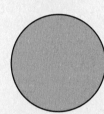

○ circle
○ triangle
○ rectangle

8.

How many more apples than oranges are there?

○ 8
○ 10
○ 16

9. Solve.

How many juice cans are there altogether?

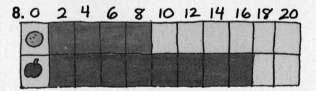
18 grape juice
12 apple juice

○ 30
○ 17
○ 7

# ANOTHER LOOK

Subtract the ones.

$$\begin{array}{r} 3\,6 \\ -\,1\,2 \\ \hline 4 \end{array}$$

Then subtract the tens.

$$\begin{array}{r} 3\,6 \\ -\,1\,2 \\ \hline 2\,4 \end{array}$$

Trade 1 ten for 10 ones.

$$\begin{array}{r} {}^{3}\cancel{4}{}^{12}\cancel{2} \\ -\,2\,8 \\ \hline \end{array}$$

Subtract the ones. Subtract the tens.

$$\begin{array}{r} {}^{3}\cancel{4}{}^{12}\cancel{2} \\ -\,2\,8 \\ \hline 1\,4 \end{array}$$

**Subtract.**

1.
$$\begin{array}{r} 47 \\ -23 \\ \hline \end{array}\qquad \begin{array}{r} 36 \\ -\ 4 \\ \hline \end{array}\qquad \begin{array}{r} 52 \\ -21 \\ \hline \end{array}$$

2.
$$\begin{array}{r} 63 \\ -33 \\ \hline \end{array}\qquad \begin{array}{r} 61 \\ -20 \\ \hline \end{array}\qquad \begin{array}{r} 58 \\ -13 \\ \hline \end{array}$$

**Trade. Then subtract.**

3.
$$\begin{array}{r} 35 \\ -17 \\ \hline \end{array}\qquad \begin{array}{r} 42 \\ -\ 6 \\ \hline \end{array}\qquad \begin{array}{r} 50 \\ -24 \\ \hline \end{array}$$

4.
$$\begin{array}{r} 63 \\ -39 \\ \hline \end{array}\qquad \begin{array}{r} 80 \\ -\ 7 \\ \hline \end{array}\qquad \begin{array}{r} 74 \\ -58 \\ \hline \end{array}$$

**Trade if necessary. Then subtract.**

5.
$$\begin{array}{r} 43 \\ -23 \\ \hline \end{array}\quad \begin{array}{r} 56 \\ -47 \\ \hline \end{array}\quad \begin{array}{r} 30 \\ -14 \\ \hline \end{array}\quad \begin{array}{r} 65 \\ -\ 4 \\ \hline \end{array}\quad \begin{array}{r} 89 \\ -29 \\ \hline \end{array}$$

6.
$$\begin{array}{r} 72 \\ -\ 7 \\ \hline \end{array}\quad \begin{array}{r} 83 \\ -41 \\ \hline \end{array}\quad \begin{array}{r} 64 \\ -58 \\ \hline \end{array}\quad \begin{array}{r} 80 \\ -29 \\ \hline \end{array}$$

# ENRICHMENT

Add "in your head." Use **counting on.**

(49, 50, 51, 52)      (38, 39, 40)      (68, 69, 70, 71)

1. $49 + 3 = \underline{52}$    2. $38 + 2 = \underline{40}$    3. $68 + 3 = \underline{71}$

(78, 79, 80)      (89, 90, 91)      (17, 18, 19, 20)

4. $78 + 2 = \underline{\hspace{1cm}}$    5. $89 + 2 = \underline{\hspace{1cm}}$    6. $17 + 3 = \underline{\hspace{1cm}}$

7. $59 + 3 = \underline{\hspace{1cm}}$    8. $48 + 2 = \underline{\hspace{1cm}}$    9. $39 + 2 = \underline{\hspace{1cm}}$

10. $67 + 3 = \underline{\hspace{1cm}}$    11. $68 + 3 = \underline{\hspace{1cm}}$    12. $29 + 3 = \underline{\hspace{1cm}}$

Subtract "in your head." Use **counting back.**

(32, 31, 30, 29)      (70, 69, 68)      (51, 50, 49, 48)

13. $32 - 3 = \underline{29}$    14. $70 - 2 = \underline{68}$    15. $51 - 3 = \underline{48}$

(52, 51, 50, 49)      (41, 40, 39)      (90, 89, 88)

16. $52 - 3 = \underline{\hspace{1cm}}$    17. $41 - 2 = \underline{\hspace{1cm}}$    18. $90 - 2 = \underline{\hspace{1cm}}$

19. $41 - 3 = \underline{\hspace{1cm}}$    20. $60 - 1 = \underline{\hspace{1cm}}$    21. $32 - 3 = \underline{\hspace{1cm}}$

22. $71 - 2 = \underline{\hspace{1cm}}$    23. $82 - 3 = \underline{\hspace{1cm}}$    24. $40 - 3 = \underline{\hspace{1cm}}$

Name _____

# MEASUREMENT—METRIC UNITS

This is 4 paper clip units long.

_4_ paper-clip units

Find the lengths. Count the paper clips.

**1.**

_5_ paper-clip units

**2.**

_____ paper-clip units

**3.**

_____ paper-clip units

**4.**

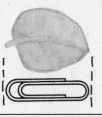

_____ paper-clip unit

**5.**

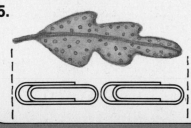

_____ paper-clip units

Measuring length—nonstandard units

Use your paper clip ruler. Find the lengths.

**1.**

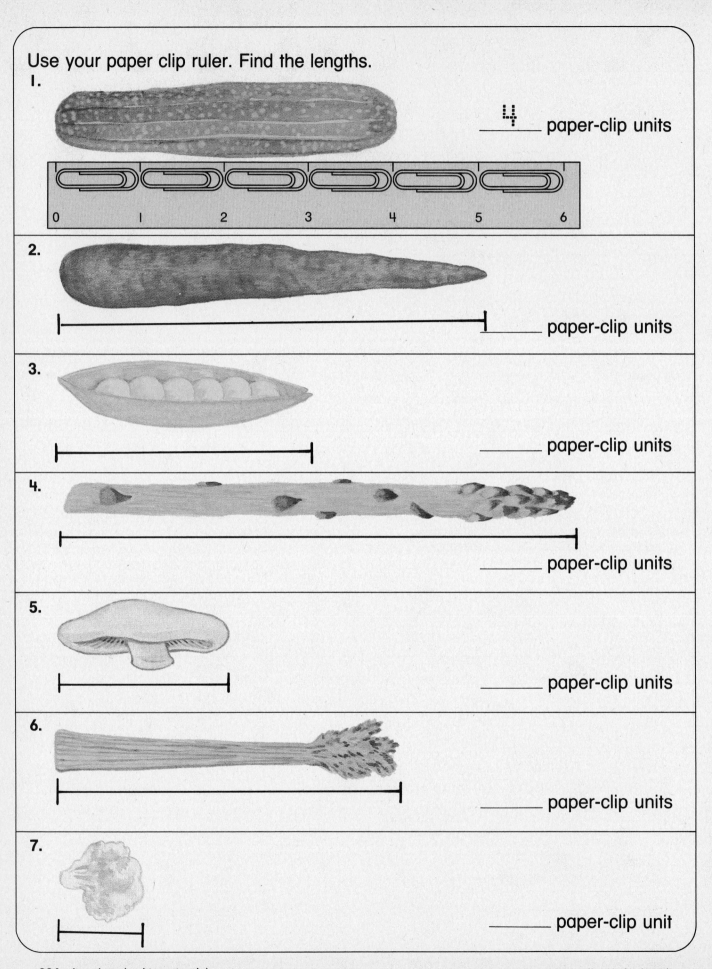

_4_ paper-clip units

| 0 | 1 | 2 | 3 | 4 | 5 | 6 |

**2.** _____ paper-clip units

**3.** _____ paper-clip units

**4.** _____ paper-clip units

**5.** _____ paper-clip units

**6.** _____ paper-clip units

**7.** _____ paper-clip unit

Nonstandard units for length

This is a **centimeter** (cm) unit. ▬

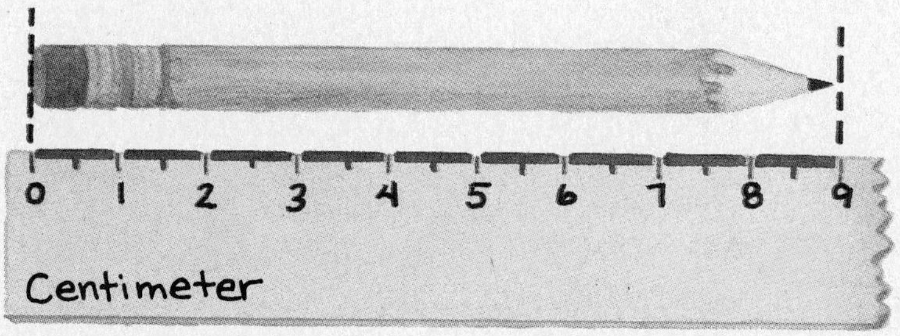

Centimeter

0 1 2 3 4 5 6 7 8 9

9 ____ cm

Use your centimeter ruler. Find the lengths.

**1.**

____ cm

**2.**

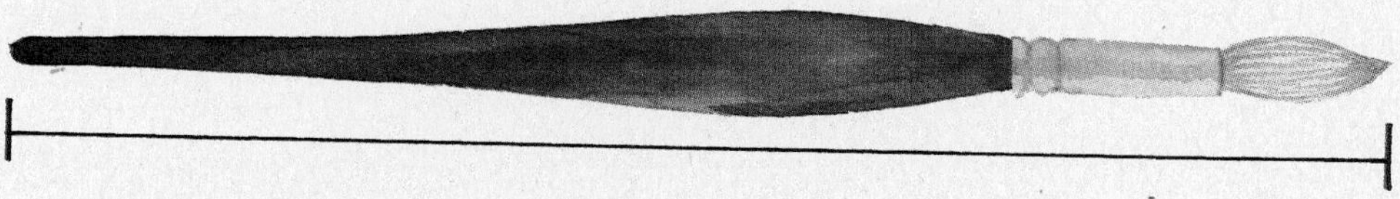

____ cm

**3.**

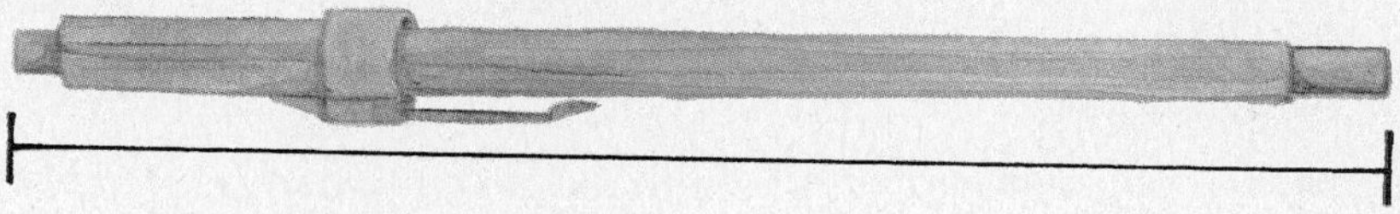

____ cm

**4.**

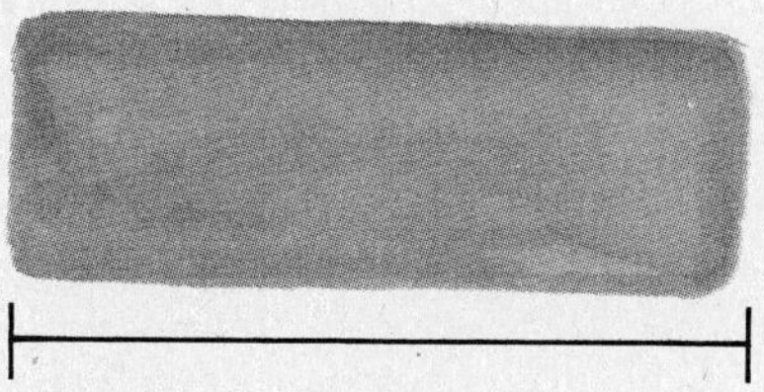

____ cm

**5.**

____ cm

**6.**

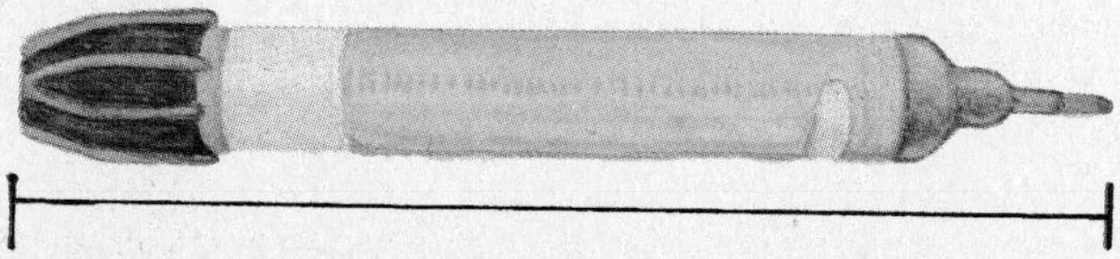

____ cm

Measuring length—using a centimeter ruler

Use your centimeter ruler. Find the lengths.

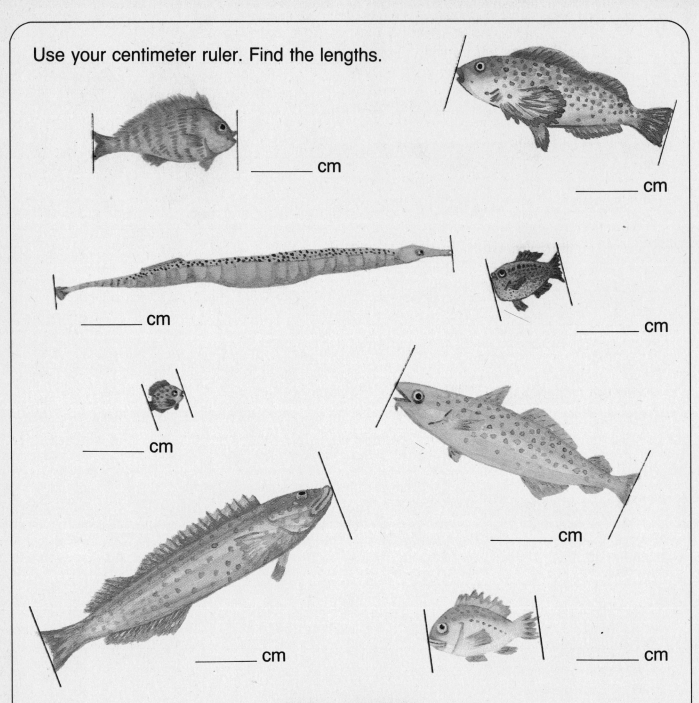

_____ cm

_____ cm

_____ cm

_____ cm

_____ cm

_____ cm

_____ cm

_____ cm

## SKILLKEEPER

Subtract.

$$\begin{array}{r} 89 \\ -72 \\ \hline \end{array} \qquad \begin{array}{r} 64 \\ -38 \\ \hline \end{array} \qquad \begin{array}{r} 57 \\ -19 \\ \hline \end{array} \qquad \begin{array}{r} 20 \\ -10 \\ \hline \end{array} \qquad \begin{array}{r} 48 \\ -9 \\ \hline \end{array} \qquad \begin{array}{r} 41 \\ -30 \\ \hline \end{array}$$

Measuring length—using a centimeter ruler

It is between 6 cm and 7 cm.

It is closer to 7 cm.

$$7$$
Nearest cm

## Use your centimeter ruler. Give the length to the nearest centimeter.

**1.**

It is between __10__ and __11__ cm.

$$10$$
Nearest cm

**2.**

It is between _____ and _____ cm.

Nearest cm

**3.**

It is between _____ and _____ cm.

Nearest cm

Nearest centimeter

Use your centimeter ruler. Give the length to the nearest centimeter.

**1.**

Nearest cm

**2.**

Nearest cm

**3.**

Nearest cm

**4.**

Nearest cm

**5.**

Nearest cm

**6.**

Nearest cm

---

## SKILLKEEPER

How many are there?

_____

_____

_____

Name _____

First estimate each length. Then measure with your centimeter ruler.

**1.**

_____    _____ cm
Your estimate    Your measure

**2.**

_____    _____ cm
Your estimate    Your measure

**3.**

_____    _____ cm
Your estimate    Your measure

**4.**

_____    _____ cm
Your estimate    Your measure

**5.**

_____    _____ cm
Your estimate    Your measure

Estimating length in centimeters

First estimate each length.
Then measure with your
centimeter ruler.

**2.** Your book

**1.** Your pencil

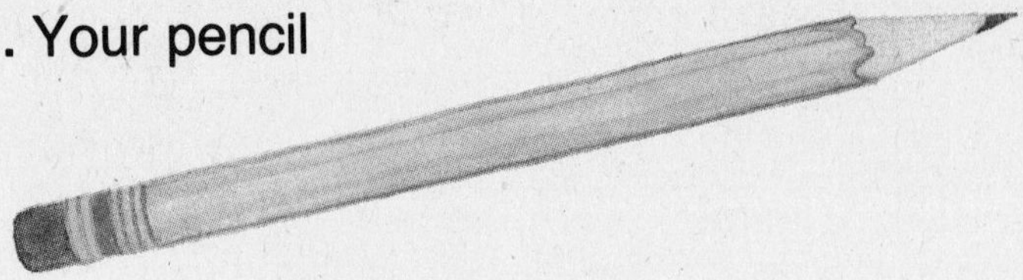

——————     ——————
Your estimate     Your measure

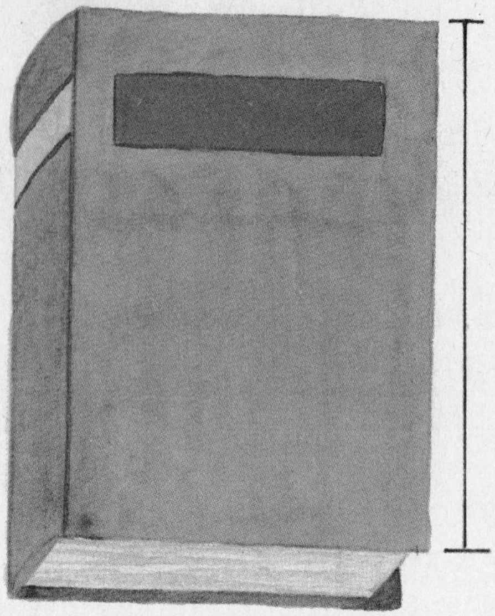

——————     ——————
Your estimate     Your measure

**3.** Your hand

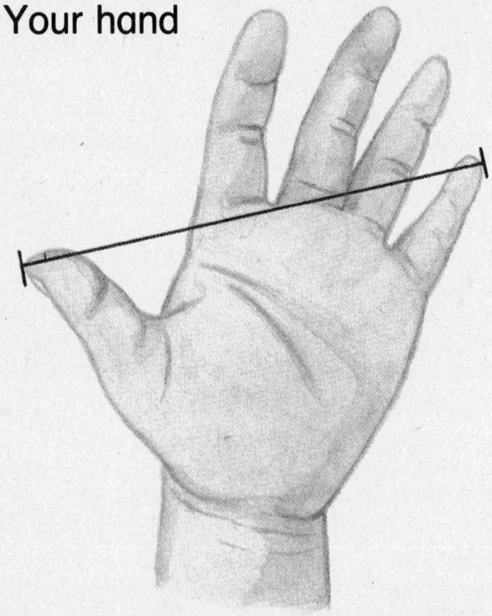

**4.** Your shoe

——————     ——————
Your estimate     Your measure

——————     ——————
Your estimate     Your measure

# THINK MATH

This is the unit ⬭ . 
Estimate how many units long
the pencil is.

Find a way to check your estimate. _____ units

Estimating length in centimeters

Name _____

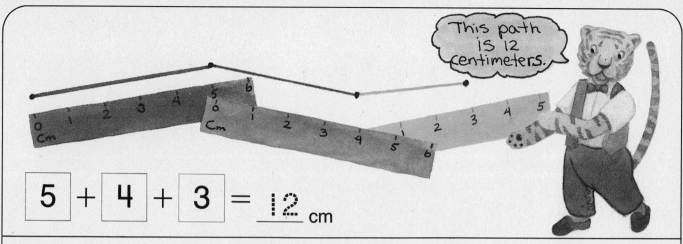

This path is 12 centimeters.

$$\boxed{5} + \boxed{4} + \boxed{3} = \underline{12}\ \text{cm}$$

Use your centimeter ruler. Find the length of each path.

**1.**

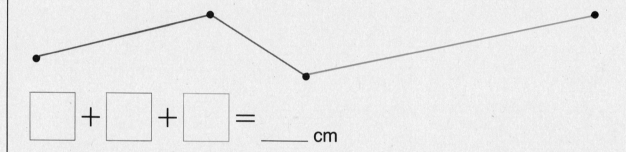

$$\boxed{\phantom{0}} + \boxed{\phantom{0}} + \boxed{\phantom{0}} = \underline{\phantom{00}}\ \text{cm}$$

**2.**

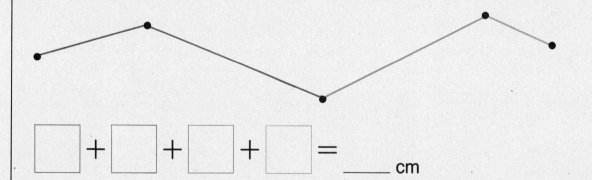

$$\boxed{\phantom{0}} + \boxed{\phantom{0}} + \boxed{\phantom{0}} + \boxed{\phantom{0}} = \underline{\phantom{00}}\ \text{cm}$$

**3.**

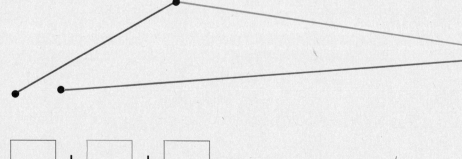

$$\boxed{\phantom{0}} + \boxed{\phantom{0}} + \boxed{\phantom{0}} = \underline{\phantom{00}}\ \text{cm}$$

Length of paths

1. Use your centimeter ruler. Measure around each figure.

$\boxed{\phantom{0}} + \boxed{\phantom{0}} + \boxed{\phantom{0}} = \underline{\phantom{000}}$ cm

2.

$\boxed{\phantom{0}} + \boxed{\phantom{0}} + \boxed{\phantom{0}} + \boxed{\phantom{0}} = \underline{\phantom{000}}$ cm

3.

$\boxed{\phantom{0}} + \boxed{\phantom{0}} + \boxed{\phantom{0}} + \boxed{\phantom{0}} = \underline{\phantom{000}}$ cm

4.

$\boxed{\phantom{0}} + \boxed{\phantom{0}} + \boxed{\phantom{0}} + \boxed{\phantom{0}} = \underline{\phantom{000}}$ cm

5. **DATA BANK**  How far is it around the red triangle?
(See page 344.)

\_\_\_\_\_ cm

## THINK MATH

Mario spent 59¢
Ring the price tags.

20¢    29¢    39¢

Perimeter

Name _____

A meter is 100 centimeters.

About 1 meter (m)

Ring the better estimate.

**1.**

Greater than 1 meter

Less than 1 meter

**2.**

Greater than 1 meter

Less than 1 meter

**3.**

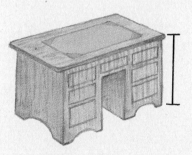

Greater than 1 meter

Less than 1 meter

**4.**

Greater than 1 meter

Less than 1 meter

**5.**

Greater than 1 meter

Less than 1 meter

**6.**

Greater than 1 meter

Less than 1 meter

Meter—estimating length

You can walk a **kilometer** (km) in about 10 minutes.

Ring the better estimate.

1. A walk around your school

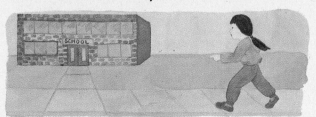

Greater than 1 kilometer

Less than 1 kilometer

2. A 10-minute bike ride

Greater than 1 kilometer

Less than 1 kilometer

3. A walk to your home from school

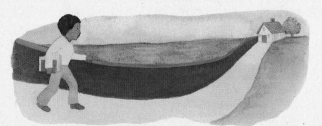

Greater than 1 kilometer

Less than 1 kilometer

4. A walk from your school to the post office

Greater than 1 kilometer

Less than 1 kilometer

# SKILLKEEPER

Add or subtract.

$$\begin{array}{r} 8 \\ +7 \\ \hline \end{array} \qquad \begin{array}{r} 17 \\ -9 \\ \hline \end{array} \qquad \begin{array}{r} 6 \\ +7 \\ \hline \end{array} \qquad \begin{array}{r} 15 \\ -6 \\ \hline \end{array} \qquad \begin{array}{r} 12 \\ -7 \\ \hline \end{array} \qquad \begin{array}{r} 5 \\ +9 \\ \hline \end{array}$$

Kilometers—estimating length

Square
Centimeter
Unit

10 square centimeters are needed to cover this space.

Give the number of square centimeters for each.

**1.**

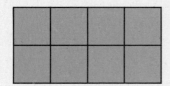

_____ square centimeters

**2.**

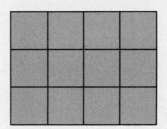

_____ square centimeters

**3.**

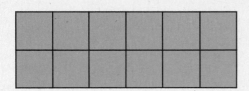

_____ square centimeters

**4.**

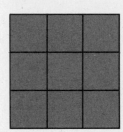

_____ square centimeters

**5.**

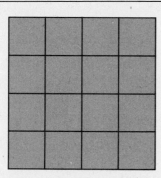

_____ square centimeters

**6.**

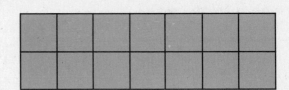

_____ square centimeters

Concept of area

Find how many square centimeters are in each figure.
Color the figures as shown in the table.

| Square centimeters | | 4 | 6 | 9 | 10 | 12 | 15 |
|---|---|---|---|---|---|---|---|
| Color | | | | | | | |

## THINK MATH

About how many
square centimeters
are there in the
orange figure?

There are about _____ square centimeters.

Concept of area—using a table

I **liter** (L) will fill 4 large glasses.

Ring the better estimate.

**1.**

More than I liter

Less than I liter

**2.**

More than I liter

Less than I liter

**3.**

More than I liter

Less than I liter

**4.**

More than I liter

Less than I liter

**5.**

More than I liter

Less than I liter

**6.**

More than I liter

Less than I liter

Liter—estimating capacity

## Ring the better estimate.

**1.**

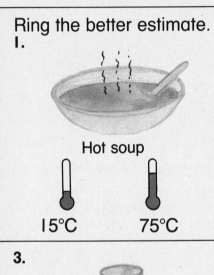

Hot soup

15°C     75°C

**2.**

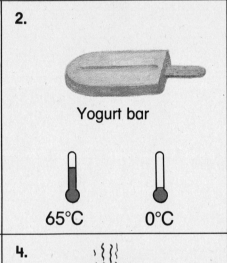

Yogurt bar

65°C     0°C

**3.**

Milk

5°C     50°C

**4.**

Hot cocoa

5°C     80°C

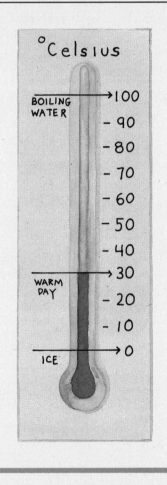

°Celsius

BOILING WATER → 100
- 90
- 80
- 70
- 60
- 50
- 40
WARM DAY → 30
- 20
- 10
ICE → 0

## SKILLKEEPER

### Draw the hands on the clocks.

4:00     4:30     10:15     10:45

     Degrees Celsius—estimating temperature

Two math books weigh about 1 kilogram (kg).

1 kg.

Ring the better estimate.

**1.**

More than 1 kilogram

Less than 1 kilogram

**2.**

More than 1 kilogram

Less than 1 kilogram

**3.**

More than 1 kilogram

Less than 1 kilogram

**4.**

More than 1 kilogram

Less than 1 kilogram

Kilogram—estimating weight

paper clip

About 1 **gram** (g)

About 5 grams

Ring the better estimate.

**1.**

8 grams

8 kilograms

**2.**

2 grams

2 kilograms

**3.**

7 grams

7 kilograms

**4.**

1 gram

1 kilogram

# THINK MATH

Fill the blanks.

Together, _____ and _____ weigh 60 kilograms.

Jan — 30 kilograms    Sue — 29 kilograms

Bill — 32 kilograms    Tom — 31 kilograms

Gram—estimating weight

# CHAPTER REVIEW/TEST

**1.** Use your centimeter ruler.
Give the length to the nearest centimeter.

‾‾‾‾‾‾
Nearest cm

‾‾‾‾‾‾
Nearest cm

‾‾‾‾‾‾
Nearest cm

**2.** Measure around the figure.

☐ + ☐ + ☐ = ‾‾‾‾ cm

**3.** Ring the better estimate. How tall are you?

Greater than I meter
Less than I meter

**4.** Count the number of square centimeters.

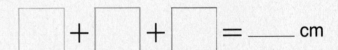

‾‾‾‾ Square centimeters

**5.** Ring the better estimate.

More than I liter
Less than I liter

0°C    10°C

More than I kilogram
Less than I kilogram

# CUMULATIVE REVIEW

1. Name the shape.

   ○ Square
   ○ Circle
   ○ Triangle

5. Subtract.  57
              − 26

   ○ 83
   ○ 31
   ○ 42

2. How many sides does the figure below have?

   ○ 4
   ○ 2
   ○ 3

6.  88
   −  6

   ○ 15
   ○ 94
   ○ 82

3. Which one is the same on both sides?

   1    2    3

   ○ 1
   ○ 2
   ○ 3

7.  74
   −  6

   ○ 68
   ○ 139
   ○ 39

4. How many flowers were sold on Tuesday?

   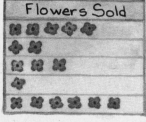
   Flowers Sold
   Monday
   Tuesday
   Wednesday
   Thursday
   Friday

   ○ 2
   ○ 5
   ○ 6

8.  80
   − 63

   ○ 20
   ○ 143
   ○ 17

9. Solve.

   There are 24 nuts in a bag.
   15 children each take one nut.
   How many nuts are left?

   PEANUTS

   ○ 29

   ○ 19

   ○ 9

# ANOTHER LOOK

It is between 2 and 3.
It is closer to

**2**
_ _ _ _ Nearest cm

Measure the sides.
Fill in the boxes.

| **2** | + | **4** | + | **3** | = | **9** ___ cm |

Count the squares.

| 1 | 2 | 3 |
| 4 | 5 | 6 |
| 7 | 8 | 9 |

**9** ___ square centimeters

Use your centimeter ruler.

1. Give the length to the nearest centimeter.

_____
Nearest cm

_____
Nearest cm

2. Measure around the figure.

☐ + ☐ + ☐ + ☐ = ___ cm

3. Give the number of square centimeters.

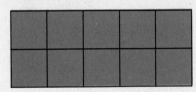

___ square centimeters

___ square centimeters

# ENRICHMENT

Margo delivered 47 letters in the morning. She delivered 38 in the afternoon. How many letters did Margo deliver that day?

Add to find how many altogether.

## 47 + 38

Use your  .

To start, always ⟶ press C .

 |  |  |  |  |

Press 4     Press 7     Press +     Press 3     Press 8     Press =

Margo delivered 85 letters that day.

Try this one. **92 − 57**

 |  |  |  |

Press 9     Press 2     Press −     Press 5     Press 7     Press =

Add or subtract. Use your 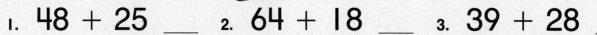 .

1. 48 + 25 ___    2. 64 + 18 ___    3. 39 + 28 ___

4. 70 − 35 ___    5. 81 − 36 ___    6. 93 − 54 ___

7. 62 + 19 ___    8. 62 − 19 ___    9. 47 − 16 ___

     Enrichment—using a calculator

Name _____

# 3-DIGIT PLACE VALUE

10 tens

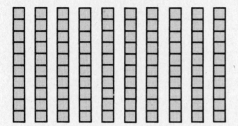  

This is one hundred.

10 tens = 1 hundred

How many hundreds, tens, and ones are there?

1.
   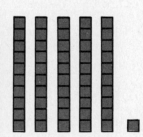

__3__ hundreds __5__ tens __2__ ones

2.
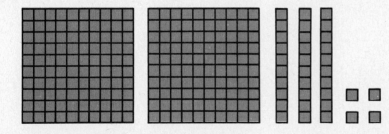

_____ hundreds _____ tens _____ ones

3.
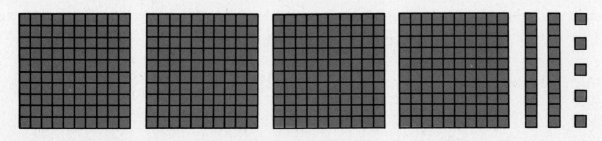

_____ hundreds _____ tens _____ ones

Hundreds, tens, and ones

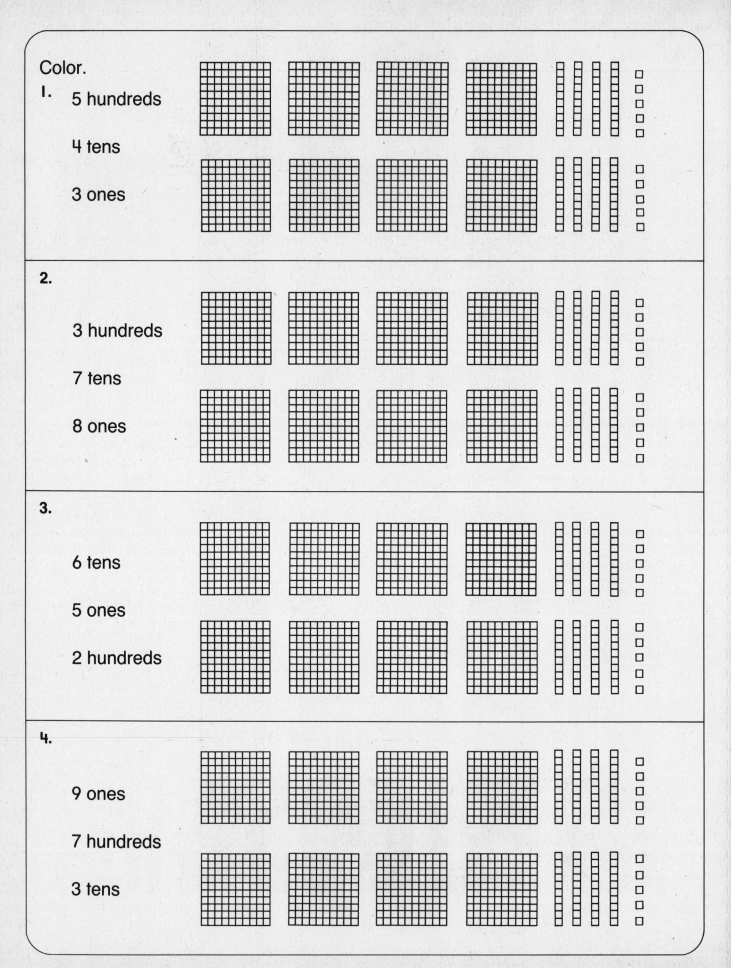

Color.

1. 5 hundreds

   4 tens

   3 ones

2. 3 hundreds

   7 tens

   8 ones

3. 6 tens

   5 ones

   2 hundreds

4. 9 ones

   7 hundreds

   3 tens

Hundreds, tens, and ones

Name _____

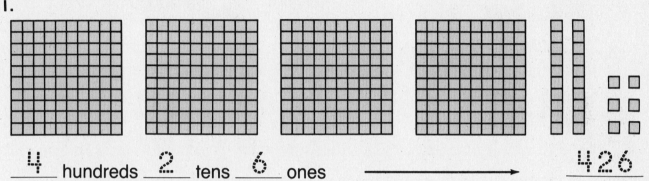

There are one hundred forty-three.

143

___1___ hundred ___4___ tens ___3___ ones

**How many are there? Write the number.**

**1.**

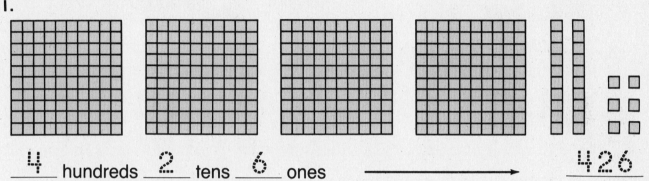

___4___ hundreds ___2___ tens ___6___ ones ⟶ 426

**2.**

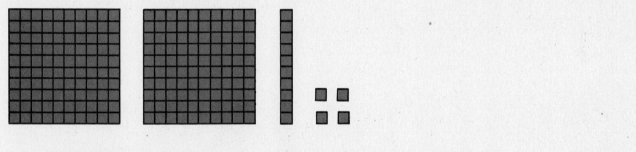

_____ hundreds _____ ten _____ ones ⟶ _____

**3.**

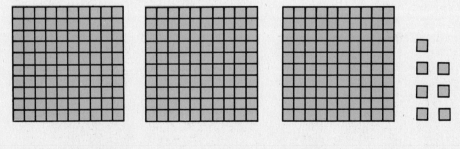

_____ hundreds _____ tens _____ ones ⟶ _____

Writing 3-digit numbers

How many are there? Write the number.

**1.**

| Hundreds | Tens | Ones |
|----------|------|------|
| 3 | 4 | 7 |

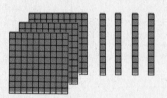

347

**2.**

| Hundreds | Tens | Ones |
|----------|------|------|
|          |      |      |

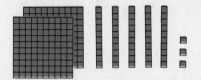

_____

**3.**

| Hundreds | Tens | Ones |
|----------|------|------|
|          |      |      |

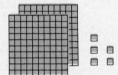

_____

**4.**

| Hundreds | Tens | Ones |
|----------|------|------|
|          |      |      |

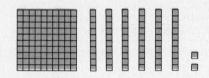

_____

**5.**

| Hundreds | Tens | Ones |
|----------|------|------|
|          |      |      |

_____

**6.**

| Hundreds | Tens | Ones |
|----------|------|------|
|          |      |      |

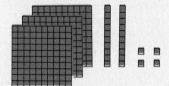

_____

## THINK MATH

Ring Brad's room number.
It has 5 tens.
It has 8 hundreds.

| | |
|---|---|
| 538 | 385 |
| 583 | 853 |
| 358 | 835 |

Writing 3-digit numbers

Name _____

How many are there? Write the number.

**1.**

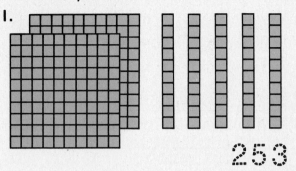

2 5 3

**2.**

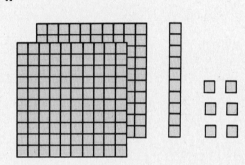

_____

**3.**

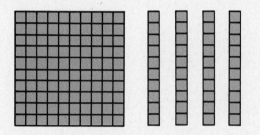

_____

**4.**

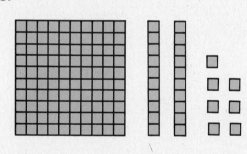

_____

**5.**

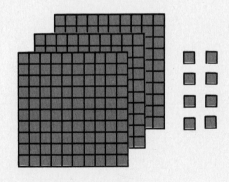

_____

**6.**

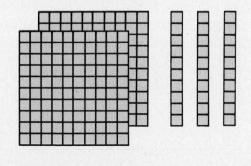

_____

**7.**

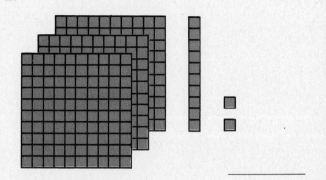

_____

**8.**

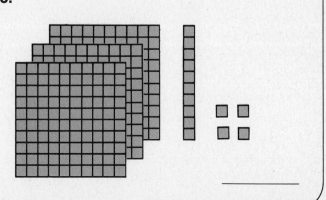

_____

Writing 3-digit numbers

(two hundred fifty-one) **251**

Color.

**1.**

546

**2.**

625

**3.**

430

## SKILLKEEPER

Add or subtract.

$$
\begin{array}{r} 73 \\ +25 \\ \hline \end{array}
\qquad
\begin{array}{r} 87 \\ -52 \\ \hline \end{array}
\qquad
\begin{array}{r} 58 \\ +17 \\ \hline \end{array}
\qquad
\begin{array}{r} 68 \\ -32 \\ \hline \end{array}
\qquad
\begin{array}{r} 63 \\ +\ 8 \\ \hline \end{array}
\qquad
\begin{array}{r} 91 \\ -\ 7 \\ \hline \end{array}
$$

Interpreting 3-digit numbers

Name _____

## How many pencils are there?

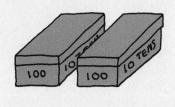 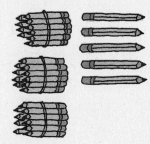 

2̈3̈5̈

**1.**

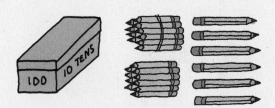

_____

**2.**

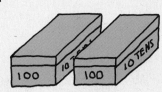

_____

**3.**

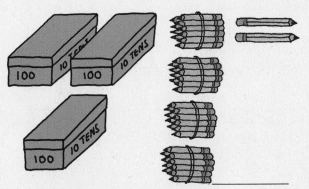

_____

**4.**

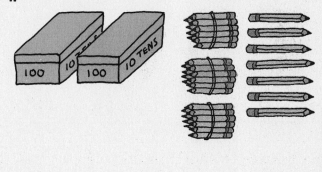

_____

**5.**

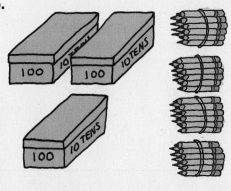

_____

**6.**

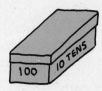

_____

3-digit numbers—varied models                    (two hundred fifty-three) **253**

How many are there?

**1.** 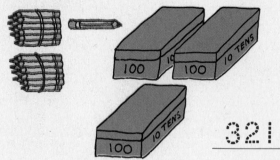 321

**2.** 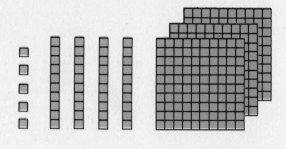 _____

**3.** 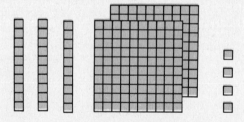 _____

**4.** 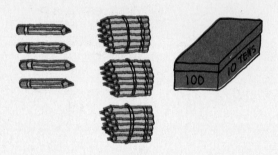 _____

**5.**  _____

**6.**  _____

---

## THINK MATH

Write the numbers in order from smallest to largest.

512      489      503

492      478

_____ _____ _____ _____ _____
Smallest                                  Largest

3 digit numbers—varied models

Name _____

The red digit means 5 tens.

352

5 hundreds    (5 tens)    5 ones

**What does the red digit mean?**

**1.**

385

3 hundreds    3 tens    3 ones

**2.**

372

7 hundreds    7 tens    7 ones

**3.**

637

6 hundreds    6 tens    6 ones

**4.**

814

4 hundreds    4 tens    4 ones

**5.**

250

2 hundreds    2 tens    2 ones

**6.**

394

9 hundreds    9 tens    9 ones

Understanding place value

Fill in the blanks.

**1.**

356

_3_ hundreds

_5_ tens

_6_ ones

**2.**

792

——— tens

——— hundreds

——— ones

**3.**

401

——— one

——— hundreds

——— tens

**4.**

837

——— tens

——— ones

——— hundreds

**5.**

920

——— hundreds

——— ones

——— tens

**6.**

162

——— tens

——— hundred

——— ones

**7.**

800

——— ones

——— hundreds

——— tens

**8.**

531

——— hundreds

——— one

——— tens

## THINK MATH

Patty's hat has a spinner.
It is not green. It has dots.
Put a ring around Patty's hat.

Understanding place value

Name _____

Finish each row. Follow the pattern.

**1.** | 97 | 98 | 99 | 100 | 101 | | |

↓ ↓ ↓ ↓ ↓ ↓ ↓

**2.** | 397 | 398 | 399 | 400 | | | |

↓ ↓ ↓ ↓ ↓ ↓ ↓

**3.** | 597 | 598 | 599 | | | | |

Finish the counting.

**4.** | 337 | 338 | 339 | | | | |

**5.** | 797 | 798 | 799 | | | | |

**6.** | 421 | 422 | 423 | | | | |

**7.** | 216 | 217 | 218 | | | | |

**8.** | 496 | 497 | 498 | | | | |

**9.** | 626 | 627 | 628 | | | | |

Counting                              (two hundred fifty-seven) **257**

Finish each row. Follow the pattern.

**1.**

| 47 | 48 | 49 | 50 | 51 | 52 |
|----|----|----|----|----|----|
| ↓  | ↓  | ↓  | ↓  | ↓  | ↓  |
| 647 | 648 | 649 | 650 |  |  |

**2.**

| 87 | 88 | 89 |  |  |  |
|----|----|----|----|----|----|
| ↓  | ↓  | ↓  | ↓  | ↓  | ↓  |
| 387 | 388 | 389 |  |  |  |

**3.**

| 26 | 27 | 28 |  |  |  |
|----|----|----|----|----|----|
| ↓  | ↓  | ↓  | ↓  | ↓  | ↓  |
| 826 | 827 | 828 |  |  |  |

**4.**

| 65 | 66 | 67 |  |  |  |
|----|----|----|----|----|----|
| ↓  | ↓  | ↓  | ↓  | ↓  | ↓  |
| 565 | 566 | 567 |  |  |  |

## SKILLKEEPER

Count the money.

_____    _____    _____

Counting patterns

Name _____

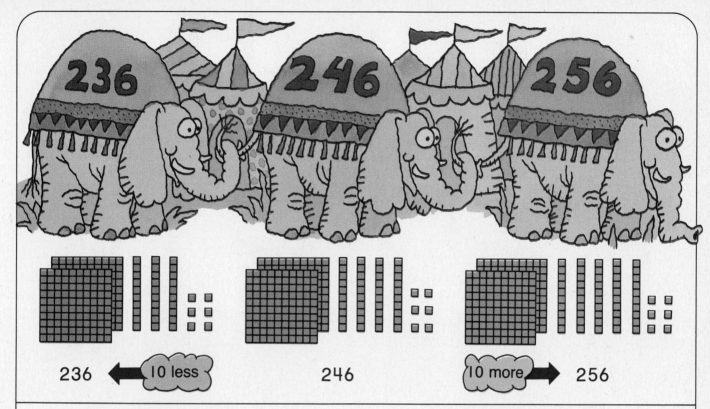

236 ← **10 less**     246     **10 more** → 256

Write the numbers.

**10 less**     **10 more**         **10 less**     **10 more**

1. _364_ , 374 , _384_       ____ , 258 , ____

2. ____ , 527 , ____       ____ , 936 , ____

3. ____ , 387 , ____       ____ , 156 , ____

4. ____ , 218 , ____       ____ , 304 , ____

5. ____ , 295 , ____       ____ , 708 , ____

6. ____ , 319 , ____       ____ , 490 , ____

10 less and 10 more than a number        (two hundred fifty-nine) **259**

146 ← 100 less    246    100 more → 346

Write the numbers.

| 100 less | 100 more | | 100 less | 100 more |

1.  523 , 623, 723  _____ , 764, _____

2. _____ , 386, _____  _____ , 735, _____

3. _____ , 248, _____ _____ , 570, _____

4. _____ , 637, _____  _____ , 759, _____

## THINK MATH

Ring the better estimate.

30 pages or 300 pages

50 beads or 500 beads

40 grapes or 400 grapes

Name _____

100¢

$1.00

This is one dollar.

One dollar and twenty-five cents.

Dollars Cents

$1.25

Match.

**1.**

$1.32

**2.**

$1.07

**3.**

$1.37

**4.**

$1.12

Larry the Crazy Duck

Dollar and cent notation

Write the amounts.

**1.**

dollars cents

$1.16

**2.**

_____

**3.**

_____

**4.**

_____

**5.**

_____

**6.**

_____

## SKILLKEEPER

Add or subtract.

$$
\begin{array}{r} 62 \\ +17 \\ \hline \end{array}
\qquad
\begin{array}{r} 86 \\ -12 \\ \hline \end{array}
\qquad
\begin{array}{r} 65 \\ +18 \\ \hline \end{array}
\qquad
\begin{array}{r} 62 \\ -17 \\ \hline \end{array}
\qquad
\begin{array}{r} 32 \\ +24 \\ \hline \end{array}
\qquad
\begin{array}{r} 42 \\ -28 \\ \hline \end{array}
$$

Dollar and cent notation

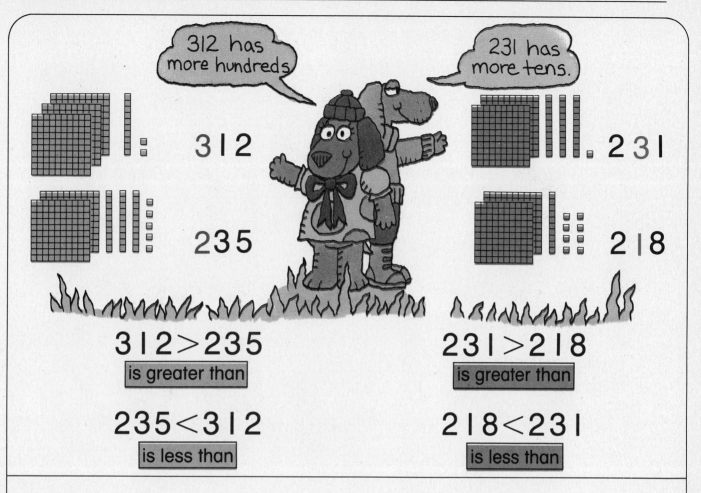

312 has more hundreds

231 has more tens.

312

235

231

218

312 > 235
| is greater than |

231 > 218
| is greater than |

235 < 312
| is less than |

218 < 231
| is less than |

Put > or < in each ◯.

1. 426 ◯ 326    583 ◯ 783    927 ◯ 627

2. 635 ◯ 645    318 ◯ 308    629 ◯ 649

3. 382 ◯ 386    427 ◯ 420    257 ◯ 256

4. 275 ◯ 257    348 ◯ 384    276 ◯ 267

5. 394 ◯ 934    287 ◯ 278    316 ◯ 136

6. 615 ◯ 797    527 ◯ 510    430 ◯ 420

Comparing numbers with > and <

# Problem-Solving Strategy

Solve.

1. Jan, Kim, and Lyn had a race.

Kim came in last.
Lyn did not win.
Who won the race?

_____

2. There are 3 houses on Clover Drive.

   Sue, Jeff, and Carlos live in these houses.

Sue does not live next to Jeff.
Jeff lives on a corner.
Who lives in the middle house?

_____

Problem solving strategy—use a picture

Name _____

# ANOTHER LOOK

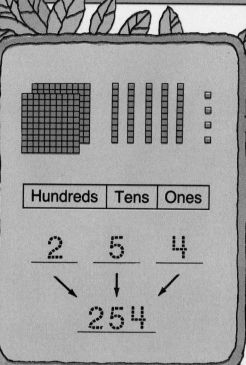

| Hundreds | Tens | Ones |
|----------|------|------|

2     5     4

254

$1.35

One dollar and
thirty-five cents.

**1. How many are there?**

| Hundreds | Tens | Ones |
|----------|------|------|

_____  _____  _____

**2.**

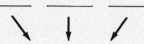

| Hundreds | Tens | Ones |
|----------|------|------|

_____  _____  _____

**Write the amounts.**

**3.**
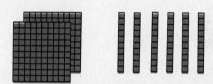

_____

**4.**

_____

# ENRICHMENT

Work the puzzle.

**Down**

1. 10 more than 347
2. 2 hundreds, 3 ones
4. 100 less than 927
8. 28 + 28 + 28
9. 10 more than 694
11. 1 more than 679
13. 74 − 48
14. 10 more than 296
16. 732, 733, 734, ___?___
17. after 579

**Across**

1. 10 less than 330
3. 67 − 29
5. 49, ___?___, 51
6. 2 tens
7. 100 more than 638
9. seven hundred seventy-seven
10. 4 hundreds, 6 tens
12. 10 more than 832
14. three hundreds
15. 660, 665, 670, ___?___
18. 10 less than 100
19. 19 + 19
20. 20, 30, 40, 50, ___?___
21. 100 less than 350

Enrichment—crossnumber puzzle

Cows: 326    Horses: 138

Sheep: 145    Rabbits: 137

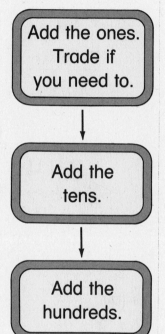

Add the ones. Trade if you need to.

↓

Add the tens.

↓

Add the hundreds.

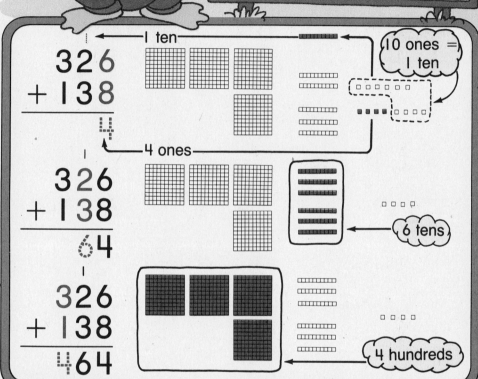

```
  326
+ 138
    4
```
4 ones

```
  326
+ 138
   64
```
6 tens

```
  326
+ 138
  464
```
4 hundreds

10 ones = 1 ten

1 ten

There were 464 horses and cows.

Add. Trade if you need to.

1.
```
  238      107      544      613      357
+ 145    + 623    + 238    + 254    + 224
```

2.
```
  355      436      824      206      516
+  28    + 126    +   5    + 368    + 345
```

Add. Trade if you need to.

1.
$$325 + 247$$   $$109 + 65$$   $$424 + 163$$

2.
$$236 + 48$$   $$165 + 626$$   $$942 + 36$$   $$224 + 628$$   $$175 + 7$$

3.
$$664 + 227$$   $$458 + 133$$   $$547 + 26$$   $$338 + 422$$   $$344 + 7$$

4. 145 sheep were at the fair.
137 rabbits were at the fair.
Altogether how many sheep and
rabbits were at the fair?

_____ in all

5. 326 cows were at the fair.
137 rabbits were at the fair.
What was the total number of
cows and rabbits at the fair?

_____ in all

## SKILLKEEPER

Count the money.

_____

Name _____

253 white mice are in the parade.
372 brown mice are in the parade.
What is the total number of mice
in the parade?

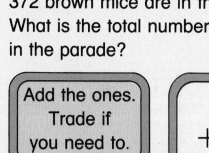

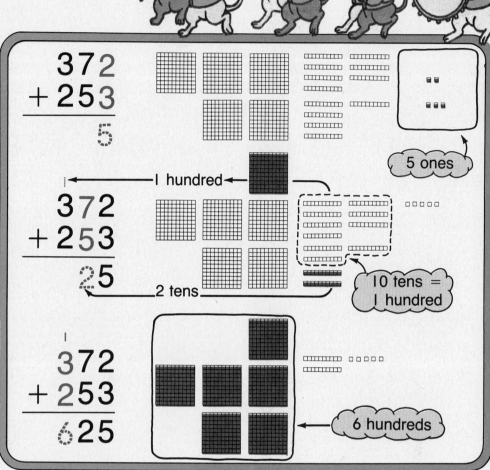

Add the ones.
Trade if
you need to.

$$\begin{array}{r} 372 \\ +253 \\ \hline 5 \end{array}$$

5 ones

Add the tens.
Trade if
you need to.

1 hundred

$$\begin{array}{r} 372 \\ +253 \\ \hline 25 \end{array}$$

2 tens

10 tens =
1 hundred

Add the
hundreds.

$$\begin{array}{r} 372 \\ +253 \\ \hline 625 \end{array}$$

6 hundreds

There are 625 mice altogether.

Add.

1.
$$\begin{array}{r} 472 \\ +263 \\ \hline \end{array}$$
$$\begin{array}{r} 238 \\ +591 \\ \hline \end{array}$$
$$\begin{array}{r} 370 \\ +\ 24 \\ \hline \end{array}$$
$$\begin{array}{r} 582 \\ +173 \\ \hline \end{array}$$
$$\begin{array}{r} 675 \\ +183 \\ \hline \end{array}$$

2.
$$\begin{array}{r} 146 \\ +693 \\ \hline \end{array}$$
$$\begin{array}{r} 83 \\ +285 \\ \hline \end{array}$$
$$\begin{array}{r} 637 \\ +281 \\ \hline \end{array}$$
$$\begin{array}{r} 90 \\ +360 \\ \hline \end{array}$$
$$\begin{array}{r} 364 \\ +243 \\ \hline \end{array}$$

Adding 3-digit numbers with trading (tens to hundreds)

(two hundred seventy-one) 271

Add. Trade if you need to.

1.
$$324 + 191$$
$$233 + 625$$
$$472 + 118$$
$$633 + 92$$

2.
$$252 + 507$$
$$88 + 171$$
$$392 + 184$$
$$747 + 182$$
$$71 + 838$$

3.
$$28 + 29$$
$$460 + 440$$
$$276 + 23$$
$$188 + 21$$
$$364 + 482$$

4.
$$103 + 808$$
$$711 + 209$$
$$973 + 19$$
$$79 + 7$$
$$248 + 191$$

5.
$$534 + 26$$
$$207 + 103$$
$$822 + 134$$
$$548 + 124$$
$$777 + 115$$

## THINK MATH

Add "in your head." Look for 100s.

1.
$$\begin{array}{r} 80 \\ 67 \\ + 20 \\ \hline 167 \end{array}$$
(100)

2.
$$\begin{array}{r} 79 \\ 50 \\ + 50 \end{array}$$
(100)

3.
$$\begin{array}{r} 20 \\ 34 \\ + 80 \end{array}$$

4.
$$\begin{array}{r} 70 \\ 30 \\ + 89 \end{array}$$

5.
$$\begin{array}{r} 50 \\ 98 \\ + 50 \end{array}$$

Addition practice

Name _____

350 ladybugs went to the park.
124 flew home.
How many bugs did not go home?

| Subtract the ones. Trade if you need to. |
| :-: |

↓

| Subtract the tens. |
| :-: |

↓

| Subtract the hundreds. |
| :-: |

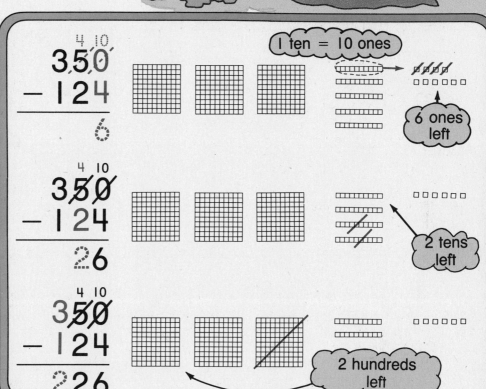

$$\begin{array}{r} {}^{4}\;\;{}^{10}\\ 3\,5\!\!\!/\,0 \\ -\;1\,2\,4 \\ \hline 6 \end{array}$$

1 ten = 10 ones

6 ones left

$$\begin{array}{r} {}^{4}\;\;{}^{10}\\ 3\,5\!\!\!/\,0 \\ -\;1\,2\,4 \\ \hline 2\,6 \end{array}$$

2 tens left

$$\begin{array}{r} {}^{4}\;\;{}^{10}\\ 3\,5\!\!\!/\,0 \\ -\;1\,2\,4 \\ \hline 2\,2\,6 \end{array}$$

2 hundreds left

226 ladybugs did not go home.

Subtract.

1.
$$\begin{array}{r} 762 \\ -235 \\ \hline \end{array} \qquad \begin{array}{r} 410 \\ -206 \\ \hline \end{array} \qquad \begin{array}{r} 546 \\ -\;\;28 \\ \hline \end{array} \qquad \begin{array}{r} 821 \\ -615 \\ \hline \end{array} \qquad \begin{array}{r} 327 \\ -219 \\ \hline \end{array}$$

2.
$$\begin{array}{r} 565 \\ -\;\;27 \\ \hline \end{array} \qquad \begin{array}{r} 972 \\ -755 \\ \hline \end{array} \qquad \begin{array}{r} 831 \\ -824 \\ \hline \end{array} \qquad \begin{array}{r} 743 \\ -224 \\ \hline \end{array} \qquad \begin{array}{r} 663 \\ -618 \\ \hline \end{array}$$

Subtract. Trade if you need to.

1.
$$\begin{array}{r} 473 \\ -134 \\ \hline \end{array}$$
$$\begin{array}{r} 626 \\ -418 \\ \hline \end{array}$$
$$\begin{array}{r} 545 \\ -521 \\ \hline \end{array}$$
$$\begin{array}{r} 736 \\ -717 \\ \hline \end{array}$$

2.
$$\begin{array}{r} 864 \\ -524 \\ \hline \end{array}$$
$$\begin{array}{r} 226 \\ -\phantom{0}7 \\ \hline \end{array}$$
$$\begin{array}{r} 464 \\ -249 \\ \hline \end{array}$$
$$\begin{array}{r} 587 \\ -528 \\ \hline \end{array}$$
$$\begin{array}{r} 644 \\ -\phantom{0}18 \\ \hline \end{array}$$

3.
$$\begin{array}{r} 342 \\ -237 \\ \hline \end{array}$$
$$\begin{array}{r} 410 \\ -108 \\ \hline \end{array}$$
$$\begin{array}{r} 562 \\ -351 \\ \hline \end{array}$$
$$\begin{array}{r} 786 \\ -628 \\ \hline \end{array}$$
$$\begin{array}{r} 850 \\ -\phantom{0}7 \\ \hline \end{array}$$

4. 673 bugs were on the curb.
348 crossed the street.
How many bugs did not cross
the street?

_____ bugs

5. 58 of the 124 ladybugs
went back to the park.
How many did not go
back?

_____ ladybugs

## SKILLKEEPER

Fill in the _____ .

110, _____ , 130          321, _____ , 521

265, _____ , 465          538, _____ , 558

Subtraction practice

## Problem Solving    Name _____

**Going to School**

| | | | | | | | | | |
|---|---|---|---|---|---|---|---|---|---|
| Walk: | ♣ | ♣ | ♣ | ♣ | ♣ | ♣ | ♣ | ♣ | ♣ |
| Ride a Bike: | ♣ | ♣ | ♣ | ♣ | ♣ | ♣ | | | |
| Ride the Bus: | ♣ | ♣ | ♣ | ♣ | ♣ | | | | |
| Ride in a car: | ♣ | ♣ | ♣ | ♣ | | | | | |

Each ♣ means 5 students

Solve. Use the graph.

1. How many walk to school?

_____ students

2. How many ride the bus to school?

_____ students

3. How many more students walk to school than ride a bike?

_____

_____

_____ more

4. How many fewer ride in cars than ride the bus?

_____

_____

_____ fewer

5. Altogether, how many students ride the bus or ride in a car to school?

_____

_____

_____ in all

6. What is the total number who walk or ride a bike to school?

_____

_____

_____ students

Problem solving—using data from a graph                    (two hundred seventy-nine)  **279**

## Problem Solving

Solve.

1. 12 model airplanes were bought.
   21 model boats were bought.
   Altogether, how many models were bought?

   __33__ models

   9 models were put together.
   How many have not been put together?

   __24__ models

$$
\begin{array}{r}
12 \\
+21 \\
\hline
33
\end{array}
\qquad
\begin{array}{r}
2\ 13 \\
\cancel{33} \\
-\ 9 \\
\hline
24
\end{array}
$$

2. 40 old nickels were collected.
   35 old pennies were collected.
   Altogether, how many coins were collected?

   _____ coins

   28 coins were given away.
   How many were not given away?

   _____ coins

3. 65 stamps were bought.
   38 were sold.
   How many stamps were not sold?

   _____ stamps

   37 more stamps were bought.
   What is the total number of stamps now?

   _____ stamps

About how much does the bear cost?

That is about 50¢

The bear costs about 50¢.

Ring the amount that is closer to the cost.

1.
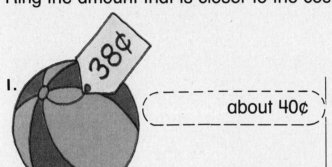

(about 40¢)

about 30¢

2.

about 40¢

(about 30¢)

3.
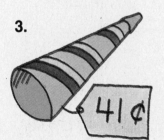

about 40¢

about 50¢

4.

about 40¢

about 50¢

5.

about 20¢

about 30¢

6.

about 20¢

about 30¢

That is about $3.00.

$2.98

Ring the amount that is closer to the cost.

**1.**
$3.05

about $3.00

about $4.00

**2.**
$4.98

about $4.00

about $5.00

**3.**
$2.10

about $2.00

about $3.00

**4.**
$3.99

about $3.00

about $4.00

**5.**
$2.90

about $2.00

about $3.00

**6.**
$1.95

about $1.00

about $2.00

## THINK MATH

Ed and Sue have the same amount of money. Ed has more coins than Sue. Put a mark on Ed's money.

Rounding

Name _____

40 ants were carrying the hamburger.
30 ants were carrying the bun.
How many ants were there
altogether?

$4$ tens $\quad + \quad 3$ tens $\quad = \quad 7$ tens

$40 \quad + \quad 30 \quad = \quad 70$

There were 70 ants altogether.

Find the sums.

1. $3 + 2 =$ ___  $\quad 30 + 20 =$ ___  $\quad 300 + 200 =$ ___

2. $5 + 2 =$ ___  $\quad 50 + 20 =$ ___  $\quad 500 + 200 =$ ___

3. $3 + 6 =$ ___  $\quad 30 + 60 =$ ___  $\quad 300 + 600 =$ ___

4. $4 + 4 =$ ___  $\quad 40 + 40 =$ ___  $\quad 400 + 400 =$ ___

5. $7 + 2 =$ ___  $\quad 70 + 20 =$ ___  $\quad 700 + 200 =$ ___

6. $3 + 5 =$ ___  $\quad 30 + 50 =$ ___  $\quad 300 + 500 =$ ___

Mental math—special sums

(two hundred eighty-three) **283**

Ring the amounts that are close.
Add these amounts to **estimate** the total.

**1.**

about 20¢

(about 30¢)

29¢

42¢

(about 40¢)

about 50¢

The total is about __70__ ¢.

**2.**

31¢

about 30¢

about 40¢

58¢

about 50¢

about 60¢

The total is about _____ ¢.

**3.**

$2.95

about $2.00

about $3.00

$1.12

about $1.00

about $2.00

The total is about $_____.

**4.**

$4.10

about $4.00

about $5.00

$1.98

about $1.00

about $2.00

The total is about $_____.

## SKILLKEEPER

Write the number.

_____          _____          _____

Name _____

60 children went to the zoo.
20 parents went to the zoo.
How many more children than
parents went to the zoo?

$$6 \text{ tens} - 2 \text{ tens} = 4 \text{ tens}$$
$$60 - 20 = 40$$

40 more children went to the zoo.

Find the differences.

1.

$$7 - 4 = \underline{\hspace{1cm}} \quad 70 - 40 = \underline{\hspace{1cm}} \quad 700 - 400 = \underline{\hspace{1cm}}$$

2. $$8 - 3 = \underline{\hspace{1cm}} \quad 80 - 30 = \underline{\hspace{1cm}} \quad 800 - 300 = \underline{\hspace{1cm}}$$

3. $$7 - 2 = \underline{\hspace{1cm}} \quad 70 - 20 = \underline{\hspace{1cm}} \quad 700 - 200 = \underline{\hspace{1cm}}$$

4. $$9 - 3 = \underline{\hspace{1cm}} \quad 90 - 30 = \underline{\hspace{1cm}} \quad 900 - 300 = \underline{\hspace{1cm}}$$

5. $$10 - 6 = \underline{\hspace{1cm}} \quad 100 - 60 = \underline{\hspace{1cm}} \quad 100 - 40 = \underline{\hspace{1cm}}$$

6. $$10 - 3 = \underline{\hspace{1cm}} \quad 100 - 30 = \underline{\hspace{1cm}} \quad 100 - 70 = \underline{\hspace{1cm}}$$

Mental math—special differences

First write how much money.
Then ring the amount that is close to the cost of the toy.
Subtract to estimate how much money is left.

**1.**   ___70___ ¢   39¢   about 30¢

About ___30___ ¢ is left.   (about 40¢)

**2.**   _____ ¢   58¢   about 50¢

About _____ ¢ is left.   about 60¢

**3.**   _100_ ¢   72¢   about 70¢

About _____ ¢ is left.   about 80¢

**4.**   _____ ¢   49 ¢   about 40¢

About _____ ¢ is left.   about 50¢

**5.**   $ _5.00_   $2.95   about $2.00

About $_____ is left.   about $3.00

**6.**   $_____   $4.12   about $4.00

About $_____ is left.   about $5.00

Name _____

# CHAPTER REVIEW/TEST

Add or subtract.

1.
$$542 + 423$$   $$124 + 737$$   $$638 + 21$$   $$292 + 483$$   $$272 + 433$$

2.
$$237 - 114$$   $$526 - 241$$   $$873 - 564$$   $$346 - 23$$   $$474 - 255$$

3.
$$\$3.24 - 2.11$$   $$\$2.47 + 1.29$$   $$\$6.48 - 3.29$$   $$\$5.25 + 1.30$$   $$\$8.32 - 2.50$$

---

4. Ring the amounts that are close. Then add.

about 20¢

about 30¢

about 40¢

about 50¢

The total is about _____ ¢.

---

5. First write how much money. Ring the amount that is close to the price. Subtract to estimate your change.

_____ ¢

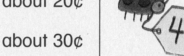

about 10¢

about 20¢

Your change is about _____ ¢

---

6. 178 girls went to camp. 215 boys went to camp.

How many went to camp in all?

_____ in all

7. 325 big tents were used. 108 small tents were used.

How many more big tents were used?

_____ more

# CUMULATIVE REVIEW

1. The pencil is between _____ centimeters long.

○ 1 and 2
○ 3 and 4
○ 4 and 5

5. What does the red digit mean?

274

○ 2 hundreds
○ 2 tens
○ 2 ones

2. Which is greater than a meter?

○ door
○ pencil
○ hammer

6. What comes next?

452, 453, 454, ___

○ 449
○ 456
○ 455

3. Hot soup is about _____.

○ 75°C
○ 50°C
○ 30°C

7. 557, 558 559, ___

○ 570
○ 560
○ 510

4. How many are there?

○ 256
○ 472
○ 351

8. Count.

○ $1.07
○ $2.36
○ $3.65

9. Solve.

John's pen was 18 centimeters long. Holly's pen was 15 centimeters long. How many centimeters longer was John's pen than Holly's pen?

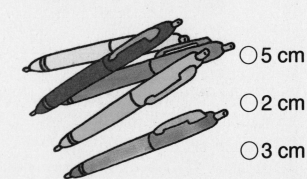

○ 5 cm
○ 2 cm
○ 3 cm

# ANOTHER LOOK

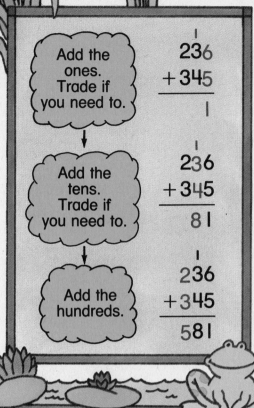

Add the ones. Trade if you need to.

$$\begin{array}{r} ^1 \\ 236 \\ +345 \\ \hline 1 \end{array}$$

Add the tens. Trade if you need to.

$$\begin{array}{r} ^1 \\ 236 \\ +345 \\ \hline 81 \end{array}$$

Add the hundreds.

$$\begin{array}{r} ^1 \\ 236 \\ +345 \\ \hline 581 \end{array}$$

Subtract the ones. Trade if you need to.

$$\begin{array}{r} ^{5\ 13} \\ 5\cancel{6}\cancel{3} \\ -125 \\ \hline 8 \end{array}$$

Subtract the tens. Trade if you need to.

$$\begin{array}{r} ^{5\ 13} \\ 5\cancel{6}\cancel{3} \\ -125 \\ \hline 38 \end{array}$$

Subtract the hundreds.

$$\begin{array}{r} ^{5\ 13} \\ 5\cancel{6}\cancel{3} \\ -125 \\ \hline 438 \end{array}$$

Add.

1.
$$\begin{array}{r} 225 \\ +468 \end{array} \qquad \begin{array}{r} 507 \\ +\ 29 \end{array} \qquad \begin{array}{r} 314 \\ +233 \end{array}$$

2.
$$\begin{array}{r} 124 \\ +748 \end{array} \qquad \begin{array}{r} 8 \\ +167 \end{array} \qquad \begin{array}{r} 534 \\ +436 \end{array}$$

Subtract.

3.
$$\begin{array}{r} 337 \\ -218 \end{array} \qquad \begin{array}{r} 870 \\ -255 \end{array} \qquad \begin{array}{r} 463 \\ -261 \end{array}$$

4.
$$\begin{array}{r} 588 \\ -\ 79 \end{array} \qquad \begin{array}{r} 642 \\ -129 \end{array} \qquad \begin{array}{r} 775 \\ -248 \end{array}$$

Add or subtract. Trade if you need to.

5.
$$\begin{array}{r} 462 \\ +129 \end{array} \qquad \begin{array}{r} 583 \\ -281 \end{array} \qquad \begin{array}{r} 746 \\ +222 \end{array}$$

6.
$$\begin{array}{r} 624 \\ -216 \end{array} \qquad \begin{array}{r} 537 \\ -\ 19 \end{array} \qquad \begin{array}{r} 762 \\ +\ 28 \end{array}$$

7.
$$\begin{array}{r} 821 \\ -510 \end{array} \qquad \begin{array}{r} 163 \\ +727 \end{array} \qquad \begin{array}{r} 325 \\ +224 \end{array}$$

# ENRICHMENT

Mental Math

Color pairs of tags that add to $1.00 (100¢) the same color.
Use a different color for each pair.

Enrichment—mental math (compatible numbers)

Name_____

# MULTIPLICATION

2
2
+ 2
___
6

3 twos = __6__

---

How many are there? Use counters.

**1.**

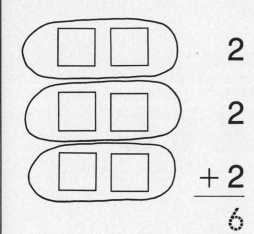

3
3
+ 3
___
9

3 threes = __9__

**2.**

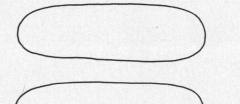

2
+ 2
___

2 twos = _____

---

**3.**

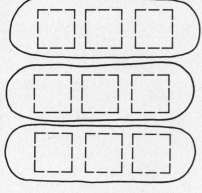

4
4
+ 4
___

3 fours = _____

**4.**

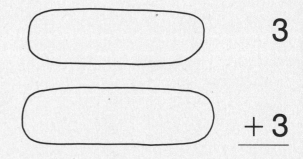

3
+ 3
___

2 threes = _____

---

Multiplication—repeated addition

How many are there?

**1.**

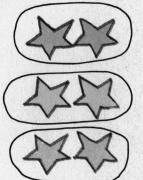

2
2
+2
___

3 twos = _____

**2.**

5

+5
___

2 fives = _____

**3.**

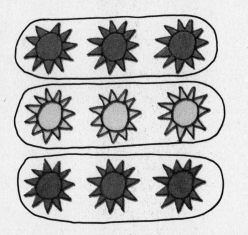

3
3
+3
___

3 threes = _____

**4.**

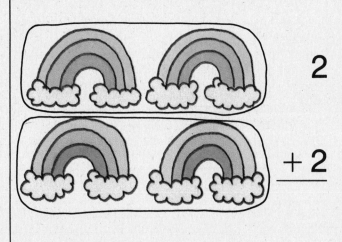

2

+2
___

2 twos = _____

## SKILLKEEPER

Add or subtract.

$$\begin{array}{r} 958 \\ -142 \\ \hline \end{array} \quad \begin{array}{r} 623 \\ +\ 75 \\ \hline \end{array} \quad \begin{array}{r} 785 \\ -323 \\ \hline \end{array} \quad \begin{array}{r} 615 \\ +\ 37 \\ \hline \end{array} \quad \begin{array}{r} 891 \\ -\ 27 \\ \hline \end{array} \quad \begin{array}{r} 29 \\ +438 \\ \hline \end{array}$$

Multiplication—repeated addition

Read, "Two times four equals eight."

2 fours = 8        2 × 4 = 8
↑
Product

## Find the products.

**1.**

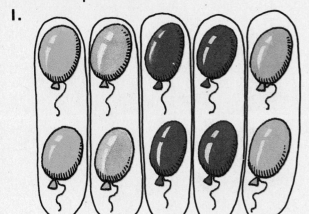

5 twos = _____        5 × 2 = _____

**2.**

3 threes = _____        3 × 3 = _____

**3.**

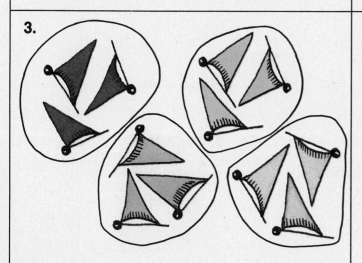

4 threes = _____        4 × 3 = _____

**4.**

3 twos = _____        3 × 2 = _____

2 and 3 as factors

Find the products.

**1.**

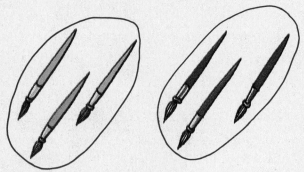

2 threes = _____     $2 \times 3 =$ _____

**2.**

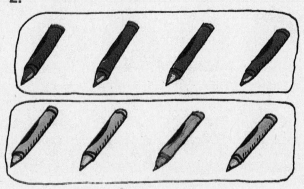

2 fours = _____     $2 \times 4 =$ _____

**3.**

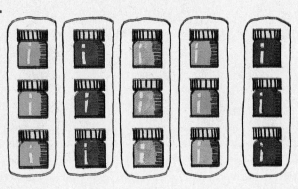

5 threes = _____     $5 \times 3 =$ _____

**4.**

2 twos = _____     $2 \times 2 =$ _____

## THINK MATH

Vera uses a large tube of toothpaste every month. Each tube costs $1.79. How much does she spend for toothpaste in a year?

Use your  _____

Name _____

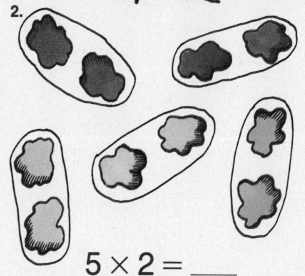

3 fours

$3 \times 4 = 12$

Multiply.

1.

$2 \times 4 = \underline{8}$

2.

$5 \times 2 = \underline{\hphantom{00}}$

3.

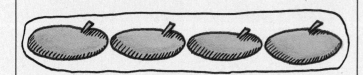

$4 \times 4 = \underline{\hphantom{00}}$

4.

$3 \times 4 = \underline{\hphantom{00}}$

2, 3, and 4 as factors

**Draw and multiply.**

**1.**

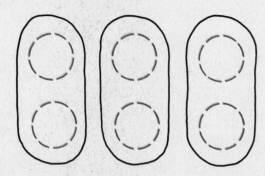

3 twos

$$3 \times 2 = \underline{\quad}$$

**2.**

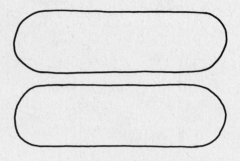

2 fours

$$2 \times 4 = \underline{\quad}$$

**3.**

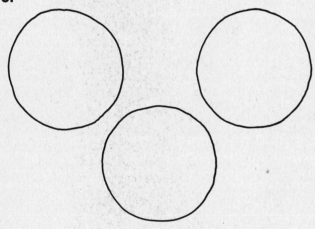

3 threes

$$3 \times 3 = \underline{\quad}$$

**4.**

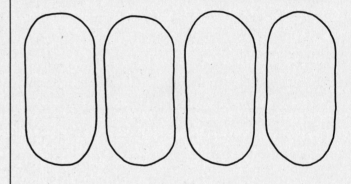

4 twos

$$4 \times 2 = \underline{\quad}$$

## SKILLKEEPER

Count the money.

$\underline{50}$ $\underline{\quad}$ $\underline{\quad}$ $\underline{\quad}$ $\underline{\quad}$ $\underline{\quad}$ ¢

2, 3, and 4 as factors

Name _____

$3 \times 5 = 15$

$$\begin{array}{r} 5 \\ \times\, 3 \\ \hline 15 \end{array}$$

Find the products.

**1.**

$$\begin{array}{r} 5 \\ \times\, 2 \\ \hline 10 \end{array}$$

**2.**

$$\begin{array}{r} 3 \\ \times\, 4 \\ \hline \end{array}$$

**3.**

$$\begin{array}{r} 4 \\ \times\, 2 \\ \hline \end{array}$$

**4.**

$$\begin{array}{r} 4 \\ \times\, 5 \\ \hline \end{array}$$

Vertical notation—2–5 as factors

(two hundred ninety-seven)   **297**

Multiply.

1.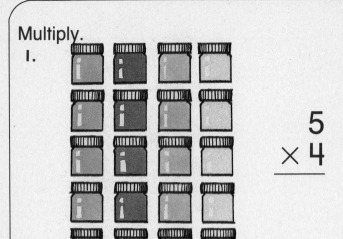

$$\begin{array}{r} 5 \\ \times\, 4 \\ \hline \end{array}$$

2.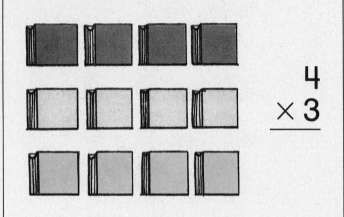

$$\begin{array}{r} 4 \\ \times\, 3 \\ \hline \end{array}$$

3.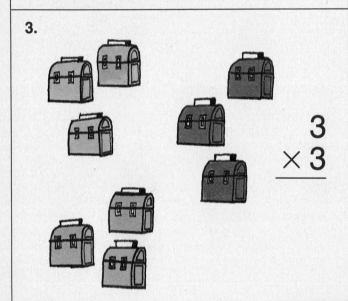

$$\begin{array}{r} 3 \\ \times\, 3 \\ \hline \end{array}$$

4.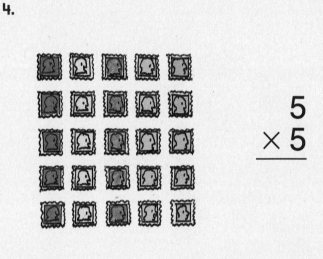

$$\begin{array}{r} 5 \\ \times\, 5 \\ \hline \end{array}$$

## THINK MATH

Continue the pattern.

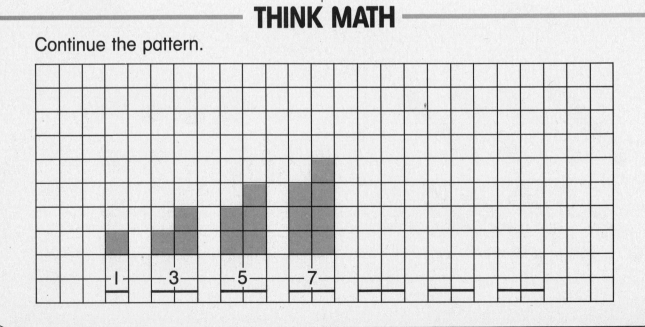

1    3    5    7

Vertical notation—2–5 as factors

Name _____

## Draw and multiply.

**1.**

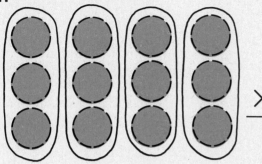

$$\begin{array}{r} 3 \\ \times\, 4 \\ \hline \end{array}$$

4 threes

**2.**

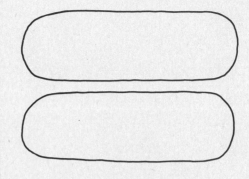

$$\begin{array}{r} 5 \\ \times\, 2 \\ \hline \end{array}$$

2 fives

**3.**

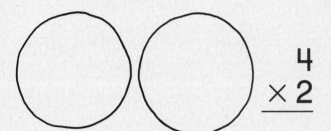

$$\begin{array}{r} 4 \\ \times\, 2 \\ \hline \end{array}$$

2 fours

**4.**

$$\begin{array}{r} 3 \\ \times\, 3 \\ \hline \end{array}$$

3 threes

**5.**

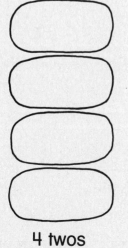

$$\begin{array}{r} 2 \\ \times\, 4 \\ \hline \end{array}$$

4 twos

**6.**

$$\begin{array}{r} 3 \\ \times\, 5 \\ \hline \end{array}$$

5 threes

2–5 as factors

Match and mutiply.

1.

$3 \times 2 =$ \_\_\_\_

2.

$3 \times 3 =$ \_\_\_\_

3.

$2 \times 4 = \underline{8}$

4.
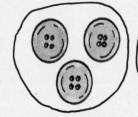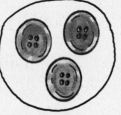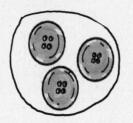
$4 \times 3 =$ \_\_\_\_

5.

$2 \times 5 =$ \_\_\_\_

---

## THINK MATH

Pretend you buy two of these.
You spend about $1.00. What
did you buy? Ring them.

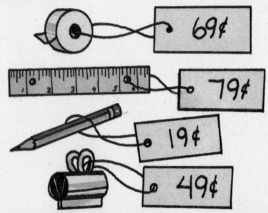

69¢

79¢

19¢

49¢

2–5 as factors

Name _____

$3 \times 4 = 12$  $4 \times 3 = 12$

Multiply.

1. $2 \times 3 = $ ___  $2 \times 4 = $ ___  $3 \times 5 = $ ___

   $3 \times 2 = $ ___  $4 \times 2 = $ ___  $5 \times 3 = $ ___

2. $2 \times 5 = $ ___  $5 \times 4 = $ ___  $3 \times 4 = $ ___

   $5 \times 2 = $ ___  $4 \times 5 = $ ___  $4 \times 3 = $ ___

3.
$$\begin{array}{r} 2 \\ \times 3 \\ \hline \end{array} \qquad \begin{array}{r} 3 \\ \times 2 \\ \hline \end{array} \qquad \begin{array}{r} 4 \\ \times 2 \\ \hline \end{array} \qquad \begin{array}{r} 2 \\ \times 4 \\ \hline \end{array} \qquad \begin{array}{r} 5 \\ \times 3 \\ \hline \end{array} \qquad \begin{array}{r} 3 \\ \times 5 \\ \hline \end{array}$$

4.
$$\begin{array}{r} 5 \\ \times 2 \\ \hline \end{array} \qquad \begin{array}{r} 2 \\ \times 5 \\ \hline \end{array} \qquad \begin{array}{r} 5 \\ \times 4 \\ \hline \end{array} \qquad \begin{array}{r} 4 \\ \times 5 \\ \hline \end{array} \qquad \begin{array}{r} 4 \\ \times 3 \\ \hline \end{array} \qquad \begin{array}{r} 3 \\ \times 4 \\ \hline \end{array}$$

Order in multiplication

$$4 \times 1 = 4 \qquad 4 \times 0 = 0$$

Multiply.

1. $5 \times 1 = \underline{\phantom{00}}$  $3 \times 1 = \underline{\phantom{00}}$  $2 \times 1 = \underline{\phantom{00}}$

   $1 \times 5 = \underline{\phantom{00}}$  $1 \times 3 = \underline{\phantom{00}}$  $1 \times 2 = \underline{\phantom{00}}$

2. $5 \times 0 = \underline{\phantom{00}}$  $4 \times 0 = \underline{\phantom{00}}$  $2 \times 0 = \underline{\phantom{00}}$

   $0 \times 5 = \underline{\phantom{00}}$  $0 \times 4 = \underline{\phantom{00}}$  $0 \times 2 = \underline{\phantom{00}}$

## SKILLKEEPER

Add or subtract.

$$
\begin{array}{cccccc}
64 & 86 & 45 & 50 & 38 & 91 \\
+23 & -15 & +\phantom{0}5 & -39 & +48 & +\phantom{0}9 \\
\hline
\end{array}
$$

0 and 1 as factors

# Problem Solving

Name _____

**1.** Find the total cost.

2 ¢
× 3
_____
6 ¢

Total _____

3  _____

_____

Total _____

4  _____

_____

Total _____

**2.**

3  _____

_____

Total _____

2  _____

_____

Total _____

5 _____

_____

Total _____

**3.**

5  _____

_____

Total _____

4 _____

_____

Total _____

4 _____

_____

Total _____

**4.**

4  _____

_____

Total _____

3  _____

_____

Total _____

2 _____

_____

Total _____

Problem solving—using data from a stamp

# Problem Solving

 5¢  3¢ 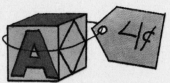 2¢ 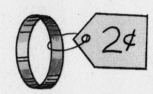 4¢

## Find the total cost.

**1.**

$$\begin{array}{r} 2¢ \\ \times\ 4 \\ \hline 8¢ \end{array}$$

_____

**2.**

_____

**3.**

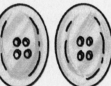

_____

**4.**

_____

**5.**

_____

**6.**

_____

**7.**

_____

**8. DATA BANK**

**(See page 344.)**

_____

Problem solving—using data from a price tag

Multiply.

1. $4 \times 2 =$ ___   $4 \times 3 =$ ___   $1 \times 1 =$ ___

2. $4 \times 4 =$ ___   $1 \times 4 =$ ___   $2 \times 4 =$ ___

3. $2 \times 3 =$ ___   $5 \times 5 =$ ___   $0 \times 2 =$ ___

4. $5 \times 1 =$ ___   $2 \times 5 =$ ___   $3 \times 3 =$ ___

5. $2 \times 2 =$ ___   $3 \times 0 =$ ___   $5 \times 4 =$ ___

6.
$$\begin{array}{r} 3 \\ \times 5 \\ \hline \end{array} \quad \begin{array}{r} 1 \\ \times 4 \\ \hline \end{array} \quad \begin{array}{r} 4 \\ \times 3 \\ \hline \end{array} \quad \begin{array}{r} 4 \\ \times 4 \\ \hline \end{array} \quad \begin{array}{r} 0 \\ \times 2 \\ \hline \end{array} \quad \begin{array}{r} 3 \\ \times 2 \\ \hline \end{array}$$

7.
$$\begin{array}{r} 4 \\ \times 2 \\ \hline \end{array} \quad \begin{array}{r} 1 \\ \times 0 \\ \hline \end{array} \quad \begin{array}{r} 4 \\ \times 5 \\ \hline \end{array} \quad \begin{array}{r} 0 \\ \times 0 \\ \hline \end{array} \quad \begin{array}{r} 5 \\ \times 2 \\ \hline \end{array} \quad \begin{array}{r} 2 \\ \times 2 \\ \hline \end{array}$$

8.
$$\begin{array}{r} 3 \\ \times 0 \\ \hline \end{array} \quad \begin{array}{r} 2 \\ \times 4 \\ \hline \end{array} \quad \begin{array}{r} 5 \\ \times 1 \\ \hline \end{array} \quad \begin{array}{r} 3 \\ \times 3 \\ \hline \end{array} \quad \begin{array}{r} 3 \\ \times 4 \\ \hline \end{array} \quad \begin{array}{r} 5 \\ \times 5 \\ \hline \end{array}$$

## THINK MATH

Terry bought a bat and 3 balls.
How much did he spend?

_____

$4.00   $3.00

Multiplication practice

# Problem Solving

Solve.

**1.**

Pam has 2 dolls. Each doll
has 3 dresses. How many
dresses in all?

_____6_____ dresses

$$\begin{array}{r} 2 \\ \times\ 3 \\ \hline 6 \end{array}$$

**2.**

Teri has 30 baseball cards.
Ted has 16 baseball cards.
How many more baseball cards
does Teri have than Ted?

_____ more cards

**3.**

Dora scored 26 points in one
game. She scored 35 points
in another. How many points
did she score in all?

_____ points

**4.**

Boyd has 3 boxes of pencils.
Each box has 5 pencils.
How many pencils altogether?

_____ pencils

5
pencils

Problem solving—story problems

Name _____

There are 4 twos in eight.

How many twos?          8 in all

---

1. Ring twos.

How many twos in 4? _____

2. Ring threes.

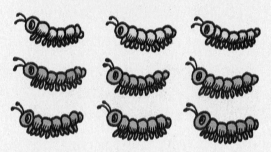

How many threes in 9? _____

---

3. Ring twos.

How many twos in 10? _____

4. Ring threes.

How many threes in 12? _____

---

5. Ring twos.

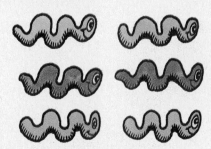

How many twos in 6? _____

6. Ring threes.

How many threes in 6? _____

---

Division readiness

1. Jason bought a baseball hat.

He does not like green hats.
He has never liked the Birds.
Ring the hat Jason bought.

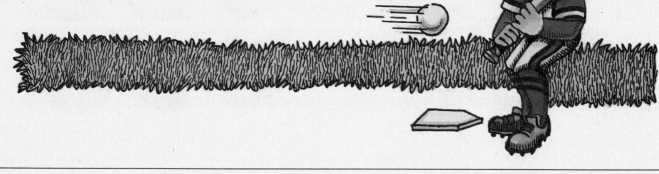

2. Amy lost a number from her locker.
It is greater than her last number.
It is smaller than her first number.
You say it when you count by 2s.
Ring Amy's missing number.

Problem solving strategy—use logical reasoning

Name _____

## CHAPTER REVIEW/TEST

Find the products.

**1.**  $2 \times 3 =$ ___

**2.** 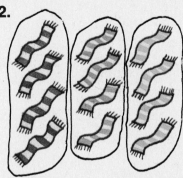 $3 \times 4 =$ ___

**3.**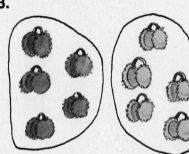
$\begin{array}{r} 5 \\ \times 2 \\ \hline \end{array}$

**4.**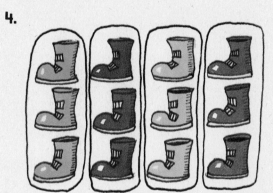
$\begin{array}{r} 3 \\ \times 4 \\ \hline \end{array}$

Multiply.

**5.** $3 \times 2 =$ ___   $3 \times 5 =$ ___   $2 \times 4 =$ ___

**6.**
$\begin{array}{r} 3 \\ \times 3 \\ \hline \end{array}$
$\begin{array}{r} 2 \\ \times 1 \\ \hline \end{array}$
$\begin{array}{r} 4 \\ \times 3 \\ \hline \end{array}$
$\begin{array}{r} 2 \\ \times 2 \\ \hline \end{array}$
$\begin{array}{r} 5 \\ \times 4 \\ \hline \end{array}$
$\begin{array}{r} 3 \\ \times 0 \\ \hline \end{array}$

**7.** Ring threes. Answer the question.

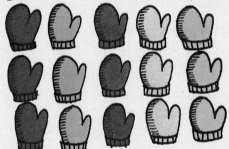

How many threes in 15? ___

**8.** Jane has 2 plants. Each plant has 4 flowers. How many flowers in all? ___

___ flowers

**Name** _____

## How many are there?

1.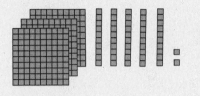
   - ○ 352
   - ○ 451
   - ○ 361

2.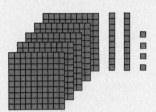
   - ○ 524
   - ○ 254
   - ○ 462

3.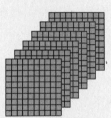
   - ○ 16
   - ○ 6
   - ○ 600

4.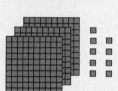
   - ○ 390
   - ○ 309
   - ○ 39

## Add or subtract.

5.
$$277 + 413$$
   - ○ 552
   - ○ 690
   - ○ 164

6.
$$786 - 54$$
   - ○ 745
   - ○ 840
   - ○ 732

7.
$$543 - 29$$
   - ○ 514
   - ○ 523
   - ○ 751

8.
$$\$8.34 - 2.17$$
   - ○ \$7.25
   - ○ \$6.17
   - ○ \$5.51

9. Solve.

   The teacher had 341 pencils.
   She gave 240 to the class.
   How many did she have left?

   - ○ 581
   - ○ 101
   - ○ 421

# ANOTHER LOOK

2 threes = 6

$$\begin{array}{r} 3 \\ \times 2 \\ \hline 6 \end{array}$$

4 twos = 8

$$\begin{array}{r} 2 \\ \times 4 \\ \hline 8 \end{array}$$

$$\begin{array}{r} 4 \\ \times 3 \\ \hline 12 \end{array}$$

$$\begin{array}{r} 5 \\ \times 2 \\ \hline 10 \end{array}$$

Multiply.

1.
$$\begin{array}{r} 2 \\ \times 2 \\ \hline \end{array} \quad \begin{array}{r} 3 \\ \times 1 \\ \hline \end{array} \quad \begin{array}{r} 3 \\ \times 4 \\ \hline \end{array} \quad \begin{array}{r} 2 \\ \times 5 \\ \hline \end{array}$$

2.
$$\begin{array}{r} 2 \\ \times 0 \\ \hline \end{array} \quad \begin{array}{r} 3 \\ \times 3 \\ \hline \end{array} \quad \begin{array}{r} 2 \\ \times 3 \\ \hline \end{array} \quad \begin{array}{r} 3 \\ \times 5 \\ \hline \end{array}$$

3.
$$\begin{array}{r} 5 \\ \times 1 \\ \hline \end{array} \quad \begin{array}{r} 4 \\ \times 5 \\ \hline \end{array} \quad \begin{array}{r} 5 \\ \times 3 \\ \hline \end{array} \quad \begin{array}{r} 5 \\ \times 4 \\ \hline \end{array}$$

4.
$$\begin{array}{r} 4 \\ \times 2 \\ \hline \end{array} \quad \begin{array}{r} 4 \\ \times 4 \\ \hline \end{array} \quad \begin{array}{r} 5 \\ \times 0 \\ \hline \end{array} \quad \begin{array}{r} 4 \\ \times 1 \\ \hline \end{array}$$

5.
$$\begin{array}{r} 0 \\ \times 2 \\ \hline \end{array} \quad \begin{array}{r} 4 \\ \times 3 \\ \hline \end{array} \quad \begin{array}{r} 1 \\ \times 2 \\ \hline \end{array} \quad \begin{array}{r} 3 \\ \times 5 \\ \hline \end{array}$$

6.
$$\begin{array}{r} 2 \\ \times 5 \\ \hline \end{array} \quad \begin{array}{r} 3 \\ \times 4 \\ \hline \end{array} \quad \begin{array}{r} 1 \\ \times 1 \\ \hline \end{array} \quad \begin{array}{r} 5 \\ \times 2 \\ \hline \end{array}$$

Name _____

Check (✔) each wrong answer.
Mark the number correct.
Finish coloring the bar graph.

**Mike**

Add.

```
  1           1
 38    45    375
+27   +39   +116
 65    74    491
```

Subtract.

```
            6 10
 82    7̶0̶    463
-39   -28   -127
 57    42    344
```

Multiply.

```
  3     5     2
 ×5    ×4    ×5
 15    25    10
```

**Susan**

Add.

```
  1           1
 63    38    375
+26   +27   +116
 99    65    491
```

Subtract.

```
 6 16   7 12   5 13
 76    82    463
-31   -39   -127
 35    43    336
```

Multiply.

```
  4     3     5     2
 ×3    ×5    ×4    ×5
 12    15    20     8
```

**Marco**

Add.

```
 63    38    45    375
+26   +27   +39   +116
 89    65    84    491
```

Subtract.

```
       7 12   6 10   5 13
 76    8̶2̶    7̶0̶    4̶6̶3̶
-31   -39   -28   -127
 45    43    42    336
```

Multiply.

```
  4     3     5     2
 ×3    ×5    ×4    ×5
 12    16    20    10
```

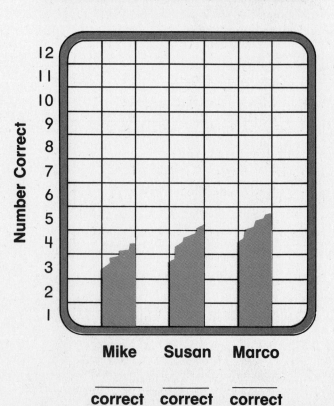

Number Correct

12
11
10
9
8
7
6
5
4
3
2
1

Mike   Susan   Marco

correct   correct   correct

Enrichment—graphing

Name _____

**2 equal parts**
**Halves**

Ring the figures that show equal parts.

**1.** 2 equal parts
Halves

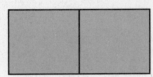

**2.**

3 equal parts
Thirds

  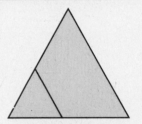

**3.**

4 equal parts
Fourths

 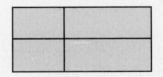 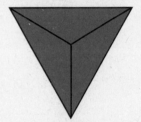

**4.**

5 equal parts
Fifths

 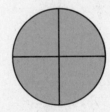 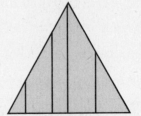

**5.**

6 equal parts
Sixths

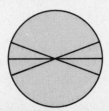 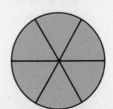 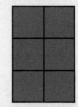

Concept of equal parts for fractions

(three hundred thirteen) **313**

Color the figures that show the correct parts.

1. Thirds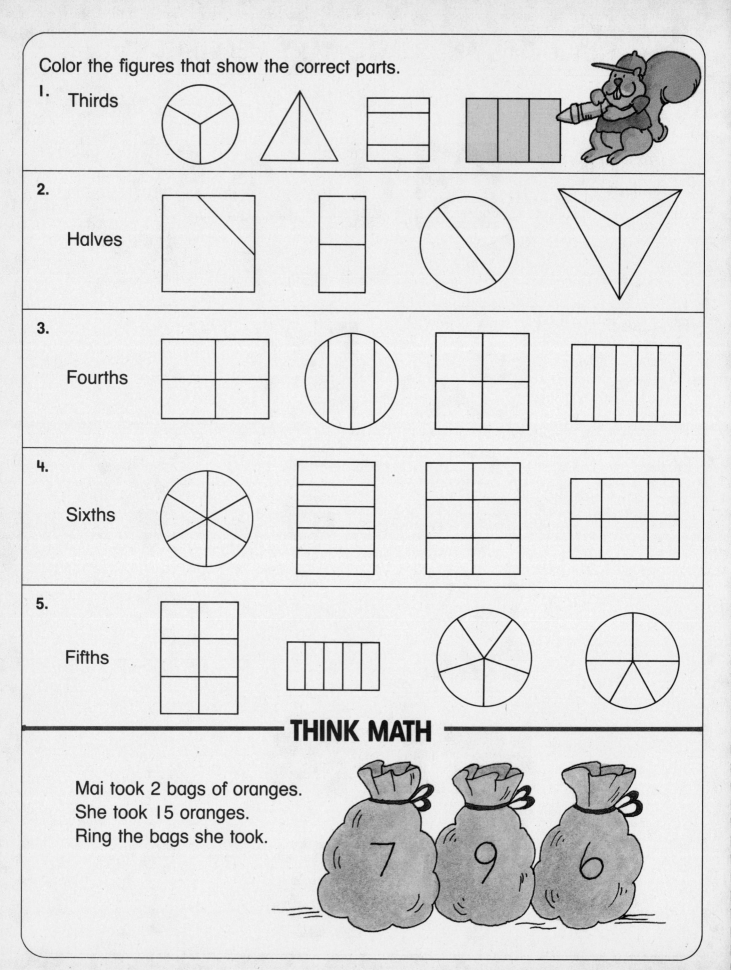

2. Halves

3. Fourths

4. Sixths

5. Fifths

**THINK MATH**

Mai took 2 bags of oranges.
She took 15 oranges.
Ring the bags she took.

7   9   6

Concept of equal parts for fractions

This is a fraction.

$$\frac{2}{3}$$ of the equal parts

**Color the figures. Write the fractions.**

**1.** Color 1 fourth.

$$\frac{\phantom{0}}{\phantom{0}}$$ of the equal parts

**2.** Color 2 fifths.

$$\frac{\phantom{0}}{\phantom{0}}$$ of the equal parts

**3.** Color 1 half.

$$\frac{\phantom{0}}{\phantom{0}}$$ of the equal parts

**4.** Color 2 fourths.

$$\frac{\phantom{0}}{\phantom{0}}$$ of the equal parts

**5.** Color 4 sixths.

$$\frac{\phantom{0}}{\phantom{0}}$$ of the equal parts

**6.** Color 1 third.

$$\frac{\phantom{0}}{\phantom{0}}$$ of the equal parts

**7.** Color 2 thirds.

$$\frac{\phantom{0}}{\phantom{0}}$$ of the equal parts

**8.** Color 5 sixths.

$$\frac{\phantom{0}}{\phantom{0}}$$ of the equal parts

Fraction names

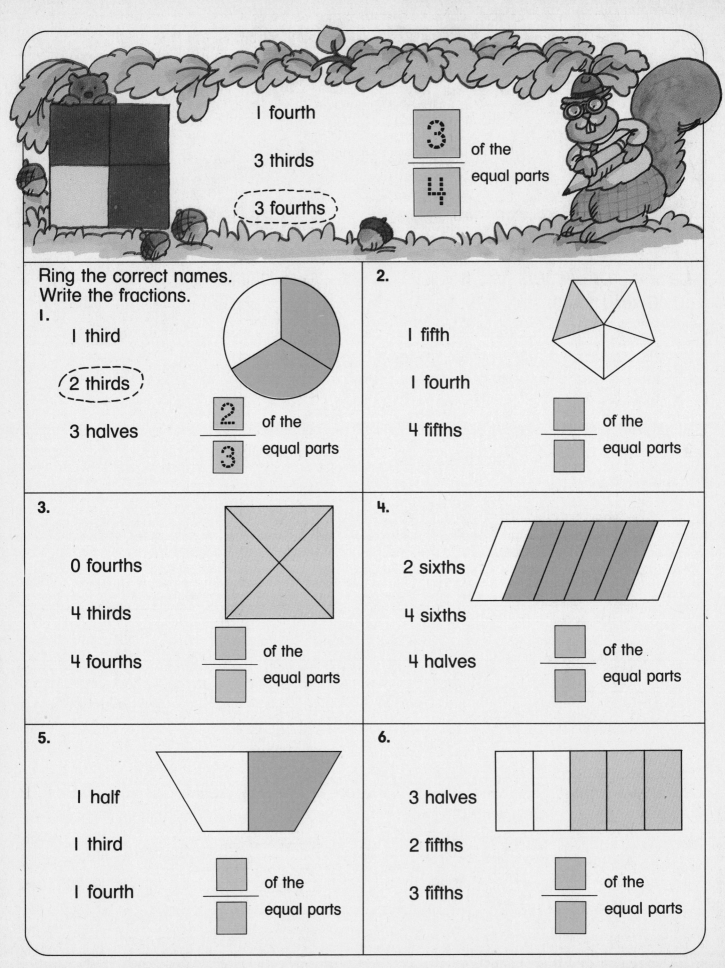

I fourth

3 thirds

(3 fourths)

$\dfrac{3}{4}$ of the equal parts

Ring the correct names.
Write the fractions.

**1.**

I third

(2 thirds)

3 halves

$\dfrac{2}{3}$ of the equal parts

**2.**

I fifth

I fourth

4 fifths

$\dfrac{\phantom{0}}{\phantom{0}}$ of the equal parts

**3.**

0 fourths

4 thirds

4 fourths

$\dfrac{\phantom{0}}{\phantom{0}}$ of the equal parts

**4.**

2 sixths

4 sixths

4 halves

$\dfrac{\phantom{0}}{\phantom{0}}$ of the equal parts

**5.**

I half

I third

I fourth

$\dfrac{\phantom{0}}{\phantom{0}}$ of the equal parts

**6.**

3 halves

2 fifths

3 fifths

$\dfrac{\phantom{0}}{\phantom{0}}$ of the equal parts

Fraction names

Name _____

This is 2 fourths.

**1.** Color $\dfrac{1}{3}$.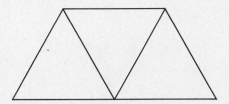

**2.** Color $\dfrac{1}{6}$.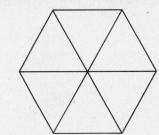

**3.** Color $\dfrac{3}{4}$.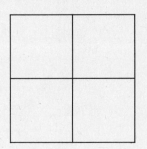

**4.** Color $\dfrac{4}{5}$.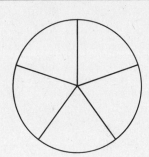

**5.** Color $\dfrac{2}{6}$.

**6.** Color $\dfrac{1}{2}$.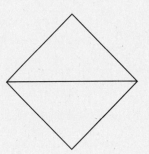

**7.** Color $\dfrac{1}{4}$.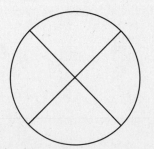

**8.** Color $\dfrac{2}{3}$.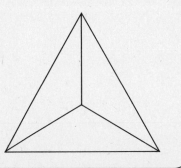

Recognizing and writing fractions

$\dfrac{3}{4}$

Write the fraction that tells what part is colored.

**1.**

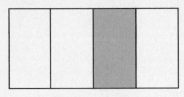

$\dfrac{1}{4}$

**2.**

___

**3.**

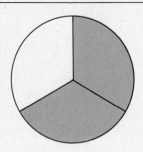

___

**4.**

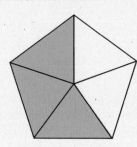

___

**5.**

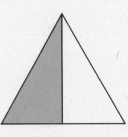

___

**6.**

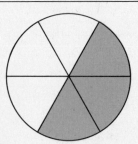

___

## SKILLKEEPER

Multiply.

$$\begin{array}{r} 3 \\ \times 2 \\ \hline \end{array} \qquad \begin{array}{r} 4 \\ \times 1 \\ \hline \end{array} \qquad \begin{array}{r} 2 \\ \times 5 \\ \hline \end{array} \qquad \begin{array}{r} 4 \\ \times 3 \\ \hline \end{array} \qquad \begin{array}{r} 5 \\ \times 0 \\ \hline \end{array} \qquad \begin{array}{r} 2 \\ \times 4 \\ \hline \end{array}$$

Recognizing and writing fractions

$\dfrac{4}{10}$

$\dfrac{6}{10}$

**Color the figures to show the parts.**

**1.** $\dfrac{1}{3}$

$\dfrac{2}{3}$

**2.** $\dfrac{2}{5}$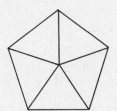

$\dfrac{3}{5}$

**3.** $\dfrac{1}{10}$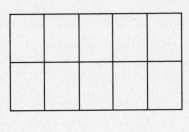

$\dfrac{9}{10}$

**4.** $\dfrac{1}{8}$

$\dfrac{7}{8}$

**5.** $\dfrac{2}{4}$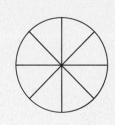

$\dfrac{2}{4}$

**6.** $\dfrac{4}{6}$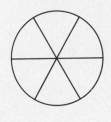

$\dfrac{2}{6}$

**7.** $\dfrac{7}{10}$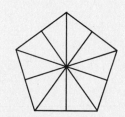

$\dfrac{3}{10}$

**8.** $\dfrac{4}{8}$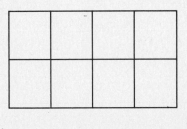

$\dfrac{4}{8}$

Fractional parts of regions

Write the fractions that tell what parts are colored.

**1.** 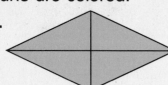 $\dfrac{1}{4}$

$\dfrac{3}{4}$

**2.**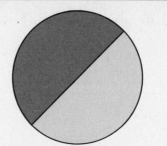

**3.**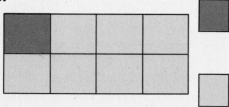

**4.**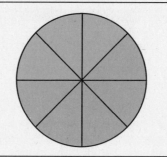

**5.**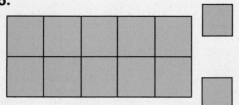

**6.**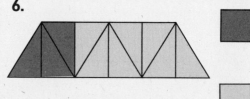

---

## SKILLKEEPER

Add or subtract.

$$\begin{array}{r} 576 \\ -258 \\ \hline \end{array} \qquad \begin{array}{r} 429 \\ +\ 67 \\ \hline \end{array} \qquad \begin{array}{r} 527 \\ +291 \\ \hline \end{array} \qquad \begin{array}{r} 416 \\ +340 \\ \hline \end{array} \qquad \begin{array}{r} 682 \\ -291 \\ \hline \end{array}$$

Fractional parts of regions

$\dfrac{2}{3}$

$\dfrac{2}{3}$ — 2 baskets colored
$\dfrac{3}{3}$ — 3 baskets in all

two thirds

**1.** Color one third.

$\dfrac{1}{3}$

**2.** Color one half.

$\dfrac{1}{2}$

**3.** Color two fourths.

$\dfrac{2}{4}$

**4.** Color three fifths.

$\dfrac{3}{5}$

**5.** Color one sixth.

$\dfrac{1}{6}$

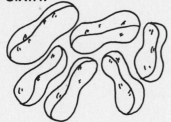

**6.** Color two thirds.

$\dfrac{2}{3}$

**7.** Color five eighths.

$\dfrac{5}{8}$

**8.** Color seven tenths.

$\dfrac{7}{10}$

Fractional parts of sets

**1.** Ring $\frac{1}{2}$.

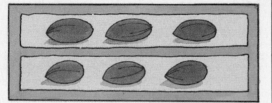

**2.** Ring $\frac{1}{3}$.

**3.** Ring $\frac{1}{4}$.

**4.** Ring $\frac{1}{2}$.

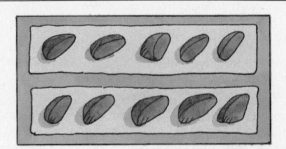

**5.** Ring $\frac{1}{3}$.

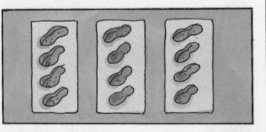

**6.** Ring $\frac{1}{4}$.

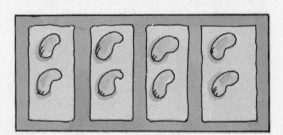

## THINK MATH

The large box holds 8 erasers.
Each small box holds 2 erasers.
How many erasers are there in all?

_____ erasers

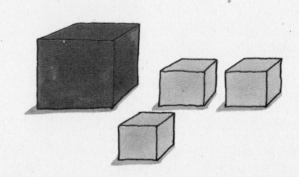

Fractional parts of sets

Name _____

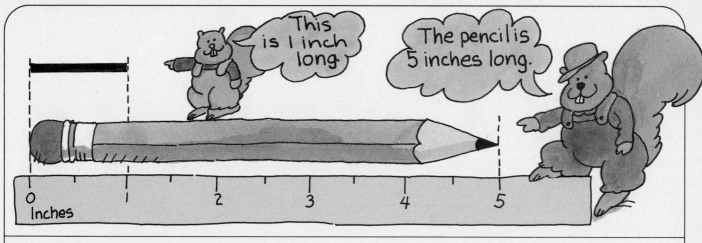

Use your inch ruler. Find the lengths.

**1.**

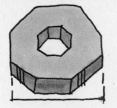

_4_ inches

**2.**

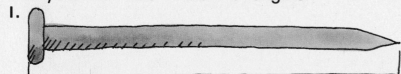

_____ inch

**3.**

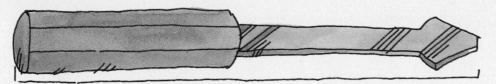

_____ inches

**4.**

_____ inches

**5.**

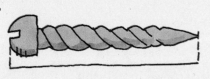

_____ inches

**6.**

_____ inches

Measuring length using an inch-ruler

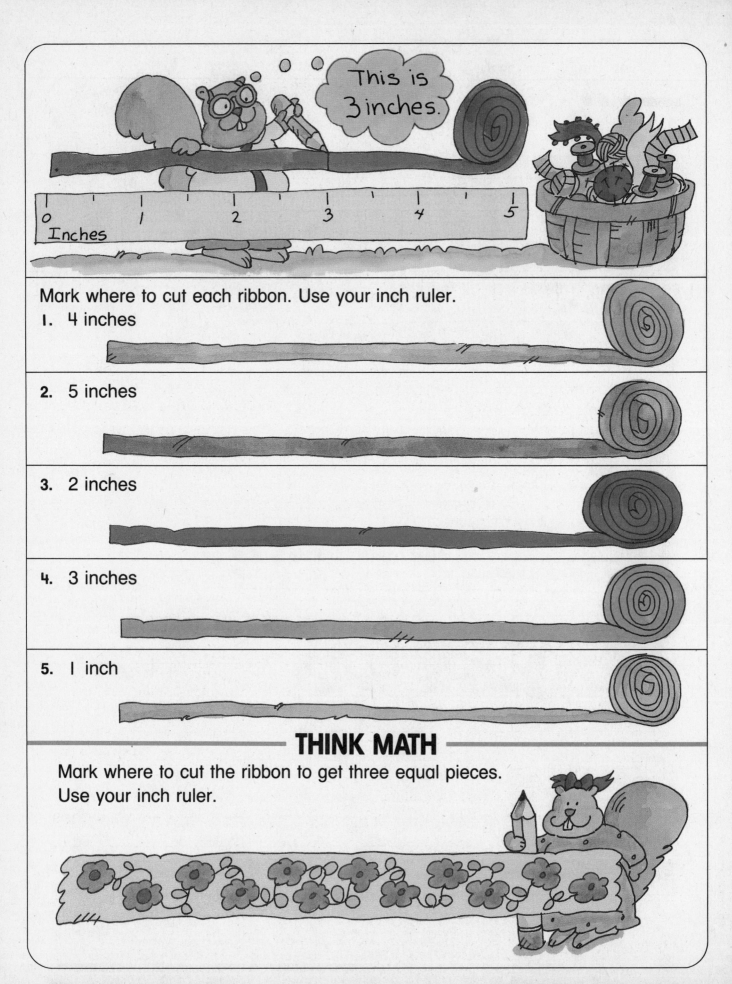

This is 3 inches.

Inches
0  1  2  3  4  5

Mark where to cut each ribbon. Use your inch ruler.

1. 4 inches

2. 5 inches

3. 2 inches

4. 3 inches

5. 1 inch

## THINK MATH

Mark where to cut the ribbon to get three equal pieces.
Use your inch ruler.

Measuring length using an inch-ruler

Name _____

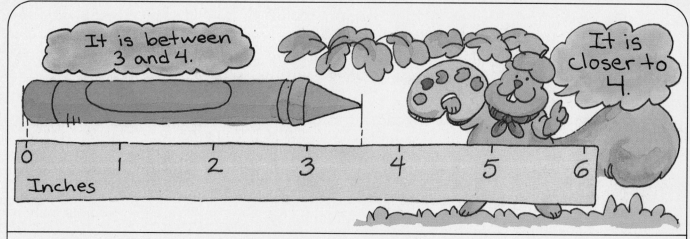

Use your inch ruler. Find the length to the nearest inch.

**1.**

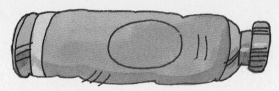

**4**
_____
Nearest inch

It is between ___4___ and ___5___ inches.

**2.**

**_____**
Nearest inch

It is between _____ and _____ inches.

**3.**

**_____**
Nearest inch

It is between _____ and _____ inches.

**4.**

**_____**
Nearest inch

It is between _____ and _____ inches.

Use your inch ruler. Find the length to the nearest inch.

**1.**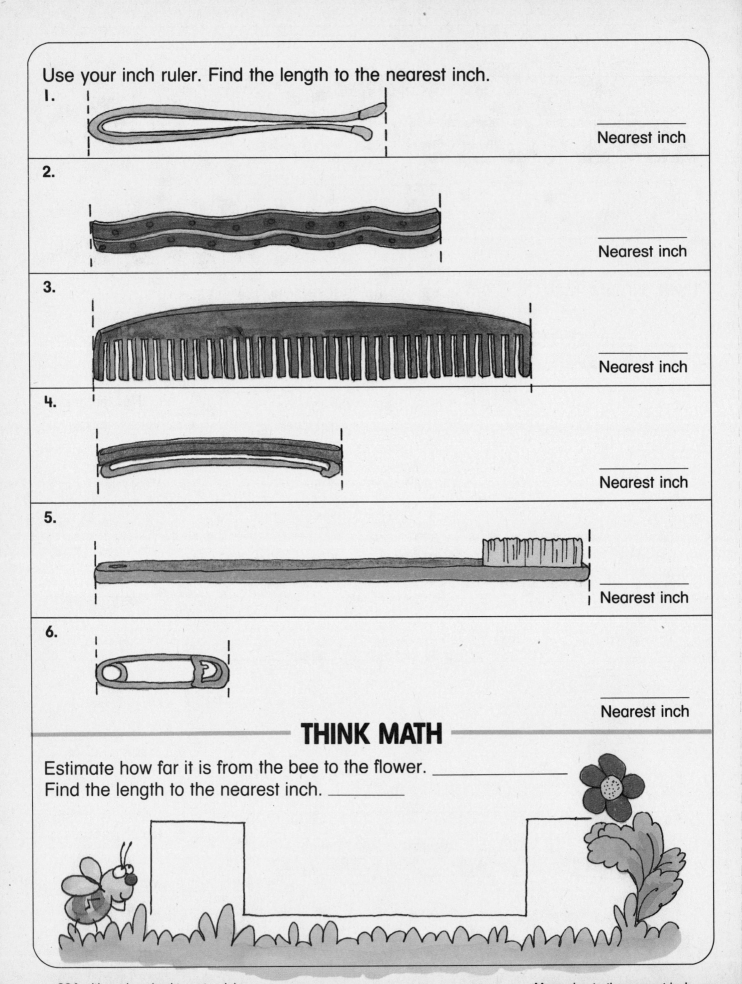

_____
Nearest inch

**2.**

_____
Nearest inch

**3.**

_____
Nearest inch

**4.**

_____
Nearest inch

**5.**

_____
Nearest inch

**6.**

_____
Nearest inch

## THINK MATH

Estimate how far it is from the bee to the flower. _____
Find the length to the nearest inch. _____

Name _____

$\boxed{2} + \boxed{2} + \boxed{2} = \underline{\phantom{6}6} $ inches

## Use your ruler. Measure around each figure.

**1.**

$\square + \square + \square + \square = $ _____ inches

**2.**

$\square + \square + \square + \square = $ _____ inches

**3.**

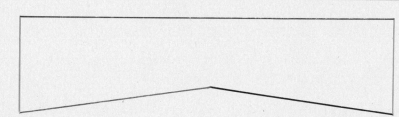

$\square + \square + \square + \square + \square = $ _____ inches

**4.**

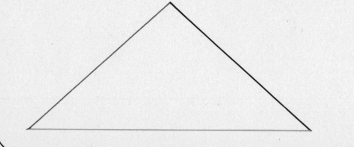

$\square + \square + \square = $ _____ inches

Perimeter                                    (three hundred twenty-seven) **327**

Finish drawing the lines.
How many square inches
are in each figure?

This is
1 square inch.

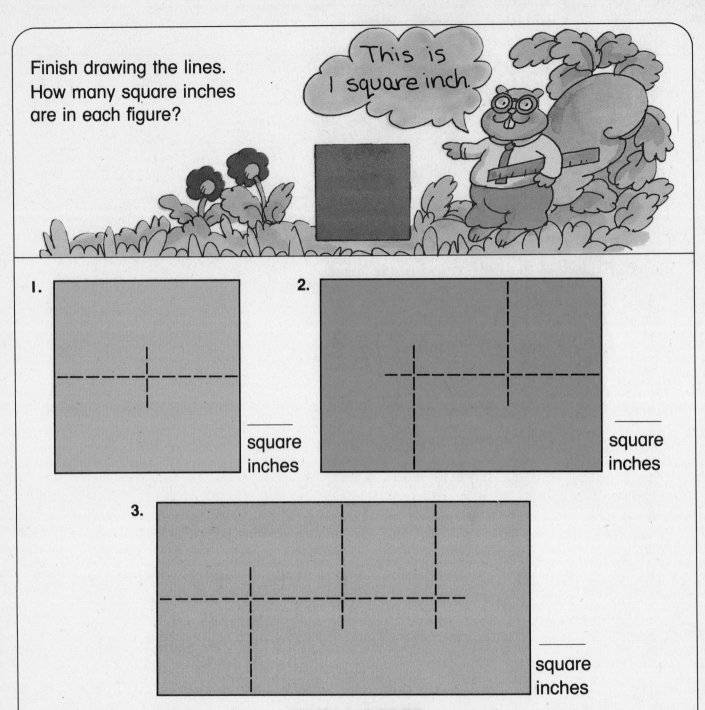

**1.**

_____ square
inches

**2.**

_____ square
inches

**3.**

_____ square
inches

## SKILLKEEPER

Write the times.

_____  _____  _____  _____

Ring the better estimate.

**1.**

More than 1 pint

Less than 1 pint

**2.**

More than 1 quart

Less than 1 quart

**3.**

More than 1 pint

Less than 1 pint

**4.**

More than 1 quart

Less than 1 quart

**5.**

More than 1 pint

Less than 1 pint

**6.**

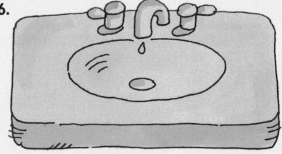

More than 1 quart

Less than 1 quart

Cups, pints and quarts

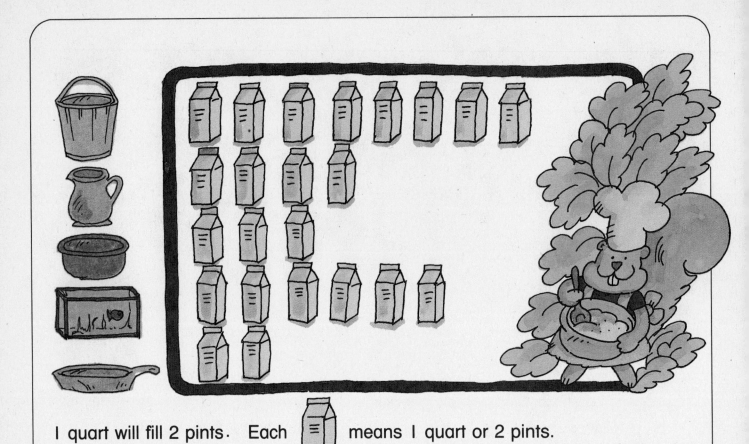

I quart will fill 2 pints. Each  means I quart or 2 pints.

---

| 1. How many quarts will it hold? | 2. How many pints will it hold? |
|---|---|
|  $\underline{8}$ quarts |  $\underline{16}$ pints |
|  _____ quarts |  _____ pints |
|  _____ quarts |  _____ pints |
|  _____ quarts |  _____ pints |
|  _____ quarts |  _____ pints |

Quarts and pints

Name _____

This can weighs about 1 pound.

Ring the better estimate.

**1.**

More than 1 pound
Less than 1 pound

**2.**

More than 1 pound
Less than 1 pound

**3.**

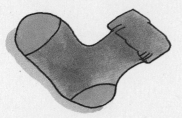

More than 1 pound
Less than 1 pound

**4.**

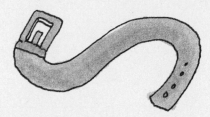

More than 1 pound
Less than 1 pound

**5.**

More than 1 pound
Less than 1 pound

**6.**

More than 1 pound

Less than 1 pound

Pounds

100°F    40°F

°fahrenheit

Boiling water — 210

Warm day — 80

Ice — 30

240
230
220
210
200
190
180
170
160
150
140
130
120
110
100
90
80
70
60
50
40
30
20
10
0

Ring the better estimate.

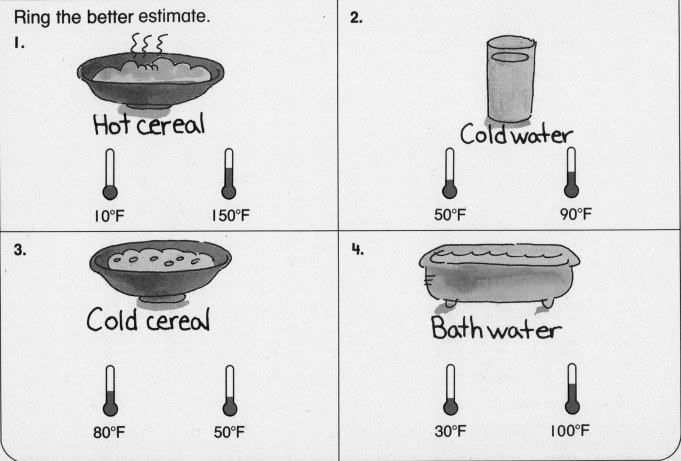

1.

Hot cereal

10°F       150°F

2.

Cold water

50°F       90°F

3.

Cold cereal

80°F       50°F

4.

Bath water

30°F       100°F

Degrees Fahrenheit—estimating temperature

Name _____

**1.** Ring the correct figure.

Thirds 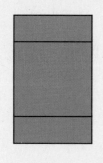 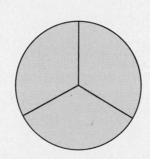        Fourths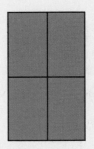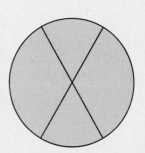

**2.** Ring the fraction that tells what part is shaded.

            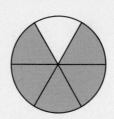            

$\dfrac{1}{3}$  $\dfrac{2}{3}$  $\dfrac{1}{2}$            $\dfrac{1}{5}$  $\dfrac{1}{6}$  $\dfrac{5}{6}$            $\dfrac{1}{3}$  $\dfrac{3}{4}$  $\dfrac{3}{5}$

**3.** Give the length to the nearest inch.

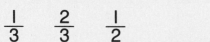

_____
Nearest inch

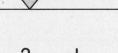

_____
Nearest inch

**4.** Measure around the figure.

 = _____ inches

**5.** Ring the better guess.

            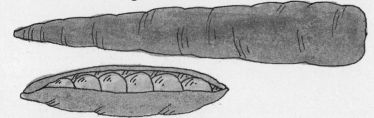            

More than 1 quart        More than 1 pound        150°   20°
Less than 1 quart        Less than 1 pound

Name _____

# CUMULATIVE REVIEW

Multiply.

1.
$3 \times 3 = $ _____

- ○ 6
- ○ 12
- ○ 9

2.
$\begin{array}{r} 4 \\ \times\, 4 \\ \hline \end{array}$

- ○ 12
- ○ 8
- ○ 16

3.
$\begin{array}{r} 5 \\ \times\, 2 \\ \hline \end{array}$

- ○ 10
- ○ 5
- ○ 15

4.
$\begin{array}{r} 5 \\ \times\, 5 \\ \hline \end{array}$

- ○ 36
- ○ 25
- ○ 20

What part is shaded?

5.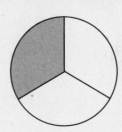

- ○ $\frac{4}{5}$
- ○ $\frac{1}{3}$
- ○ $\frac{1}{4}$

6.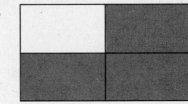

- ○ $\frac{3}{4}$
- ○ $\frac{1}{4}$
- ○ $\frac{2}{3}$

7. How many inches?

- ○ 2
- ○ 4
- ○ 8

8. A book weighs about

- ○ I pound
- ○ I quart
- ○ I inch

9. Solve.

The dog dug 4 holes. He put 2 bones in each. How many bones are there altogether?

- ○ 6 bones
- ○ 8 bones
- ○ 10 bones

Name _____

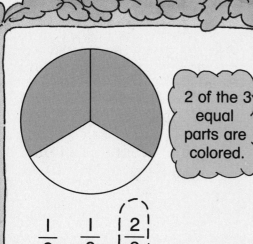

2 of the 3 equal parts are colored.

$\frac{1}{2}$  $\frac{1}{3}$  $\boxed{\frac{2}{3}}$

Color 1 of the 3 equal parts red.

$\frac{1}{3}$ is colored red.

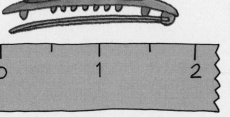

It is between 1 and 2.
It is closer to 2.

_2_ Nearest inch

1. Ring the fraction that tells what part is shaded.

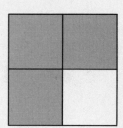

$\frac{1}{2}$  $\frac{1}{3}$  $\frac{1}{4}$      $\frac{1}{3}$  $\frac{3}{4}$  $\frac{1}{4}$

2. Color 2 of the 3 equal parts green.

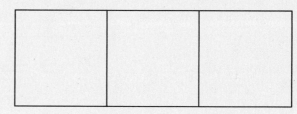

You colored $\frac{2}{3}$ of the figure.

3. How long to the nearest inch?

between _____ and _____

closer to _____

_____
Nearest inch

# ENRICHMENT

Can you work my cross-number puzzle?

Have fun!

## Across

1. 56 + 68
3. 70 − 39
5. 25 + 25 + 25
6. 100 + 50 + 6
7. 6 tens, 4 ones
9. 29 + 77
11. Two hundred eighty-one
13. One less than 100
15. 146 + 67
18. Half of one hundred
19. 100 − 22
20. 2 hundreds, 3 tens, and 4

## Down

1. 3 × 5
2. 27 + 13
3. Five more than 30
4. 4 × 4
5. 730 − 4
6. smallest 3-digit number
8. 7 × 6
10. 70 − 1
12. Eight hundred forty-three
14. 9 hundreds
15. 3 × 3 × 3
16. 2 × 3 × 3
17. 4 + 4 + 4
18. 18 + 18 + 18

# COMPUTER INSTRUCTION—LOGO

**Guiding the Turtle**    For use after page 134

You can "move" your turtle.

● You can make it go forward.
● You can turn it left.
● You can turn it right.

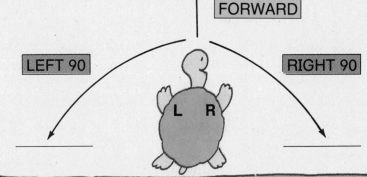

Example:

1. FORWARD 3
2. RIGHT 90, FORWARD 4
3. RIGHT 90, FORWARD 2
4. LEFT 90, FORWARD 5
5. RIGHT 90, FORWARD 2

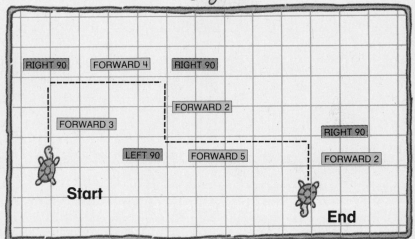

Follow the steps. Use a crayon to show the turtle's path.

1. FORWARD 9
2. RIGHT 90, FORWARD 4
3. RIGHT 90, FORWARD 3
4. LEFT 90, FORWARD 4
5. RIGHT 90, FORWARD 3
6. LEFT 90, FORWARD 4
7. RIGHT 90, FORWARD 3
8. RIGHT 90, FORWARD 12

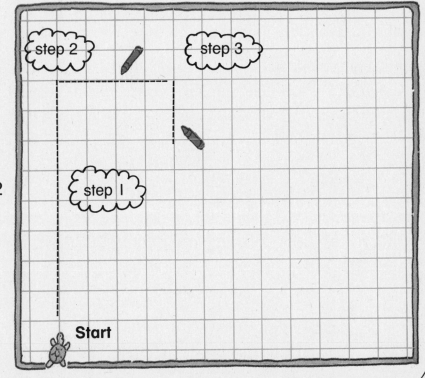

# COMPUTER INSTRUCTION—LOGO

**Length of a Path**     For use after page 233

Show the turtle's path. How far did it walk?

1. FORWARD 2
   RIGHT 90, FORWARD 8
   LEFT 90, FORWARD 5
   RIGHT 90, FORWARD 6
   RIGHT 90, FORWARD 3
   RIGHT 90, FORWARD 4

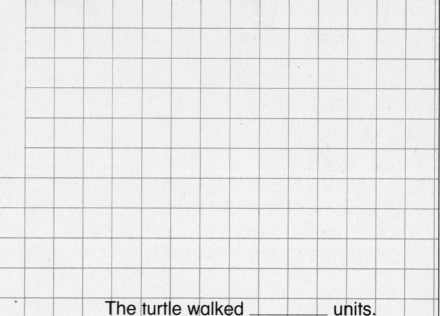

**Start**

The turtle walked _____ units.

**Finding Area**     For use after page 305

Show the turtle's path. Give the area of the figure.

1. FORWARD 4
   RIGHT 90, FORWARD 5
   RIGHT 90, FORWARD 4
   RIGHT 90, FORWARD 5

2. FORWARD 5
   LEFT 90, FORWARD 5
   LEFT 90, FORWARD 5
   LEFT 90, FORWARD 5

Area _____ units

Area _____ units

# CALCULATOR-ASSISTED PROBLEM SOLVING

## Guess and Check     For use after page 246

Which three numbers add to 73?

_____ + _____ + _____ = 73

Which three numbers add to 91?

_____ + _____ + _____ = 91

## Patterns     For use after page 258

What step has a sum over 500?     Step _____

| **Step 1** | **Step 2** | **Step 3** | **Step 4** | **Step 5** | |
|---|---|---|---|---|---|
| 1<br>+ 1<br>――<br>2 | 2<br>+ 2<br>――<br>4 | 4<br>+ 4<br>――<br>8 | 8<br>+ 8<br>――<br>16 | | and so on |

## Make a List     For use after page 272

You get two tosses.
What scores can you get?

380
270
160

lowest _____     _____     _____ highest

# CALCULATOR-ASSISTED PROBLEM SOLVING

## Doubles    For use after page 276

What number doubled is 134?

| Number | 7 | 8 | 9 | 10 | 11 | ... | _____ |
|--------|---|---|---|----|----|-----|--------|
| Double | 14 | 16 | 18 | 20 | 22 | ... | 134 |

## Estimation    For use after page 306

Multiply   $2 \times 2 \times 2 \times 2$ . . . and so on.
Stop when you get to 512.

Estimate how many 2s it will take. _____

How many did it take? _____

## Logical Reasoning    For use after page 312

      3   4   5   ×   −   =

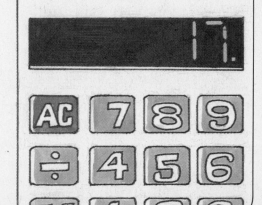

Use each key only once.
Use no other key.

Make your calculator read _____

# DATA BANK

Friday afternoon classes

Spelling      Math      Music      Reading

## MAY    YEAR 2000

| Sunday | Monday | Tuesday | Wednesday | Thursday | Friday | Saturday |
|--------|--------|---------|-----------|----------|--------|----------|
|        | 1      | 2       | 3         | 4        | 5      | 6        |
| 7      | 8      | 9       | 10        | 11       | 12     | 13       |
| 14     | 15     | 16      | 17        | 18       | 19     | 20       |
| 21     | 22     | 23      | 24        | 25       | 26     | 27       |
| 28     | 29     | 30      | 31        |          |        |          |

# DATA BANK

## Gorkeys

48 sitting down
24 standing

75 walking
36 running

26 on the long swings
38 on the short swings

15 climbing
18 jumping

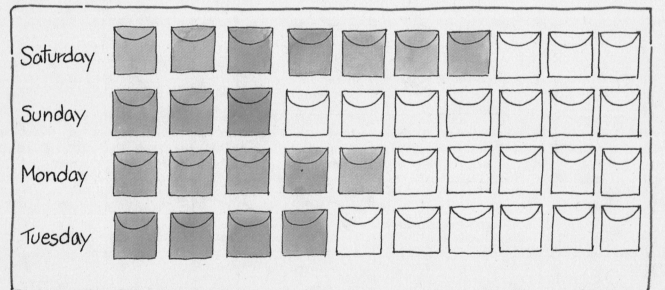

Pencils Sold

Saturday
Sunday
Monday
Tuesday

Each colored box means 5 pencils sold.

92¢    57¢    38¢

# DATA BANK

## FAVORITE GAMES

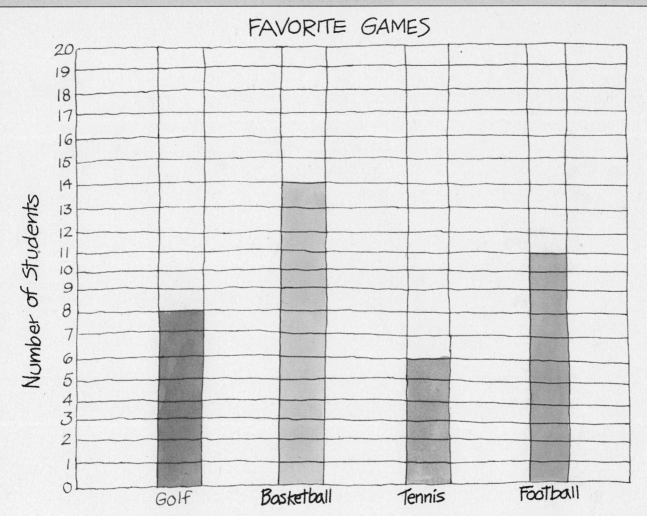

Number of Students vs. Golf, Basketball, Tennis, Football

### Guests at the Skating Party

| | | | |
|---|---|---|---|
| Grandfathers | 7 | Mothers | 17 |
| Grandmothers | 8 | Uncles | 5 |
| Fathers | 24 | Aunts | 3 |

Menu

| | | | |
|---|---|---|---|
| Egg Sandwich | $1.20 | Grape Juice | $1.15 |
| Peanut Butter Sandwich | $1.15 | Pineapple Juice | $1.10 |
| Beef Sandwich | $1.90 | Grapefruit Juice | $1.25 |

# MORE PRACTICE

**Set A**   For use after page 26

Add or subtract.

1.
$$\begin{array}{r} 5 \\ -1 \\ \hline \end{array}\qquad \begin{array}{r} 6 \\ -0 \\ \hline \end{array}\qquad \begin{array}{r} 1 \\ +6 \\ \hline \end{array}\qquad \begin{array}{r} 2 \\ +3 \\ \hline \end{array}\qquad \begin{array}{r} 12 \\ -3 \\ \hline \end{array}\qquad \begin{array}{r} 0 \\ +4 \\ \hline \end{array}$$

2.
$$\begin{array}{r} 10 \\ -2 \\ \hline \end{array}\qquad \begin{array}{r} 7 \\ +3 \\ \hline \end{array}\qquad \begin{array}{r} 4 \\ +0 \\ \hline \end{array}\qquad \begin{array}{r} 9 \\ -0 \\ \hline \end{array}\qquad \begin{array}{r} 2 \\ +8 \\ \hline \end{array}\qquad \begin{array}{r} 3 \\ -3 \\ \hline \end{array}$$

3.
$$\begin{array}{r} 5 \\ +1 \\ \hline \end{array}\qquad \begin{array}{r} 8 \\ -1 \\ \hline \end{array}\qquad \begin{array}{r} 3 \\ +6 \\ \hline \end{array}\qquad \begin{array}{r} 7 \\ -2 \\ \hline \end{array}\qquad \begin{array}{r} 11 \\ -3 \\ \hline \end{array}\qquad \begin{array}{r} 2 \\ +9 \\ \hline \end{array}$$

**Set B**   For use after page 38

1.  What does the digit with the line under it mean?

   78          43          12          85

   7 tens   7 ones      3 tens   3 ones      2 tens   2 ones      8 tens   8 ones

2.  How many are there?

_____ tens                _____ tens                _____ tens

_____ ones   in all       _____ ones   in all       _____ ones   in all

Name _____

## MORE PRACTICE

**Set A**    For use after page 50

Count on to find how many in all.

1.   _____ paper clips

2.  _____ marbles

3.   _____ muffins

4.   _____ pencils

**Set B**    For use after page 56

Put > or < in each ◯

1. 5◯8      12◯10      6◯3      15◯17

2. 50◯40      30◯70      20◯80      85◯95

3. 47◯27      63◯68      29◯27      56◯51

4. 49◯52      45◯38      73◯37      89◯98

Name _____

# MORE PRACTICE

**Set A**  For use after page 68

Add.

1.
$$3 + 2 \qquad 1 + 4 \qquad 2 + 2 \qquad 5 + 6 \qquad 2 + 1 \qquad 4 + 5$$

2.
$$6 + 2 \qquad 1 + 1 \qquad 5 + 4 \qquad 3 + 4 \qquad 5 + 5 \qquad 2 + 3$$

3.
$$3 + 3 \qquad 1 + 2 \qquad 6 + 5 \qquad 4 + 4 \qquad 2 + 5 \qquad 4 + 3$$

**Set B**  For use after page 72

Add.

1.
$$6 + 2 \qquad 6 + 6 \qquad 8 + 7 \qquad 3 + 7 \qquad 7 + 6 \qquad 9 + 9$$

2.
$$1 + 8 \qquad 7 + 8 \qquad 7 + 7 \qquad 8 + 9 \qquad 4 + 4 \qquad 9 + 2$$

3.
$$8 + 8 \qquad 9 + 8 \qquad 5 + 5 \qquad 5 + 1 \qquad 6 + 7 \qquad 7 + 2$$

# MORE PRACTICE

**Set A**    For use after page 78

Add.

1.  $\begin{array}{r} 9 \\ +3 \\ \hline \end{array}$    $\begin{array}{r} 9 \\ +5 \\ \hline \end{array}$    $\begin{array}{r} 8 \\ +9 \\ \hline \end{array}$    $\begin{array}{r} 9 \\ +1 \\ \hline \end{array}$    $\begin{array}{r} 4 \\ +9 \\ \hline \end{array}$    $\begin{array}{r} 7 \\ +9 \\ \hline \end{array}$

2.  $\begin{array}{r} 9 \\ +6 \\ \hline \end{array}$    $\begin{array}{r} 2 \\ +9 \\ \hline \end{array}$    $\begin{array}{r} 9 \\ +9 \\ \hline \end{array}$    $\begin{array}{r} 7 \\ +8 \\ \hline \end{array}$    $\begin{array}{r} 9 \\ +8 \\ \hline \end{array}$    $\begin{array}{r} 6 \\ +7 \\ \hline \end{array}$

3.  $\begin{array}{r} 7 \\ +7 \\ \hline \end{array}$    $\begin{array}{r} 6 \\ +9 \\ \hline \end{array}$    $\begin{array}{r} 5 \\ +6 \\ \hline \end{array}$    $\begin{array}{r} 9 \\ +7 \\ \hline \end{array}$    $\begin{array}{r} 8 \\ +8 \\ \hline \end{array}$    $\begin{array}{r} 9 \\ +4 \\ \hline \end{array}$

**Set B**    For use after page 80

Add.

1.  $\begin{array}{r} 8 \\ +4 \\ \hline \end{array}$    $\begin{array}{r} 6 \\ +6 \\ \hline \end{array}$    $\begin{array}{r} 5 \\ +8 \\ \hline \end{array}$    $\begin{array}{r} 4 \\ +7 \\ \hline \end{array}$    $\begin{array}{r} 7 \\ +5 \\ \hline \end{array}$    $\begin{array}{r} 6 \\ +4 \\ \hline \end{array}$

2.  $\begin{array}{r} 7 \\ +4 \\ \hline \end{array}$    $\begin{array}{r} 4 \\ +8 \\ \hline \end{array}$    $\begin{array}{r} 7 \\ +6 \\ \hline \end{array}$    $\begin{array}{r} 4 \\ +6 \\ \hline \end{array}$    $\begin{array}{r} 8 \\ +5 \\ \hline \end{array}$    $\begin{array}{r} 3 \\ +9 \\ \hline \end{array}$

3.  $\begin{array}{r} 8 \\ +6 \\ \hline \end{array}$    $\begin{array}{r} 8 \\ +7 \\ \hline \end{array}$    $\begin{array}{r} 3 \\ +8 \\ \hline \end{array}$    $\begin{array}{r} 6 \\ +8 \\ \hline \end{array}$    $\begin{array}{r} 7 \\ +3 \\ \hline \end{array}$    $\begin{array}{r} 5 \\ +7 \\ \hline \end{array}$

# MORE PRACTICE

## Set A    For use after page 83

Add.

1.
$\begin{array}{r} 7 \\ +6 \\ \hline \end{array}$
$\begin{array}{r} 8 \\ +4 \\ \hline \end{array}$
$\begin{array}{r} 9 \\ +5 \\ \hline \end{array}$
$\begin{array}{r} 5 \\ +5 \\ \hline \end{array}$
$\begin{array}{r} 6 \\ +9 \\ \hline \end{array}$
$\begin{array}{r} 3 \\ +8 \\ \hline \end{array}$

2.
$\begin{array}{r} 5 \\ +8 \\ \hline \end{array}$
$\begin{array}{r} 8 \\ +3 \\ \hline \end{array}$
$\begin{array}{r} 4 \\ +9 \\ \hline \end{array}$
$\begin{array}{r} 3 \\ +9 \\ \hline \end{array}$
$\begin{array}{r} 7 \\ +9 \\ \hline \end{array}$
$\begin{array}{r} 8 \\ +7 \\ \hline \end{array}$

3.
$\begin{array}{r} 9 \\ +8 \\ \hline \end{array}$
$\begin{array}{r} 7 \\ +5 \\ \hline \end{array}$
$\begin{array}{r} 8 \\ +8 \\ \hline \end{array}$
$\begin{array}{r} 6 \\ +4 \\ \hline \end{array}$
$\begin{array}{r} 4 \\ +7 \\ \hline \end{array}$
$\begin{array}{r} 5 \\ +6 \\ \hline \end{array}$

## Set B    For use after page 98

Subtract.

1.
$\begin{array}{r} 9 \\ -3 \\ \hline \end{array}$
$\begin{array}{r} 8 \\ -2 \\ \hline \end{array}$
$\begin{array}{r} 9 \\ -5 \\ \hline \end{array}$
$\begin{array}{r} 9 \\ -7 \\ \hline \end{array}$
$\begin{array}{r} 8 \\ -6 \\ \hline \end{array}$
$\begin{array}{r} 8 \\ -4 \\ \hline \end{array}$

2.
$\begin{array}{r} 8 \\ -3 \\ \hline \end{array}$
$\begin{array}{r} 9 \\ -2 \\ \hline \end{array}$
$\begin{array}{r} 9 \\ -8 \\ \hline \end{array}$
$\begin{array}{r} 8 \\ -1 \\ \hline \end{array}$
$\begin{array}{r} 9 \\ -4 \\ \hline \end{array}$
$\begin{array}{r} 9 \\ -6 \\ \hline \end{array}$

3.
$\begin{array}{r} 9 \\ -1 \\ \hline \end{array}$
$\begin{array}{r} 8 \\ -8 \\ \hline \end{array}$
$\begin{array}{r} 9 \\ -9 \\ \hline \end{array}$
$\begin{array}{r} 8 \\ -7 \\ \hline \end{array}$
$\begin{array}{r} 9 \\ -0 \\ \hline \end{array}$
$\begin{array}{r} 8 \\ -5 \\ \hline \end{array}$

# MORE PRACTICE

**Set A**     For use after page 102

Subtract.

1.
$$\begin{array}{r} 11 \\ -\ 3 \\ \hline \end{array}\qquad \begin{array}{r} 11 \\ -\ 6 \\ \hline \end{array}\qquad \begin{array}{r} 12 \\ -\ 4 \\ \hline \end{array}\qquad \begin{array}{r} 11 \\ -\ 5 \\ \hline \end{array}\qquad \begin{array}{r} 12 \\ -\ 7 \\ \hline \end{array}\qquad \begin{array}{r} 11 \\ -\ 8 \\ \hline \end{array}$$

2.
$$\begin{array}{r} 12 \\ -\ 8 \\ \hline \end{array}\qquad \begin{array}{r} 12 \\ -\ 6 \\ \hline \end{array}\qquad \begin{array}{r} 11 \\ -\ 4 \\ \hline \end{array}\qquad \begin{array}{r} 11 \\ -\ 7 \\ \hline \end{array}\qquad \begin{array}{r} 12 \\ -\ 5 \\ \hline \end{array}\qquad \begin{array}{r} 11 \\ -\ 2 \\ \hline \end{array}$$

3.
$$\begin{array}{r} 11 \\ -\ 9 \\ \hline \end{array}\qquad \begin{array}{r} 12 \\ -\ 7 \\ \hline \end{array}\qquad \begin{array}{r} 11 \\ -\ 3 \\ \hline \end{array}\qquad \begin{array}{r} 12 \\ -\ 3 \\ \hline \end{array}\qquad \begin{array}{r} 12 \\ -\ 8 \\ \hline \end{array}\qquad \begin{array}{r} 12 \\ -\ 9 \\ \hline \end{array}$$

**Set B**     For use after page 106

Subtract.

1.
$$\begin{array}{r} 14 \\ -\ 6 \\ \hline \end{array}\qquad \begin{array}{r} 13 \\ -\ 4 \\ \hline \end{array}\qquad \begin{array}{r} 13 \\ -\ 8 \\ \hline \end{array}\qquad \begin{array}{r} 14 \\ -\ 7 \\ \hline \end{array}\qquad \begin{array}{r} 13 \\ -\ 6 \\ \hline \end{array}\qquad \begin{array}{r} 14 \\ -\ 9 \\ \hline \end{array}$$

2.
$$\begin{array}{r} 13 \\ -\ 9 \\ \hline \end{array}\qquad \begin{array}{r} 13 \\ -\ 6 \\ \hline \end{array}\qquad \begin{array}{r} 13 \\ -\ 7 \\ \hline \end{array}\qquad \begin{array}{r} 14 \\ -\ 5 \\ \hline \end{array}\qquad \begin{array}{r} 13 \\ -\ 5 \\ \hline \end{array}\qquad \begin{array}{r} 14 \\ -\ 8 \\ \hline \end{array}$$

3.
$$\begin{array}{r} 14 \\ -\ 8 \\ \hline \end{array}\qquad \begin{array}{r} 14 \\ -\ 7 \\ \hline \end{array}\qquad \begin{array}{r} 13 \\ -\ 8 \\ \hline \end{array}\qquad \begin{array}{r} 13 \\ -\ 7 \\ \hline \end{array}\qquad \begin{array}{r} 14 \\ -\ 6 \\ \hline \end{array}\qquad \begin{array}{r} 14 \\ -\ 9 \\ \hline \end{array}$$

Name _____

# MORE PRACTICE

**Set A**    For use after page 112

Subtract.

1.
$$\begin{array}{r} 15 \\ -\ 6 \\ \hline \end{array} \qquad \begin{array}{r} 16 \\ -\ 9 \\ \hline \end{array} \qquad \begin{array}{r} 15 \\ -\ 7 \\ \hline \end{array} \qquad \begin{array}{r} 16 \\ -\ 7 \\ \hline \end{array} \qquad \begin{array}{r} 15 \\ -\ 8 \\ \hline \end{array} \qquad \begin{array}{r} 17 \\ -\ 9 \\ \hline \end{array}$$

2.
$$\begin{array}{r} 16 \\ -\ 8 \\ \hline \end{array} \qquad \begin{array}{r} 17 \\ -\ 8 \\ \hline \end{array} \qquad \begin{array}{r} 15 \\ -\ 9 \\ \hline \end{array} \qquad \begin{array}{r} 16 \\ -\ 7 \\ \hline \end{array} \qquad \begin{array}{r} 18 \\ -\ 9 \\ \hline \end{array} \qquad \begin{array}{r} 15 \\ -\ 7 \\ \hline \end{array}$$

3.
$$\begin{array}{r} 15 \\ -\ 9 \\ \hline \end{array} \qquad \begin{array}{r} 16 \\ -\ 8 \\ \hline \end{array} \qquad \begin{array}{r} 17 \\ -\ 8 \\ \hline \end{array} \qquad \begin{array}{r} 18 \\ -\ 9 \\ \hline \end{array} \qquad \begin{array}{r} 16 \\ -\ 9 \\ \hline \end{array} \qquad \begin{array}{r} 15 \\ -\ 8 \\ \hline \end{array}$$

**Set B**    For use after page 116

Add or subtract.

1.
$$\begin{array}{r} 14 \\ -\ 7 \\ \hline \end{array} \qquad \begin{array}{r} 8 \\ +\ 5 \\ \hline \end{array} \qquad \begin{array}{r} 12 \\ -\ 8 \\ \hline \end{array} \qquad \begin{array}{r} 4 \\ +\ 6 \\ \hline \end{array} \qquad \begin{array}{r} 18 \\ -\ 9 \\ \hline \end{array} \qquad \begin{array}{r} 15 \\ -\ 6 \\ \hline \end{array}$$

2.
$$\begin{array}{r} 4 \\ +\ 7 \\ \hline \end{array} \qquad \begin{array}{r} 17 \\ -\ 9 \\ \hline \end{array} \qquad \begin{array}{r} 9 \\ +\ 8 \\ \hline \end{array} \qquad \begin{array}{r} 11 \\ -\ 2 \\ \hline \end{array} \qquad \begin{array}{r} 16 \\ -\ 9 \\ \hline \end{array} \qquad \begin{array}{r} 14 \\ -\ 8 \\ \hline \end{array}$$

3.
$$\begin{array}{r} 5 \\ +\ 6 \\ \hline \end{array} \qquad \begin{array}{r} 13 \\ -\ 5 \\ \hline \end{array} \qquad \begin{array}{r} 7 \\ +\ 5 \\ \hline \end{array} \qquad \begin{array}{r} 15 \\ -\ 7 \\ \hline \end{array} \qquad \begin{array}{r} 9 \\ +\ 5 \\ \hline \end{array} \qquad \begin{array}{r} 3 \\ +\ 8 \\ \hline \end{array}$$

All rights reserved. Addison-Wesley

(three hundred fifty-one) **351**

# MORE PRACTICE

**Set A**    For use after page 132

Write the times.

1.

_____    _____    _____

2.

_____    _____    _____

**Set B**    For use after page 144

Is there enough money? Count, then ring **Yes** or **No**.

1.                     Yes

_____    No

2.                    Yes

_____    No

3.                 Yes

_____    No

# MORE PRACTICE

## Set A    For use after page 156

Add. Trade 10 ones for 1 ten.
Write the numbers.

1.  $\begin{array}{r} 7 \\ +5 \end{array}$ ⟶ ____ ten ____ ones

2.  $\begin{array}{r} 5 \\ +5 \end{array}$ ⟶ ____ ten ____ ones

3.  $\begin{array}{r} 6 \\ +9 \end{array}$ ⟶ ____ ten ____ ones

4.  $\begin{array}{r} 7 \\ +8 \end{array}$ ⟶ ____ ten ____ ones

## Set B    For use after page 160

Add.

1.  $\begin{array}{r} 59 \\ + 8 \end{array}$    $\begin{array}{r} 34 \\ + 5 \end{array}$    $\begin{array}{r} 17 \\ + 5 \end{array}$    $\begin{array}{r} 66 \\ + 8 \end{array}$    $\begin{array}{r} 26 \\ + 2 \end{array}$    $\begin{array}{r} 48 \\ + 5 \end{array}$

2.  $\begin{array}{r} 7 \\ +51 \end{array}$    $\begin{array}{r} 73 \\ + 8 \end{array}$    $\begin{array}{r} 3 \\ +24 \end{array}$    $\begin{array}{r} 46 \\ + 7 \end{array}$    $\begin{array}{r} 77 \\ + 7 \end{array}$    $\begin{array}{r} 7 \\ +38 \end{array}$

3.  $\begin{array}{r} 5 \\ +85 \end{array}$    $\begin{array}{r} 67 \\ + 9 \end{array}$    $\begin{array}{r} 84 \\ + 8 \end{array}$    $\begin{array}{r} 41 \\ + 4 \end{array}$    $\begin{array}{r} 5 \\ +52 \end{array}$    $\begin{array}{r} 31 \\ + 9 \end{array}$

# MORE PRACTICE

**Set A**    For use after page 164

Add. Trade if you need to.

1.  $\begin{array}{r} 37 \\ +13 \\ \hline \end{array}$

2.  $\begin{array}{r} 45 \\ +18 \\ \hline \end{array}$

3.  $\begin{array}{r} 29 \\ +22 \\ \hline \end{array}$

4.  $\begin{array}{r} 16 \\ +37 \\ \hline \end{array}$

**Set B**    For use after page 168

Add. Trade if you need to.

1.  $\begin{array}{r} 37 \\ +57 \\ \hline \end{array}$    $\begin{array}{r} 62 \\ +17 \\ \hline \end{array}$    $\begin{array}{r} 56 \\ +29 \\ \hline \end{array}$    $\begin{array}{r} 74 \\ +16 \\ \hline \end{array}$    $\begin{array}{r} 43 \\ +47 \\ \hline \end{array}$    $\begin{array}{r} 36 \\ +56 \\ \hline \end{array}$

2.  $\begin{array}{r} 27 \\ +26 \\ \hline \end{array}$    $\begin{array}{r} 15 \\ +65 \\ \hline \end{array}$    $\begin{array}{r} 38 \\ +34 \\ \hline \end{array}$    $\begin{array}{r} 47 \\ +28 \\ \hline \end{array}$    $\begin{array}{r} 26 \\ +65 \\ \hline \end{array}$    $\begin{array}{r} 44 \\ +29 \\ \hline \end{array}$

3.  $\begin{array}{r} 26 \\ +43 \\ \hline \end{array}$    $\begin{array}{r} 59 \\ +25 \\ \hline \end{array}$    $\begin{array}{r} 18 \\ +78 \\ \hline \end{array}$    $\begin{array}{r} 84 \\ +15 \\ \hline \end{array}$    $\begin{array}{r} 39 \\ +49 \\ \hline \end{array}$    $\begin{array}{r} 26 \\ +68 \\ \hline \end{array}$

Name _____

---

# MORE PRACTICE

**Set A**    For use after page 170

Add. Ring the problems where you had to trade.

1.
$$48 + 32$$    $$73 + 25$$    $$5 + 89$$    $$37 + 17$$    $$80 + 9$$    $$28 + 43$$

2.
$$24 + 44$$    $$78 + 15$$    $$57 + 29$$    $$3 + 91$$    $$39 + 52$$    $$64 + 18$$

3.
$$27 + 64$$    $$36 + 47$$    $$9 + 41$$    $$57 + 12$$    $$78 + 6$$    $$34 + 53$$

---

**Set B**    For use after page 184

Give the number of sides and corners.
Ring the correct name.

1. ____ sides          2. ____ sides          3. ____ sides

____ corners          ____ corners          ____ corners

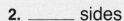                    

rectangle                circle                square

triangle                square                triangle

# MORE PRACTICE

**Set A**   For use after page 190

1. Count the tally marks.
   Color the graph to match.

||||  |          ||||  ||||          |||          ||||  |||

total _____      total _____      total _____      total _____

Kinds of Shoes

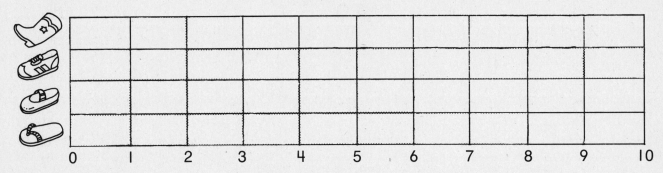

0    1    2    3    4    5    6    7    8    9    10

2. How many 🥾 and 👟 are there in all? _____

3. How many more 👟 than 👞 are there? _____

**Set B**   For use after page 202

Trade 1 ten for 10 ones. Write the numbers.

1. □□  24        □□  45        □□  71        □□  96

2. □□  43        □□  87        □□  64        □□  19

3. □□  26        □□  70        □□  38        □□  52

# MORE PRACTICE

## Set A    For use after page 204

Subtract.

1.

| Tens | Ones |
|------|------|
| ☐ | ☐ |

$$\begin{array}{r} 5\ 1 \\ -\ 2\ 8 \\ \hline \end{array}$$ Trade

| Tens | Ones |
|------|------|
| ☐ | ☐ |

$$\begin{array}{r} 6\ 5 \\ -\ 4\ 6 \\ \hline \end{array}$$ Trade

| Tens | Ones |
|------|------|
| ☐ | ☐ |

$$\begin{array}{r} 2\ 9 \\ -\ 1\ 7 \\ \hline \end{array}$$ No trade

2.

| Tens | Ones |
|------|------|
| ☐ | ☐ |

$$\begin{array}{r} 7\ 7 \\ -\ 4\ 1 \\ \hline \end{array}$$ No trade

| Tens | Ones |
|------|------|
| ☐ | ☐ |

$$\begin{array}{r} 4\ 2 \\ -\ 3\ 3 \\ \hline \end{array}$$ Trade

| Tens | Ones |
|------|------|
| ☐ | ☐ |

$$\begin{array}{r} 8\ 2 \\ -\ 2\ 1 \\ \hline \end{array}$$ No trade

## Set B    For use after page 209

Copy and subtract.
Trade if you need to. _____

1.

$$46 - 18$$

2.

_____

$$31 - 9$$

3.

$$85 - 26$$

4.

$$74 - 57$$

# MORE PRACTICE

**Set A**     For use after page 214

Trade if you need to.
Then subtract.

1.  $\begin{array}{r} 46 \\ -29 \\ \hline \end{array}$  $\begin{array}{r} 84 \\ -38 \\ \hline \end{array}$  $\begin{array}{r} 63 \\ -14 \\ \hline \end{array}$  $\begin{array}{r} 59 \\ -47 \\ \hline \end{array}$  $\begin{array}{r} 37 \\ -19 \\ \hline \end{array}$  $\begin{array}{r} 52 \\ -33 \\ \hline \end{array}$

2.  $\begin{array}{r} 78 \\ -49 \\ \hline \end{array}$  $\begin{array}{r} 95 \\ -64 \\ \hline \end{array}$  $\begin{array}{r} 36 \\ -\ 7 \\ \hline \end{array}$  $\begin{array}{r} 20 \\ -13 \\ \hline \end{array}$  $\begin{array}{r} 44 \\ -22 \\ \hline \end{array}$  $\begin{array}{r} 81 \\ -61 \\ \hline \end{array}$

3.  $\begin{array}{r} 72 \\ -34 \\ \hline \end{array}$  $\begin{array}{r} 18 \\ -16 \\ \hline \end{array}$  $\begin{array}{r} 34 \\ -\ 5 \\ \hline \end{array}$  $\begin{array}{r} 85 \\ -57 \\ \hline \end{array}$  $\begin{array}{r} 63 \\ -46 \\ \hline \end{array}$  $\begin{array}{r} 57 \\ -18 \\ \hline \end{array}$

**Set B**     For use after page 216

Add or subtract.

1.  $\begin{array}{r} 37 \\ -18 \\ \hline \end{array}$  $\begin{array}{r} 27 \\ +\ 5 \\ \hline \end{array}$  $\begin{array}{r} 40 \\ -31 \\ \hline \end{array}$  $\begin{array}{r} 94 \\ -85 \\ \hline \end{array}$  $\begin{array}{r} 52 \\ +43 \\ \hline \end{array}$  $\begin{array}{r} 29 \\ +49 \\ \hline \end{array}$

2.  $\begin{array}{r} 78 \\ +17 \\ \hline \end{array}$  $\begin{array}{r} 14 \\ +16 \\ \hline \end{array}$  $\begin{array}{r} 94 \\ -\ 6 \\ \hline \end{array}$  $\begin{array}{r} 50 \\ -\ 5 \\ \hline \end{array}$  $\begin{array}{r} 21 \\ -14 \\ \hline \end{array}$  $\begin{array}{r} 88 \\ +\ 3 \\ \hline \end{array}$

3.  $\begin{array}{r} 62 \\ -39 \\ \hline \end{array}$  $\begin{array}{r} 46 \\ +27 \\ \hline \end{array}$  $\begin{array}{r} 45 \\ +30 \\ \hline \end{array}$  $\begin{array}{r} 83 \\ -19 \\ \hline \end{array}$  $\begin{array}{r} 38 \\ -19 \\ \hline \end{array}$  $\begin{array}{r} 76 \\ +16 \\ \hline \end{array}$

# MORE PRACTICE

**Set A**   For use after page 230

Use your centimeter ruler.
Give the length to the nearest centimeter.

1.

_____
Nearest centimeter

2.

_____
Nearest centimeter

3.

_____
Nearest centimeter

4.

_____
Nearest centimeter

5.

_____
Nearest centimeter

**Set B**   For use after page 256

1. What does the underlined digit mean?

951

5 hundreds    5 tens    5 ones

136

6 hundreds    6 tens    6 ones

Fill in the blanks.

2.  764

_____ hundreds

_____ tens

_____ ones

3. 100

_____ tens

_____ hundred

_____ ones

4. 285

_____ ones

_____ hundreds

_____ tens

5. 913

_____ hundreds

_____ ones

_____ ten

# MORE PRACTICE

**Set A**   For use after page 272

Add. Trade if you need to.

1.
|  | 187 | 453 | 65 | 334 | 269 |
|---|---|---|---|---|---|
|  | +372 | +206 | +191 | +292 | +650 |

2.
|  | 728 | 261 | 290 | 9 | 583 |
|---|---|---|---|---|---|
|  | + 43 | +446 | +553 | + 65 | +274 |

3.
|  | 111 | 660 | 586 | 625 | 605 |
|---|---|---|---|---|---|
|  | +792 | + 77 | +162 | +293 | +387 |

**Set B**   For use after page 276

Add or subtract. Trade if you need to.

1.
|  | 407 | 236 | 153 | 479 | 725 |
|---|---|---|---|---|---|
|  | −182 | − 54 | + 81 | −258 | −444 |

2.
|  | 159 | 357 | 872 | 273 | 747 |
|---|---|---|---|---|---|
|  | +308 | −249 | − 9 | +165 | −474 |

3.
|  | 386 | 746 | 72 | 322 | 889 |
|---|---|---|---|---|---|
|  | +451 | −293 | +547 | −208 | + 9 |

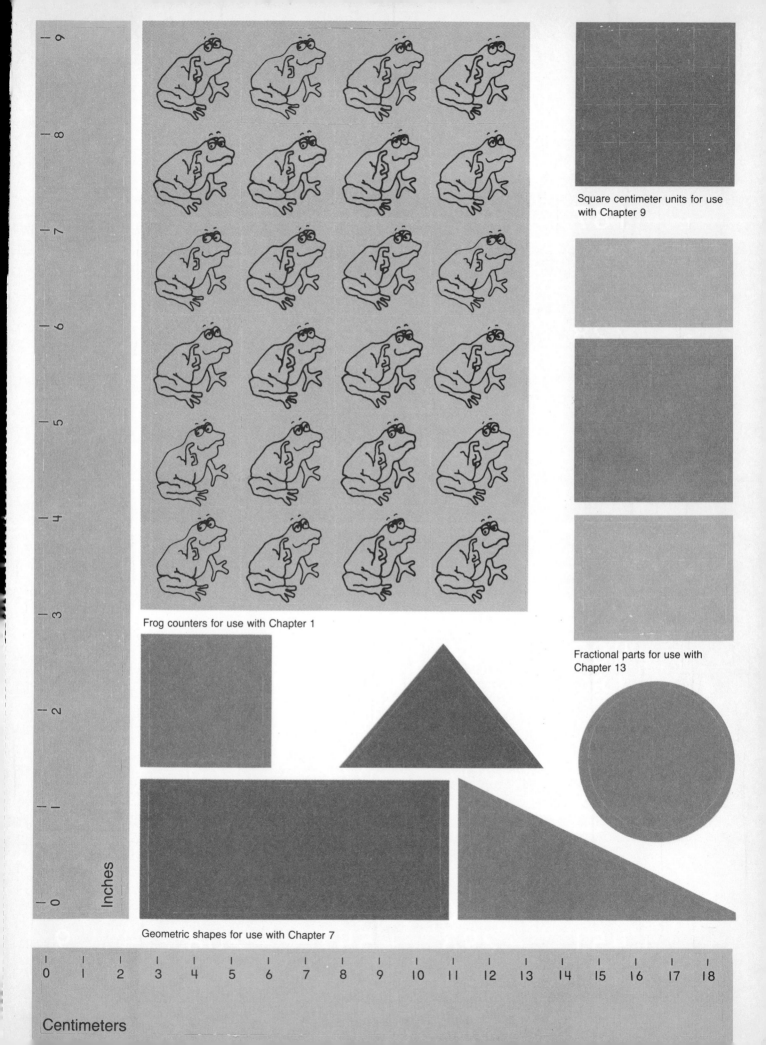

Frog counters for use with Chapter 1

Square centimeter units for use with Chapter 9

Fractional parts for use with Chapter 13

Geometric shapes for use with Chapter 7

Inches

9 8 7 6 5 4 3 2 1 0

0 1 2 3 4 5 6 7 8 9 10 11 12 13 14 15 16 17 18

Centimeters

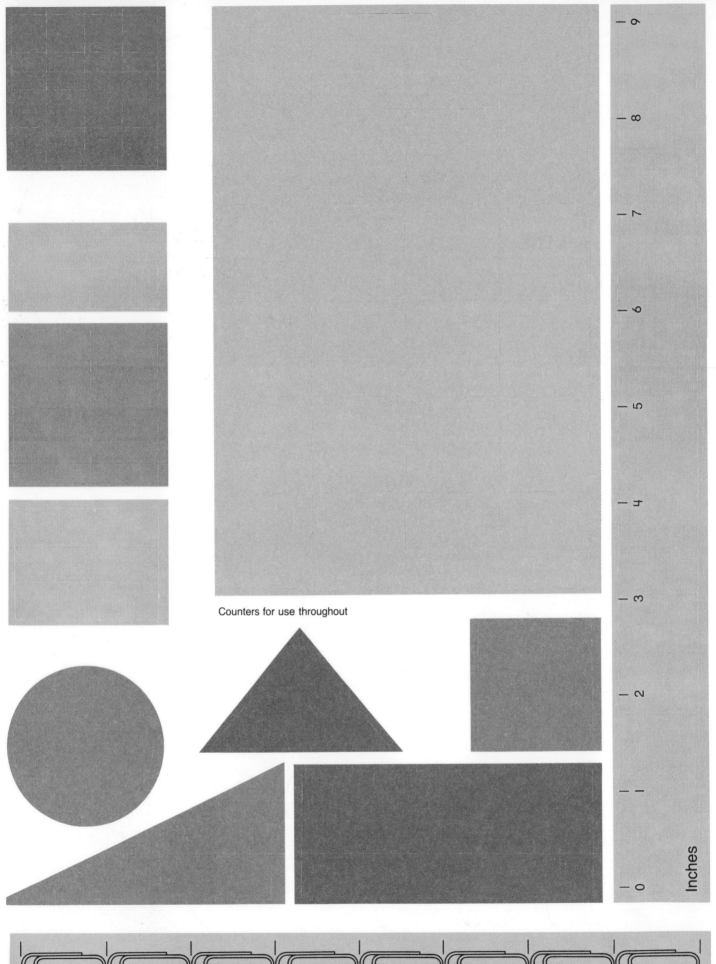

Counters for use throughout

Inches

Paper-clip units

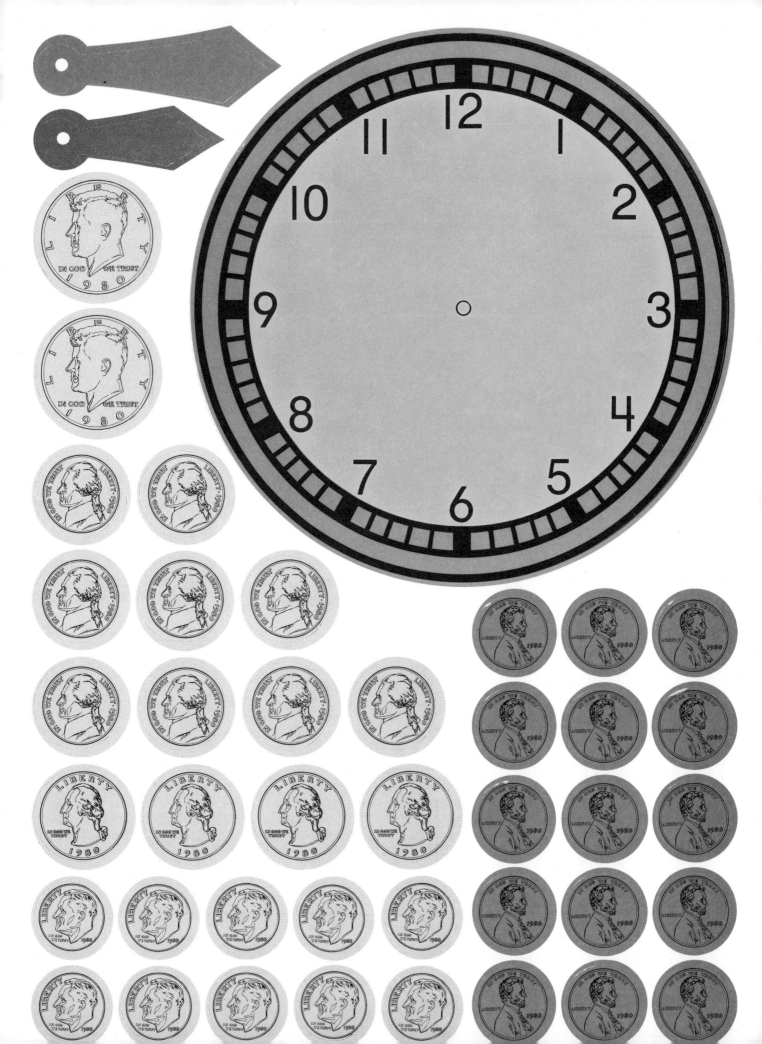